# Corporate Sustainability Assessments

Sustainable development is an internationally recognised objective for governments, businesses and societies. However, how the private sector engages with sustainability in a systematic way through their business activities remains unclear. This book evaluates the sustainability practices of the private sector by utilising a sustainability assessment framework – a method for integrating different strands of impact assessment, to better inform decision-making for the promotion of sustainable economic development.

Through a sample of leading multinational enterprises (MNEs) in Thailand, this book provides evidence on the types of sustainability approaches being utilised by the private sector, shedding light on the important relationship between FDI and sustainable development. It also clarifies the role of FDI in sustainable development, and the methods, tools and techniques that enable the private sector to engage with sustainability and sustainable development. The book will generate significant interest from sustainability practitioners in both the public and private sector.

**Jerome D. Donovan** is Senior Lecturer in International Business at Swinburne University of Technology. He is also Principal Advisor for Technology Entrepreneurship and Commercialization Development with the Ministry of Science and Technology, Vietnam.

**Cheree Topple** is Lecturer at the Department of Management and Marketing at Swinburne University of Technology. She has worked on a range of government-funded projects to support SME development in the areas of sustainability and human resource development.

**Eryadi K. Masli** is Lecturer in International Business at Swinburne University of Technology. He is also Senior Advisor for the Ministry of Planning and Investment, Social Republic of Vietnam, and Senior Advisor in Economic Development for the Ministry of Planning and Investment, Lao People's Democratic Republic.

**Teerin Vanichseni** is Lecturer at the School of Business, and Director of the Center of Business Research and Case Study at the University of the Thai Chamber of Commerce.

# Routledge Frontiers of Business Management

# Corporate Sustainability Assessments

Sustainability practices of multinational enterprises in Thailand

**Edited by Jerome D. Donovan, Cheree Topple, Eryadi K. Masli and Teerin Vanichseni**

Routledge
Taylor & Francis Group

LONDON AND NEW YORK

First published 2017 by Routledge

2 Park Square, Milton Park, Abingdon, Oxfordshire OX14 4RN
711 Third Avenue, New York, NY 10017

*Routledge is an imprint of the Taylor & Francis Group,
an informa business*

First issued in paperback 2018

*British Library Cataloguing in Publication Data*
A catalogue record for this book is available from
the British Library

*Library of Congress Cataloging-in-Publication Data*
Names: Donovan, Jerome, editor. | Topple, Cheree, editor.
Title: Corporate sustainability assessments : sustainability practices
    of multinational enterprises in Thailand / edited by Jerome
    D. Donovan, Cheree Topple, Eryadi K. Masli and Teerin Vanichseni.
Description: First Edition. | New York : Routledge, 2016. |
    Series: Routledge frontiers of business management; 3 |
    Includes bibliographical references and index.
Identifiers: LCCN 2016015418 | ISBN 9781138691766 (hardback) |
    ISBN 9781315534015 (ebook)
Subjects: LCSH: International business enterprises—Thailand. |
    Industrial management—Environmental aspects—Thailand. |
    Corporations—Environmental aspects—Thailand. | Business
    enterprises—Environmental aspects.
Classification: LCC HD2902.55 C67 2016 |
    DDC 658.4/0809593—dc23
LC record available at https://lccn.loc.gov/2016015418

ISBN: 978-1-138-69176-6 (hbk)
ISBN: 978-1-138-31783-3 (pbk)

Typeset in Galliard
by Apex CoVantage, LLC

# Contents

# Figures

# Tables

# Contributors

**Thomas Borgert** is Research Associate and PhD candidate at Swinburne University of Technology. His research interests include corporate sustainability assessments, global value chains, and development in South East Asia. He is currently working with Fairtrade ANZ on increasing ethical and sustainable supply chains into Australia, and the Global Reporting Initiative on integrating sustainability reporting into global value chains.

**Jerome D. Donovan** is Senior Lecturer in International Business at Swinburne University of Technology. He is also Principal Advisor for Technology Entrepreneurship and Commercialization Development with the Ministry of Science and Technology, Vietnam.

**Lalita Hongratanawong** graduated with PhD in Management Science from Illinois Institute of Technology, USA. Currently, she is working at University of the Thai Chamber of Commerce as Head of Finance Division in School of Business.

**Masayoshi Ike** is Research Associate at Swinburne University of Technology. His research interests include Japanese foreign direct investment, corporate social responsibility, and sustainability. He is currently working on a project with Fairtrade ANZ, and specifically looking at third party certifications for ethical products in the region.

**Jirapan Kunthawangso** was Research Associate at Swinburne University of Technology and the University of the Thai Chamber of Commerce. Her research interests include sustainability, global value chains, and international politics.

**Laddawan Lekmat** graduated with a PhD in Entrepreneurship and Innovation from Swinburne University, Australia. Currently, she is working at University of the Thai Chamber of Commerce as Director of SME Center and Institute of Trade Strategies.

**Hermann Lion** is Research Associate and PhD Candidate at Swinburne University of Technology. He specialises in the study of anthropogenic impacts, and particularly around private sector impact assessments. His work has been published in the *Journal of Business Ethics*.

**Eryadi K. Masli** is Lecturer in International Business at Swinburne University of Technology. He is also Senior Advisor for the Ministry of Planning and Investment, Social Republic of Vietnam, and Senior Advisor in Economic Development for the Ministry of Planning and Investment, Lao People's Democratic Republic.

**Cheree Topple** is Lecturer at the Department of Management and Marketing at Swinburne University of Technology. She has worked on a range of government-funded projects to support SME development in the areas of sustainability and human resource development.

**Teerin Vanichseni** is Lecturer at the School of Business, and Director of the Center of Business Research and Case Study at the University of the Thai Chamber of Commerce.

**Monica Van Wynen** is Research Assistant at Swinburne University of Technology. Her research interests include sustainability, innovation, and global value chains. She is currently working on a project with Fairtrade ANZ looking at increasing the ethical and sustainable supply chains into Australia from the Indo-Pacific region.

**Vedran Vranic** is Postdoctoral Researcher at Swinburne University of Technology. He is currently working on a project with Fairtrade ANZ, profiling supply chains in the Indo-Pacific region. He is also working on research around innovation management in Australia.

# 1 Introduction

## Sustainability practices in Thailand

*Cheree Topple, Jerome D. Donovan,*
*Eryadi K. Masli and Teerin Vanichseni*

Sustainable development is an internationally recognised objective for governments, business and society (UN, 2012; UNCTAD, 2012). While there is
agreement amongst leading scholars that sustainable development requires the
integration of economic prosperity, environmental quality and social justice
(WBCSD, 2001) it tends to be commonly described as the adoption of "business strategies and activities that meet the needs of the enterprise and its stakeholders today while protecting, sustaining and enhancing the human and natural
resources that will be needed in the future" (International Institute for Sustainable Development, 1992, p.11).

This emphasis on sustainability is also evident within the Association of South
East Asian Nations (ASEAN), with a clear direction set for the region by the
AEC (ASEAN Economic Community) Blueprint towards, not only increased
economic growth and dynamism, but also "sustained prosperity, inclusive growth
and integrated development of ASEAN" (ASEAN, 2012). However, the question remains as to how governments within the region can achieve this, particularly with regards to engaging the private sector, a key driver for economic
activity and development progress. Mobilising investment has been identified
as a key priority for achieving a sustainable development agenda. Within developing countries, foreign direct investment (FDI) is a large aspect of this priority
and generating new policies that are able to foster sustainable development
outcomes is critical (OECD, 2002; UNCTAD, 2015).

Most broadly, FDI is thought to contribute towards sustainable development
through more than just the financial resources dedicated to establishing foreign
operations. Previous research and international reports suggest it can generate
employment, drive export growth, transfer skills and knowledge to the local
private sector and contribute to revenues through taxation. Amongst other
things it is also associated with improving productivity, infrastructure and extending global value chain integration to incorporate local suppliers and producers
(UNCTAD, 2015). However, the link that is depicted between FDI and economic development is not necessarily straightforward. It is based largely on
economic growth caused by FDI and relies on different investment policies,
regulations and local characteristics from which the receiving country then sets

the ground for economic development to be achieved (Kosack and Tobin, 2006; Ranis and Stewart, 2000).

The importance and understanding of how FDI can contribute to sustainable development becomes even more pertinent when considering the sheer size and flow of FDI within the region. Over recent years, Asia has been the world's top recipient group of FDI, accounting for about 31 per cent of worldwide investment (UNCTAD, 2015). Thailand is one of the region's most successful countries to attract FDI. The Thai government, over recent decades, has recognised the significance of the private sector as a core facilitator of their economic and technological growth. Experiencing an average economic growth rate of nearly 8 per cent p.a. from 1960–1996, since 2008 Thailand has however made a slow recovery from the global financial crisis and, more recently, has seen FDI projects shelved because of political instability. Despite FDI inflows dropping 10.3 per cent between 2013 and 2014 to $12.6 billion, Thailand remains one of the top five host economies in the region (UNCTAD, 2015, p.39). Understanding the role of FDI for their economy is more critical than ever for Thailand if it is to harness the benefits of FDI for their sustainable development.

## An ambiguous relationship between FDI and sustainable development?

Private sector activity is of considerable interest to developing countries given their increasing reliance on it as a form of funding, and this includes Thailand. From the early 1990s, over 75 per cent of developing countries' external capital flows were from private sources of funding (Reiter and Steensma, 2010). FDI is often seen as a key pathway for developing countries to achieve accelerated economic development (Sachs and McArthurs, 2005). For the purpose of this research, we have drawn on the most common international definition of FDI from the OECD (2015), which describes FDI as:

> A category of investment that reflects the objective of establishing a lasting interest by a resident enterprise in one economy (direct investor) in an enterprise (direct investment enterprise) that is resident in an economy other than that of the direct investor. The lasting interest implies the existence of a long-term relationship between the direct investor and the direct investment enterprise and a significant degree of influence on the management of the enterprise. The direct or indirect ownership of 10 percent or more of the voting power of an enterprise resident in one economy by an investor resident in another economy is evidence of such a relationship.

According to the OECD (2002, p.171), FDI is a major catalyst for economic development with the potential contributing towards both economic growth, and, in turn improved living standards: "FDI has the potential to bring social and environmental benefits to the host economy through the dissemination of good practices and technologies within [multi- national enterprises] MNEs and through their subsequent spill-overs to domestic enterprises." FDI has consistently been a major source of private capital, increasing from less than 30 per cent in the early 1990s to almost two-thirds of the total private capital by 1998 (UNCTAD, 2006, 2014). More recently in 2012, for the first time in history, FDI into developing economies was larger than that invested into developed economies.

Despite the existence of a bank of research, empirical studies on the impact of FDI on economic development are inconclusive. Relationships of FDI and measures associated with economic development like industry structure and performance (see Aitken and Harrison, 1999; Blomstrom, Lipsey and Zejan, 1994; Smarzynska, 2002); human capital [education] (see Borensztein, De Gregorio and Lee, 1998; Kucera, 2002); and, technological spill-overs (see Alvarez and Molero, 2005; Blomstrom and Sjoholm, 1999; Bwayla, 2006; Konings, 2001; Tu and Tan, 2012) support the fact that the role of FDI in development progress is unknown. Looking at relationships between FDI and economic growth (see Borensztein et al., 1998; Freckleton, Wright and Craigwell, 2012), arguably a more straight-forward method of analysis, the results still remain mixed (also see Balasubramanyam, Salisu and Sapsford, 1996; Carkovic and Levin, 2005; Feeny, Iamsiraroj and McGillivray, 2014; Mirza et al., 2004). Moreover, research that has revealed a positive correlation between FDI and Gross National Product (GNP) has mentioned nothing regarding causation (Caves, 1996).

Clearly, FDI is significant to the economies of developing countries but what in fact is its role in the economic growth and development of these countries? How does FDI impact on the sustainable development of a country where there is integration between economic prosperity, environmental quality and social justice? Given the current research focus on Thailand, the next section will focus more specifically on research within the ASEAN region of which Thailand is a key member and recipient of FDI, drawing together potential insights into this relationship.

## FDI effects in ASEAN countries

With reference to the ASEAN, Table 1.1 summarises 20 of the most widely cited studies conducted on FDI effects in ASEAN countries. Within this literature, none of these studies address FDI effects on sustainable development outcomes; the majority focus on economic measures with a handful emphasising FDI impact on a mix of environmental and social aspects. Some of the studies present positive relationships between FDI and economic measures while others show a negative relationship or no relationship at all. While there are various reports published on the topic of ASEAN FDI, there is a paucity of literature providing testable relationships between FDI and economic activity and sustainable development.

*Table 1.1* Summary of findings for studies into FDI impacts on ASEAN countries

| Author(s) | Relationship(s) | Results | Countries |
|---|---|---|---|
| Ang (2009) | FDI → Financial Systems → Economic Development | Positive: Improves economic development but only through enhanced financial systems | Thailand |
| Anwar and Nguyen (2010) | FDI → Economic Growth | Positive: Improves economic growth | Viet Nam |
| Anwar and Nguyen (2011a) | FDI → Net Exports | Positive: Increases net exports | Viet Nam |
| Anwar and Nguyen (2011b) | FDI Spill-overs → Export Performance | Positive: Improves firm export performance | Viet Nam |
| Anwar and Nguyen (2014) | FDI Spill-overs → Total Factor Productivity (TFP) | Mixed: Improves TFP in some regions, not in other regions | Viet Nam |
| Athukorala and Tien (2012) | FDI → Real Output | Positive: Improves real output | Viet Nam |
| Chandran and Tang (2013) | FDI → $CO_2$ Emissions | Positive: Does not increase $CO_2$ emissions | Malaysia, Indonesia, Singapore, Philippines, Thailand |
| Chansomphou and Ichihasi (2011) | FDI → Long-Run Income Per Capita | Negative: Has negative influence on long-run income | Lao PDR |
| Choong, Liew, Chan and Ch'ng (2011) | FDI Volatility → Economic Growth | Mixed: FDI volatility reduces economic growth | Indonesia, Malaysia, Philippines, Singapore, Thailand |
| Dang (2013) | FDI → Institutional Quality | Mixed: Improves institutional quality in some regions, not in others | Viet Nam |
| Marwah and Tavakoli (2004) | FDI → Economic Growth | Positive: Improves economic growth | Indonesia, Malaysia, Philippines, Thailand |
| Mirza et al. (2004) | FDI → Poverty Reduction | Mixed: Reduces poverty in some countries and regions, not in others | Cambodia, Malaysia, Singapore, Thailand, Viet Nam |

| Author(s) | Relationship(s) | Results | Countries |
|---|---|---|---|
| Mohamed, Singh, Singh and Liew (2013) | FDI → Economic Growth | Negative: Does not improve economic growth | Malaysia |
| Nguyen and Sun (2012) | FDI Spill-overs → Export Performance | Positive: Improves firm export performance | Viet Nam |
| Phommahaxay (2013) | FDI → Economic Growth | Mixed: Improves growth in some industries, not in others | Lao PDR |
| Reiter and Steensma (2010) | FDI → Economic Growth → Human Development | Mixed/Mainly Positive: Improves economic growth and human development in most developing countries | Developing countries |
| Sermcheep (2013) | FDI → Economic Growth | Positive: Improves economic growth | Thailand |
| Suyanto, Salim and Bloch (2009) | FDI → Productivity | Positive: FDI and related spill-overs improve productivity | Indonesia |
| Tu and Tan (2012) | FDI → Technology Spill-overs → Economic Growth | Positive: Improves technology spill-overs and economic growth; enhanced by education (human capital) | Cambodia, Lao PDR, Philippines, Singapore, Thailand, Viet Nam |
| Wogbe Agbola (2014) | FDI → Economic Growth | Positive: Improves economic growth, but is enhanced by education (human capital) | Philippines |

There were positive effects found between FDI and economic measures across many of the ASEAN countries. Some studies examined FDI's effect on various economic indicators including real output (Athukorala and Tien, 2012), export performance (Nguyen and Sun, 2012) and net exports (Anwar and Nguyen, 2011a) in Viet Nam, as well as total factor productivity in both Viet Nam (Anwar and Nguyen, 2014) and Indonesia (Suyanto et al., 2009). All of these studies found evidence of positive and significant relationships. In Thailand, levels of financial development were found to enhance the impact of FDI on output growth (Ang, 2009); and inward FDI contributed to the country's economic growth and industry development (Sermcheep, 2013).

Within the Philippines, Wogbe Agbola (2014) confirmed that FDI is a driver of economic growth but only if a minimum threshold of human capital existed. Likewise, Tu and Tan (2012) also demonstrated that human capital could maximise the presence of technological spill-overs from foreign to domestic firms across Viet Nam, Thailand, Cambodia, the Philippines, Lao PDR and Singapore. Another study into the same relationship (Choong et al., 2011) revealed that FDI volatility – rapid changes in FDI inflow – negatively influenced economic growth in Indonesia, Malaysia, the Philippines and Thailand, highlighting the mixed research findings on FDI effects. This result was supported in a study by Mohamed et al. (2013) who also found negative relationships between FDI and economic growth in a Malaysian sample and between FDI and long-run income per capita in Lao PDR.

Of the studies summarised in Table 1.1, there were four that broadened the understanding of sustainable development and examined FDI effects on non-economic measures (see Chandran and Tang, 2013; Dang, 2013; Mirza et al., 2004; Reiter and Steensma, 2010). In a study of 13 developing countries Mirza et al. (2004, p.60) found a link between FDI and poverty reduction for five ASEAN countries in their sample. The authors suggested that poverty could be alleviated through employment creation and/or human capital advancement of FDI through its impact on growth and separately through the direct effect on employment and training: ". . . an increase of FDI by 10 percent is associated on average in ASEAN with a 0.17 percent growth in income per capita of the poor" (Mirza et al., 2004, p.62).

Reiter and Steensma (2010) found that FDI had a positive effect on human development indicators (e.g. life expectancy, adult literacy rate and the Human Development Index), which was further enhanced with policies that favour domestic investors over foreign investors and when restricting activities that required foreign expertise. Furthermore, the relationship was weaker if there were high levels of corruption (Reiter and Steensma, 2010). Dang (2013) found similar results where the short-term effects of FDI on institutional quality – defined as the effectiveness of their anti corruption policies – had a positive relationship in most provinces of Viet Nam (Dang, 2013). Those that received a larger disbursement of FDI tended to have better institutional quality. These findings highlight the significance of FDI policy-intervention to align FDI with the nation's objectives and build a strong case for anti-corruption to yield the positive outcomes from FDI. Last, Chandran and Tang (2013) found no significant relationship between FDI inflow and $CO_2$ emissions when investigating the impact of the transportation sector's energy consumption and FDI on $CO_2$ emissions.

While FDI is often considered a key driver of economic growth and development in developing economies, the studies above show that the relationship between FDI and development is contentious. There is the assumption that FDI will benefit a nation's economic prosperity and its people's quality of life, and its overall sustainable development; yet, there remains a significant gap in determining the positive benefits of FDI for developing economies without sufficient evidence to support this relationship. This scenario is consistent in all countries – with the difficulty of determining what the impact of FDI is, and whether it actually retains many of the benefits assumed internationally.

## Corporate sustainability assessments: a basis for understanding and determining FDI impacts?

The inability to clearly determine the impacts of FDI on development leads to substantial challenges for investment management and government policies around sustainable development, as well as how to increase private sector engagement in support of sustainable development. With the contestable relationship between FDI and sustainable development, both in ASEAN and more broadly internationally, policy-makers are increasingly concentrating on how to not only determine, but also enhance the associated positive impacts and minimise the negative impacts. Difficulty remains in how to determine the impact of FDI and once this is achieved, how to manage this relationship for better outcomes at the community level. This presents governments an opportunity to re-evaluate their policies and regulatory framework addressing sustainability challenges.

One of the key methods of addressing sustainable development challenges at the moment is through impact assessments, including through the private sector. Impact assessments are a planning tool that enables the assessment and adjustment of business activities to address associated issues and impacts across environmental, social and economic dimensions (for example, see Arce-Gomez, Donovan and Bedggood, 2015; Lion, Donovan and Bedggood, 2013). Since the emergence of environmental impact assessment (EIA) in the 1970s, there has been a broad-based acceptance and mandate across the majority of nations across the world. EIAs are now mandated in over 191 nations, with an increasing number of nations also regulating social, health or cultural impact assessments (Morgan, 2012; Pope, Bond, Morrison-Saunders and Retief, 2013).

This trend continues to happen, with the recent report on the Investment Policy Framework for Sustainable Development (UNCTAD, 2014, p.11) highlighting "new social and environmental regulations are being introduced or existing rules reinforced – all of which has implications for investment." This is particularly through the context of growing recognition of the importance corporate responsibility and private sector codes of conduct are playing on business practices. This has been paralleled by work from experts within the impact assessment field towards the introduction of sustainability assessments to address the international focus on achieving more sustainable development, including through the use of sustainability assessments by the corporate sector.

A sustainability assessment is a method for integrating the different strands of impact assessment (across environment, economic and social dimensions) to better inform decision-making for the promotion of sustainable economic development. It does so through building upon a common procedure seen within other impact assessments, but extends this to having a broader focus on all three aspects of sustainable development – environmental, social and economic.

International experts have highlighted a range of benefits associated with the use of sustainability assessments (Bond, Morrison-Saunders and Howitt, 2012; Pope et al., 2013). Sustainability assessments are a key method for addressing sustainable development in business operations and are largely voluntary and private sector driven – rather than a traditional part of the regulatory context for impact assessments (such as with EIAs or SIAs).

This research specifically engages with this topic, seeking to examine the sustainability practices implemented by leading MNEs in Thailand, through a sustainability assessment methodology. In doing so, this research will shed light on the important relationship between FDI and sustainable development, clarifying not only the role of FDI in sustainable development, but also the methods in which the private sector engages with sustainability. In identifying a method from which to better understand and determine private sector activities with regards to sustainability, this research will open up avenues in which future studies may better determine the impact of FDI on sustainable development.

Through this research focus, the private sector may not only be better equipped with an understanding on the processes in which to address sustainability (particularly when examining World Class practices being utilised), but also those methods that lead to greater impact drawing from current best practices. This will also provide pathways for greater public sector understanding of the role of FDI in sustainable development, identifying those methods beyond regulatory requirements that the private sector uses to address sustainable development, and areas where the private sector can further improve their performance.

As identified earlier, investment policies and regulations play an important role in ensuring that there are in fact positive benefits realised from inward FDI for local economic and sustainable development. With a greater understanding of current practices, and particularly best practices, the public sector will be better placed to implement supportive policies and regulations to see this relationship between FDI and sustainable development achieved. This research presents a significant step forward from existing research in this field, which has tended to be ad-hoc, focusing on individual cases, with a narrow examination of the sustainability assessment framework. One of the most recent efforts by the leading researchers in this field – Bond et al. (2012) – presented one of the first key insights towards engaging further with a private sector perspective (and at the proponent and project level), however, this was limited to examining only one empirical case detailing the private sector use of sustainability assessments.

Other studies at the project level – as opposed to the significant and growing number of studies that have examined policies and programs – have been limited to taking a public sector or government led perspective. This includes the studies by Pope, Morrison-Saunders and Annandale (2005), and Duncan and Hay (2007), who have explored the use of assessments at the project level within major government projects. Perhaps the most significant of these studies was undertaken by Pope et al. (2005). In their study, they examined the use and role of assessments in the Gorgon Gas Development in Australia. In this particular case, an assessment was used to support the selection of locations for the development, including the infrastructure required. While this study is comprehensive and illuminates various insights into how assessments are utilised (including the use of internal sustainability assessments and the different interpretations of sustainability criteria held amongst stakeholders), the research did not intend to form a basis for private sector use of sustainability assessments.

This research thus presents an interesting and highly topical area attracting significant global attention, that has received scant empirical research of the role and impact of FDI on sustainable development. This positions this work as a substantial step forward in contributing to the current understanding of systematic efforts by the private sector, and specifically multinationals engaging in FDI, in addressing sustainability and sustainable development as part of their business activities. To our knowledge, this research will be the first multi-case study and most substantial contribution towards understanding how the private sector integrates sustainability practices through the lens of a sustainability assessment.

## The evidence base: an overview of the MNEs involved in this research

Before concluding this chapter with a review of the structure of the forthcoming chapters, it is worthwhile to first briefly discuss the sample that was the basis of this research. The Thailand sample of foreign MNEs that forms the basis for the evaluation of sustainability practices is comprised of 23 organisations. In total, 57 organisations were approached for interviews at both the subsidiary (located in Thailand) and headquarter (their home country of operations, and where the investment originated from) operations. Forty-six organisations were interviewed at either the subsidiary or headquarter level, which was further refined down to 29 organisations where we had substantive data necessary to make interpretations about their performance. Only 23 organisations are presented here, reflecting the preference of six organisations not to be included in the results of the interviews (either through restrictions on confidentiality and reporting, or failure to confirm the use of data from interviews for the purpose of this research book). Furthermore, the identity of our sample has been treated with the utmost of confidentiality. In compiling our analyses for Chapters 3, 4 and 5 we have removed levels of detail relating to organisation such as positions, types of business and size, market types to ensure that the MNEs in our sample remain de-identifiable. We have also endeavoured to remove particulars around specific issues and impacts within the sustainability practices of these organisations to ensure their anonymity whilst not losing the meaning or detail behind their activities.

Of the 23 organisations that are involved in this specific sample presented in this research, 74 per cent are considered large by international standards, with over USD$100 million invested in Thailand. The remaining 26 per cent are considered within the Small to Medium Enterprise (SME) category, with roughly half being small (below USD$10 million investment). These organisations' headquarter operations are based in countries that are all in the top ten FDI sources for ASEAN, including 30 per cent from North East Asia (Japan) and Australasia (Australia), 13 per cent from North America (USA), 17 per cent from Europe (France, Switzerland, Germany) and 8 per cent from South Asia and ASEAN (India and Singapore). The spread of the sectors also reflects the dominance of manufacturing FDI in Thailand, with approximately 70 per cent of organisations in this sector. The remaining is split between services (23 per cent) and mining (5 per cent). Due to the limited sample of mining organisations, with only one organisation involved, this is not included in a specific case study chapter. It is, however, indicated in the baseline analysis of the overall performance of MNEs in addressing sustainable development in Thailand.

## The structure of this book

From this point, Chapter 2 will move on to examining the role of FDI in Thailand more specifically. This involves contextualising the amount of FDI entering into the region, the relative flows of FDI into Thailand and the comparative flows of Thailand verses other countries within the region. Following this, a review of existing and available panel data is provided, contextualising important and possible trends between FDI and development indicators. This further elaborates the compelling need for a better method to determine the impact of FDI on sustainable development, demonstrating the difficulties of showing relational links between FDI and development indicators.

In Chapter 3, a detailed review is provided of the existing research that has been undertaken on sustainability assessments, and this is integrated within our proposed conceptual framework on corporate sustainability assessments, drawing on leading research (and particularly theoretical work) within the impact assessment field. This presents both a basis that was utilised for framing the research and data collection, as well as providing an informative chapter for practitioners on the state of the art in sustainability assessment knowledge. This provides a compelling basis from which to understand how the private sector might, and can, address sustainability in their business operations. At the concluding section of this chapter, a brief overview is provided of the methods used for their research as well as some more detailed information on the sample used.

Building from this point, in Chapter 4, we proceed to the analysis of the data collected. Here a broad overview is provided of the sustainability performance of the multinational enterprises within the sample. This enables an overall benchmark to be developed, showing the distribution of MNE practices across World Class, International Practices, Host Country Compliance and Non-disclosure categories. In doing so, this evaluation highlights the general practices evident across the sustainability framework. The findings indicate a substantial proportion of MNEs are engaging with World Class practices, involving cutting-edge methods, to address sustainability – extending beyond anticipations that a regulatory or compliance focus might be evident. In fact, the vast majority of the organisations in the study, and particularly for the first six steps of the sustainability assessment framework, demonstrate a common tendency to exceed government requirements for their sustainability practices.

The subsequent two chapters provide an assessment of the sustainability practices of MNEs operating in Thailand across the manufacturing and service sectors. This provides the first detailed insights, through a large sample of case studies, on the types of sustainability practices being adopted by the private sector. Results indicate, particularly for the manufacturing sector, a heavy reliance on International Practices to inform the types and extent of activities undertaken by the private sector to address sustainability. A significant sample of manufacturing organisations also provides insights into World Class practices, drawing from global guidelines and standards, to frame how they engage with local communities and stakeholders to have a positive impact on local sustainable development. The service sector, on the other hand, shows a significant percentage of organisations are not fully engaging with sustainability in their practices. This may be through a lack of information collected through our study, or an unwillingness to reveal their practices. However, the results of this research are troubling for the transparency and likely adoption of sustainability practices within the sector. Nevertheless, Chapter 6 provides some insights into World Class practices that are adopted, including the different tools and techniques to achieve this.

Chapter 7 presents a discussion and conclusion of the results, including the presentation of the key World Class practices evident across our sample of organisations. This includes the provision of a synopsis of the key methods, tools and techniques being used, providing important practical insights into corporate sustainability assessments. This chapter concludes with potential avenues of future research for scholars in this field, to direct and open opportunities to better inform the understanding of the role of FDI in sustainable development.

## References

Aitken, B. J., and Harrison, A. E. (1999). Do domestic firms benefit from direct foreign investment? Evidence from Venezuela. *The American Economic Review*, *89*(3), 605–618.

Alvarez, I., and Molero, J. (2005). Technology and the generation of international knowledge spillovers: An application to Spanish manufacturing firms. *Research Policy*, *34*, 1440–1452.

Ang, J. B. (2009). Foreign direct investment and its impact on the Thai economy: The role of financial development. *Journal of Economics and Finance*, *33*(3), 316–323.

Anwar, S., and Nguyen, L. P. (2010). Foreign direct investment and economic growth in Vietnam. *Asia Pacific Business Review*, *16*, 183–202.

Anwar, S., and Nguyen, L. P. (2011a). Foreign direct investment and trade: The case of Vietnam. *Research in International Business and Finance*, *25*(1), 39–52.

Anwar, S., and Nguyen, L. P. (2011b). Foreign direct investment and export spillovers: Evidence from Vietnam. *International Business Review*, *20*, 177–193.

Anwar, S., and Nguyen, L. P. (2014). Is foreign direct investment productive? A case study of the regions of Vietnam. *Journal of Business Research, 67*(7), 1376–1387.

Arce-Gomez, A., Donovan, J. D., and Bedggood, R. E. (2015). Social impact assessments: Developing a consolidated conceptual framework. *Environmental Impact Assessment Review, 50,* 85–94.

ASEAN. (2012). ASEAN Economic Community Blueprint, cited from: http://www.asean.org/wp-content/uploads/archive/5187-10.pdf

Athukorala, P., and Tien, T. Q. (2012). Foreign direct investment in industrial transition: The experience of Vietnam. *Journal of the Asia Pacific Economy, 17*(3), 446–463.

Balasubramanyam, V. N., Salisu, M., and Sapsford, D. (1996). Foreign direct investment and growth in EP and IS countries. *Economic Journal, 106*(434), 92–105.

Blomstrom, M., Lipsey, R. E., and Zejan, M. (1994). What explains the growth of developing countries. In W. Baumol, R. Nelson, and E. Wolff (Eds.), *Convergence and productivity: Cross national studies and historical evidence.* Oxford: Oxford University Press, 243–262.

Blomstrom, M., and Sjoholm, F. (1999). Technology transfer and spillovers: Does local participation with multinationals matter? *European Economic Review, 43*(4–6), 915–923.

Bond, A. J., Morrison-Saunders, A., and Howitt, R. (2012). *Sustainability assessment: Pluralism, practice and progress.* London: Routledge.

Borensztein, E., De Gregorio, J., and Lee, J.-W. (1998). How does foreign direct investment affect economic growth? *Journal of International Economics, 45*(1), 115–135.

Bwayla, S. M. (2006). Foreign direct investment and technology spillovers: Evidence from panel data analysis of manufacturing firms in Zambia. *Journal of Development Economics, 81,* 514–526.

Carkovic, M., and Levine, R. (2005). Does foreign direct investment accelerate economic growth? In T. H. Moran, E. M. Graham, and M. Blomstrom (Eds.), *Does foreign direct investment promote development.* Washington, DC: Center for Global Development, 195-220.

Caves, R. E. (1996). *Multinational enterprise and economic analysis* (2nd ed.). Cambridge: Cambridge University Press.

Chandran, V. G. R., and Tang, C. F. (2013). The impacts of transport energy consumption, foreign direct investment and income on $CO_2$ emissions in ASEAN-5 economies. *Renewable and Sustainable Energy Reviews, 24,* 445–453.

Chansomphou, V., and Ichihashi, M. (2011). *Foreign aid, foreign direct investment and economic growth of Lao PDR* (No. 1–2). Hiroshima: Hiroshima University, Graduate School for International Development and Cooperation (IDEC). Hiroshima

Choong, C. K., Liew, V. K. S., Chan, S. G., and Ch'ng, H. K. (2011). Foreign direct investment volatility and economic growth in ASEAN-five countries. *International Journal of Academic Research, 3*(4), 221–224.

Dang, D. A. (2013). How foreign direct investment promote institutional quality: Evidence from Vietnam. *Journal of Comparative Economics, 41*(4), 1054–1072.

Duncan, R., and Hay, P. (2007). A question of balance in integrated impact assessment: Negotiating away the environmental interest in Australia's Basslink project. *Journal of Environmental Assessment Policy and Management, 9*(3), 273–297.

Feeny, S., Iamsiraroj, S., and McGillivray, M. (2014). Growth and foreign direct investment in the Pacific Island countries. *Economic Modelling, 37,* 332–339.

Freckleton, M., Wright, A., and Craigwell, R. (2012). Economic growth, foreign direct investment and corruption in developed and developing countries. *Journal of Economic Studies*, *39*(6), 639–652.

International Institute for Sustainable Development. (1992). *Business strategy for sustainable development: Leadership and accountability for the '90s*, International Institute for Sustainable Development, Canada.

Konings, J. (2001). The effects of foreign direct investment on domestic firms. *Economics of Transition*, *9*(3), 619–633.

Kosack, S., and Tobin, J. (2006). Funding self-sustaining development: The role of Aid, FDI and government in economic success. *International Organization*, *60*(1), 205–243.

Kucera, D. (2002). Core labour standards and foreign direct investment. *International Labour Review*, *141*(1/2), 31–69.

Lion, H., Donovan, J. D., and Bedggood, R. E. (2013). Environmental impact assessments from a business perspective: Extending knowledge and guiding business practice. *Journal of Business Ethics*, *117*(4), 789–805.

Marwah, K., and Tavakoli, A. (2004). The effect of foreign capital and imports on economic growth: Further evidence from four Asian countries (1970–1998). *Journal of Asian Economics*, *15*(2), 399–413.

Mirza, H., Giroud, A., Jalilian, H., Weiss, J., Freeman, N., and Than, M. (2004). *Regionalisation, foreign direct investment and poverty reduction: The case of ASEAN*. Bradford: University of Bradford, School of Management.

Mohamed, M. R., Singh, J., Singh, K., and Liew, C. Y. (2013). Impact of foreign direct investment and domestic investment on economic growth of Malaysia. *Malaysian Journal of Economic Studies*, *50*(1), 21–35.

Morgan, R. K. (2012). Environmental impact assessment: The state of the art. *Impact Assessment and Project Appraisal*, *30*(1), 5–14.

Nguyen, D. T. H., and Sun, S. (2012). FDI and domestic firms' export behaviour: Evidence from Vietnam. *Economic Papers*, *31*(3), 380–390.

OECD. (2002). *Foreign direct investment for development: Maximising benefits, minimising costs*, OECD Publications Service, France.

Phommahaxay, A. (2013). *Impact of FDI on economic growth of Lao PDR*, Research Working Paper Series, No. 9, Mekong Institute, Lao PDR.

Pope, J., Bond, A., Morrison-Saunders, A., and Retief, F. (2013). Advancing the theory and practice of impact assessment: Setting the research agenda. *Environmental Impact Assessment Review*, *41*, 1–9.

Pope, J., Morrison-Saunders, A., and Annandale, D. (2005). Applying sustainability assessment models. *Impact Assessment and Project Appraisal*, *23*(4), 293–302.

Ranis, G., and Stewart, F. (2000). Strategies for success in human development. *Journal of Human Development*, *1*(1), 49–69.

Reiter, S. L., and Steensma, H. K. (2010). Human development and foreign direct investment in developing countries: The influence of FDI policy and corruption. *World Development*, *38*(12), 1678–1691.

Sachs, J., and McArthur, J. (2005). The millennium project: A plan for meeting the millennium development goals. *The Lancet*, *365*, 347–353.

Sermcheep, S. (2013). *Foreign direct investment and economic growth: The case of Thailand's inward and outward FDI*, Faculty of Economics, Chulalongkorn University, Pathumwan, Bangkok.

Smarzynska, B. (2002). *Does foreign direct investment increase the productivity of domestic firms? In search of spillovers through backward linkages,* World Bank Policy Research Working Paper Series, No. 2923.

Suyanto, S., Salim, R. A., and Bloch, H. (2009). Does foreign direct investment lead to productivity spillovers? Firm level evidence from Indonesia. *World Development, 37,* 1861–1876.

Tu, Y., and Tan, X. (2012). Technology spillovers of FDI in ASEAN sourcing from local and abroad. *China Finance Review International, 2*(1), 78–94.

United Nations. (2012). Report of the United Nations Conference on Sustainable Development, cited from: http://www.uncsd2012.org/content/documents/814UNCSD%20REPORT%20final%20revs.pdf

United Nations Conference on Trade and Development (UNCTAD). (2006). *World investment report: FDI from developing and transition economies: Implications for development (No. WIR06),* United Nations, New York and Geneva.

United Nations Conference on Trade and Development (UNCTAD). (2012). *World investment report: Towards a new generation of investment policies (No. WIR2012),* United Nations, New York and Geneva.

United Nations Conference on Trade and Development (UNCTAD). (2014). *World investment report: Investing in the SDGs: An action plan (No. WIR14),* United Nations, New York and Geneva.

United Nations Conference on Trade and Development (UNCTAD). (2015). Investment Policy Framework for Sustainability Development, cited from: http://investmentpolicyhub.unctad.org/Upload/Documents/INVESTMENT%20POLICY%20FRAMEWORK%202015%20WEB_VERSION.pdf

Wogbe Agbola, F. (2014). Modelling the impact of foreign direct investment and human capital on economic growth: Empirical evidence from the Philippines. *Journal of the Asia Pacific Economy, 19*(2), 272–289.

World Business Council on Sustainable Development. (2001). *The business case for sustainable development: Making a difference toward the Johannesburg Summit 2002 and beyond.* WBCSD, Geneva.

# 2 FDI and development in Thailand

*Cheree Topple, Hermann Lion,
Vedran Vranic, Eryadi K. Masli
and Jerome D. Donovan*

This chapter will examine the role of foreign direct investment (FDI) in Thailand. Before beginning an examination of potential relationships between FDI and development within Thailand, it is first useful to look at the broader dynamics of FDI within the region relative to other countries and regions globally. This provides a broader context of the importance of FDI within the Association of South East Asian Nations (ASEAN), as well as relative competitiveness of FDI inflows internationally. It also provides some insight into potential areas where a focus should be given on the regional dynamics for FDI flows. Following this, a review of existing and available panel data is provided, which contextualises important and possible trends between FDI and development indicators for Thailand. This further elaborates the compelling need for a better method to determine the impact of FDI on sustainable development, demonstrating the difficulties of showing causal or relational links between FDI and development indicators.

## FDI trends of major recipient groups worldwide

The total size of FDI in Figure 2.1 shows that investment into Developed Economies has been volatile from 1990 to 2013. Despite a rapid decline between 2008 and 2009 – a likely result of the global financial crisis and slower global economic growth – Developed Economies was the highest recipient region of FDI up until 2012 where it was overtaken by Developing Economies. The latter region has shown steady growth even during 2011 where FDI had dropped considerably in other regions other than the ASEAN. This steady growth indicates that more money, foreign expertise and technology are potentially beginning to reach developing nations, including within the ASEAN group.

Looking more specifically within Asia, the amount of FDI received for the ASEAN region is considerably more than India (apart from the decline around the time of the global financial crisis) and has recently caught up with investments in China and is encroaching on similar investments made to the United States and the European Union (EU-28). These investments no doubt show the burgeoning interest in the ASEAN as recipients of FDI over the last decade or more. These trends also provide encouraging signs of the potential for FDI to impact positively upon the sustainable development of ASEAN countries, and it further reinforces

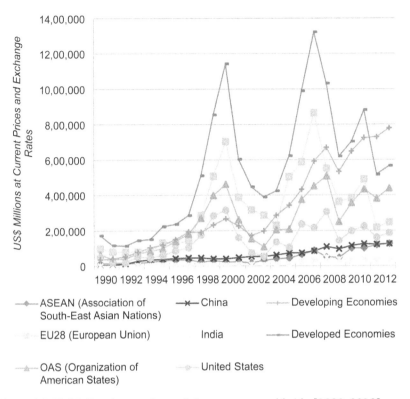

*Figure 2.1* FDI inflow into major recipient groups worldwide [1990–2013]
Source: UNCTAD 2016.

the need for a greater understanding of the associated outcomes of such investments.

Figure 2.2 provides greater context about FDI impacts on development through consideration of each recipient group's total FDI size and population. Since 2012, the results show based on total size (from Figure 2.1) that the Developing Economies receive the most investment; however, when examined on a per capita basis, Developing Economies falls from the top five recipients. In Figure 2.1, the total size of FDI into the ASEAN group was only a fraction of what was invested in the overall Developing Economies. However, when analysed based on population (per capita), as can be seen in Figure 2.2, the amount of FDI is in fact greater in ASEAN than the Developing Economies and has been since 1990. This means that there is more FDI flowing into the ASEAN per capita than all of the Developing Economies combined.

Based on this analysis, FDI in the ASEAN appears a more attractive invest-ment option than investing in other members of Developing Economies. Par-ticularly after the global financial crisis of 2008/2009, the FDI inflows into ASEAN have been steadily increasing, while China experienced slower growth

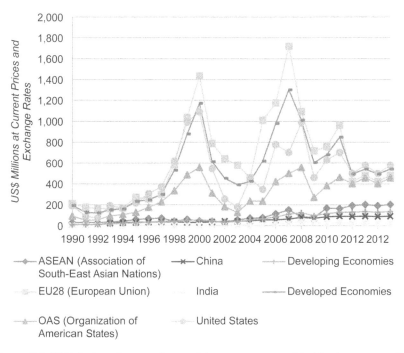

*Figure 2.2* FDI inflow into major recipient groups worldwide (as per capita) [1990–2013]
Source: UNCTAD 2016.

of FDI inflow and India was stagnant. Around 2011, yet another global financial crisis, and declining FDI in Developed Economies, the United States and the EU-28 according to total size (Figure 2.1) and per capita (Figure 2.2). Looking in more detail, Figure 2.2 shows a rather sharp drop in FDI per capita for the EU-28, the United States and the Developed Economies, which contrasts with a steady increase for the ASEAN region. The inverse trends highlight a potential relationship between the former recipient groups and the ASEAN indicating the increased attractiveness of FDI in the ASEAN compared to other regions.

Comparing major FDI recipient groups by percentage of gross domestic product (GDP), Figure 2.3 illustrates that since 2003, the largest recipient group in the world is the ASEAN region rising from 4 per cent of GDP in 2003 to 6.5 per cent in 2007 and then levelling out to just over 5 per cent in 2013. This is a healthy recovery after dropping to 3 per cent in 2008 during the global financial crisis. This highlights that although the total size of FDI in Figure 2.1 and the size of FDI per capita in Figure 2.2 are significantly smaller for the ASEAN comparatively with the United States, Organization of American State (OAS), EU-28 and the Developed Economies, it is considerably larger for the ASEAN in terms of its contribution to the economy.

This means that as a percentage of all the goods and services produced, the role of FDI in the ASEAN is most significant compared to other recipient groups worldwide. Since FDI involves a considerable degree of management control, this further highlights the influence of not only foreign money, but also foreign expertise and technology, in significantly contributing to the total production of goods and services within the ASEAN. It appears that FDI in the ASEAN is likely to have a larger impact on the proportion of goods and services produced therein.

Another point of interest relates to Figure 2.2 when looking at the size of FDI per capita, which is the highest for the United States, Developed Economies and the EU-28. What we can see in Figure 2.3 however is the inverse relationship where some of the smallest recipient groups of FDI – based on GDP – are those same three groups. This means that although the amount of FDI inflow per person is highest for the United States, Developed Economies and the EU-28, when compared to their large economies (as a percentage of GDP), it is in fact not a significant amount of FDI inflow. This contrasts directly to the case of ASEAN countries, where rather than receiving a high FDI inflow per person, the FDI inflow received is highly significant compared to the size of their economy.

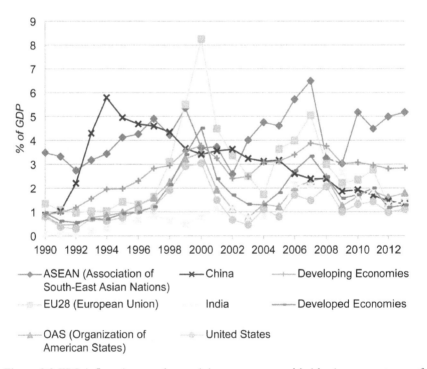

*Figure 2.3* FDI inflow into major recipient groups worldwide (as percentage of GDP) [1990–2013]

Source: UNCTAD 2016.

## FDI trends for ASEAN countries

Looking more specifically at the countries that comprise the ASEAN group, Figure 2.4 shows that the compound annual growth rate between 1990 and 2013 is highest for Cambodia at 67 per cent, followed by Brunei at 23 per cent, Lao PDR and Viet Nam at 18 per cent and finally Indonesia at 13 per cent. Second, we observe that in terms of the total size of FDI inflow, Singapore receives the largest amount of USD$539,000 million, followed by Malaysia at USD$133,783 million, Thailand at USD$133,502 million and Indonesia at USD$120,800 million.

On first glance, it appears that FDI inflow is growing faster in the ASEAN countries that receive less of it. Cambodia, Brunei and Lao PDR receive the smallest sums of FDI inflow in the ASEAN yet have the fastest growth over this period. Looking more closely, Lao PDR and Viet Nam have had the most significant compound annual growth rate of FDI, at 18 per cent. Although they have similar growth rates, Viet Nam, has received USD$81,728 million in FDI and has continued to attract FDI at the same rate as Lao PDR, which has only received USD$2,772 million. While this growth rate is a promising sign for Lao PDR and the future of FDI inflow into Lao PDR, it also highlights that Viet Nam has performed exceptionally well at attracting large amounts of FDI at a fast-growing rate. This is likely a result of the Doi Moi policy introduced in 1986, which encouraged open-door policies to attract foreign investment.

Of further interest are the comparisons between Thailand and Indonesia. While the latter has received USD$120,800 million and the former USD$133,502

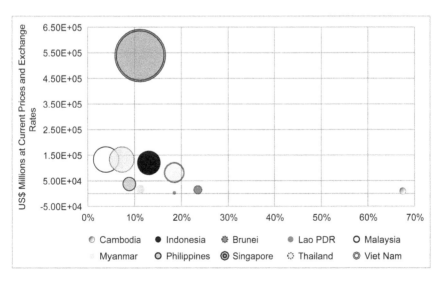

*Figure 2.4* FDI inflow into ASEAN region, by size and compound annual growth rate (US millions at current prices and exchange rates) [1990–2013]

Source: UNCTAD 2016.

million, Indonesia has performed better overall (a 13 per cent compound annual growth rate, compared to only 7 per cent in Thailand). These figures suggest that Indonesia has been the most effective at attracting FDI at an increasing rate between 1990 and 2013 (particularly in the later part of the 2000s), followed closely by Viet Nam.

Clearly, Singapore, Indonesia and Viet Nam have been the biggest winners in the ASEAN, enjoying both a steady growth rate and size of FDI inflow. Other countries in the ASEAN group thus stand to benefit from the examples of Indonesia, Viet Nam and Singapore. Whether that concerns particular regulatory, cultural or resource-related factors, remains unclear. It nevertheless provides an interesting question for what is effective in attracting FDI within the region.

Figure 2.5 looks at the size of FDI inflows into ASEAN from dialogue partners between 2005 and 2013. Over this period, FDI inflows into ASEAN have steadily increased other than the sudden drops in 2008/2009 with the global financial crisis. With recovery time extending into 2010, there is strong investment in the region from 2011. Excluding the contributions from the Rest of the World, the EU has consistently been the largest FDI contributor over this period, except in 2012 when Japan contributed USD$5,692 million more.

In fact, Japan is the next biggest contributor after the EU with strong investment over 2012/2013. Japan is followed closely by the United States and then China, who over more recent times, are catching up to the lead contributors. The increasing levels of FDI from Japan, the United States and China questions the ASEAN's reliance on the EU as a major source of FDI with the recent growing interest from these countries. This fact points to the potential importance

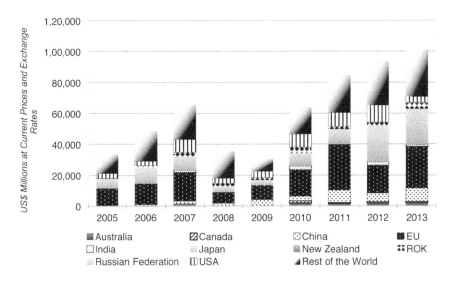

*Figure 2.5* Size of FDI inflow from dialogue partners into ASEAN (US millions at current prices and exchange rates) [2005–2013]

Source: ASEANstats 2016a.

of an understanding of particular practices of MNEs from these countries as key contributors to FDI inflows in the ASEAN region.

Of further interest are some of the smaller dialogue partner contributors – Australia, Canada, India, New Zealand, Russia and the Republic of Korea. When combined, these countries collectively contribute more than any other single country in the world. Likewise, these findings suggest an understanding of the practices in these countries is also important when profiling FDI impacts within the region.

Looking more closely at the recipients of the FDI inflows from these dialogue partners, Figure 2.6 illustrates the distribution of FDI inflows across the ASEAN countries. The biggest stand-out recipient within the ASEAN region is Singapore, receiving an exceptional level of investment between USD$50,000 and USD$60,000 million post-2010. These sums are highly disproportionate compared to other ASEAN countries.

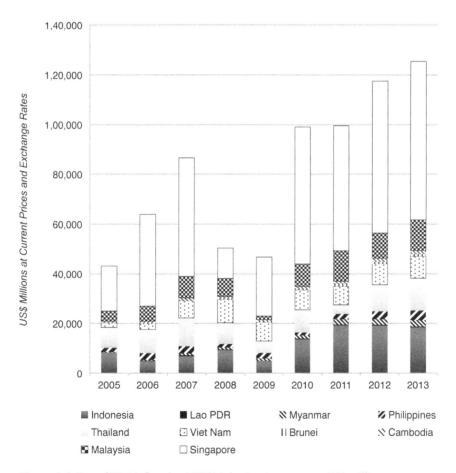

*Figure 2.6* Size of FDI inflow by ASEAN destination country (US millions at current prices and exchange rates) [2005–2013]

Source: ASEANstats 2016b.

Indonesia receives the second largest amount of investment at a range between USD$13,000 to USD$19,000 million over the same four-year period. Of particular interest was that the investment landscape was more proportionately distributed during the global financial crisis (2008/2009), which indicates the impact on the three largest contributors during this period: the EU, Japan and the United States. Accordingly, this also illustrates that the EU, Japan and the United States have also significantly invested in Singapore.

By comparison, FDI inflows from dialogue partners into Brunei, Cambodia and Lao PDR is relatively small compared to Singapore and Indonesia. In contrast to the other ASEAN countries, Figure 2.6 highlights that these three countries are small recipients of FDI.

Further examination of Figure 2.6 shows that the share of FDI into Malaysia, Viet Nam and Thailand has remained relatively consistent over the period between 2005 and 2013, while the share of FDI into the Philippines and Indonesia has fluctuated more. These fluctuations, however, appear to be more settled with increasing investment for both the Philippines and Indonesia after the global financial crisis of 2008/2009. Since 2010, FDI into Myanmar also appears to be steadily rising.

With the limited data available from the ASEAN Secretariat, Figure 2.7 demonstrates broadly the proportions of FDI flowing to specific ASEAN industries between 2005 and 2010. Unfortunately, the limitations do not provide any insight on investments into specific industries after the financial crisis.

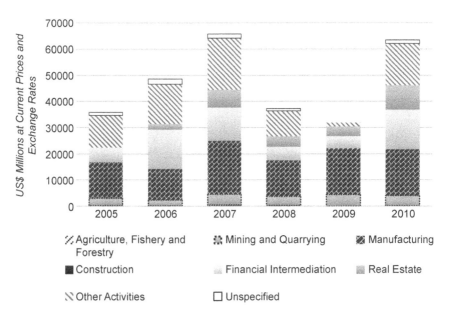

*Figure 2.7* Size of FDI inflow by ASEAN destination industry (US millions at current prices and exchange rates) [2005–2010]

Source: ASEANstats 2016c.

Reflecting multinationals' reliance on cheap labour within Manufacturing, this industry has seen the largest FDI inflows between 2005 and 2010. Manufacturing has experienced strong and relatively consistent investment even during the financial crisis, which reflects the stability of the industry within ASEAN countries. Unlike the certainty that surrounds the Manufacturing industry, it is somewhat more challenging to make inferences about further industries especially when the timeframe splits across pre- and post-financial crisis. With 'Other Activities' put aside, the Manufacturing industry is followed by Financial Intermediation, Real Estate, and Mining and Quarrying; respectively.

The data for the Financial Intermediation and Real Estate industries shows that the share of FDI into these industries has fluctuated more than with Manufacturing. However, the Mining and Quarrying industry appears to be more consistent, in terms of the amounts they have received over this five-year period (particularly from 2007). Like Manufacturing, this is an industry that has fared well over the financial crisis and perhaps also reflects a more stable environment in the ASEAN. As indicated by the large size of 'Other Activities' and the limited time-range it would be highly beneficial for policy-makers and decision-makers if additional data were collected on ASEAN FDI destination industries. Little can be inferred from such a limited data range, but it is still worth highlighting the disproportionately large FDI inflows into ASEAN Manufacturing and the potential importance of focusing on this sector in order for development impacts to reflect its significance in overall FDI inflow.

Data available from the ASEAN Secretariat in Figure 2.8 shows that there is clear progress in the quality of FDI-related policies and regulations for many of the ASEAN countries. Over this six-year period, Singapore is the outright top performer, consistently scoring higher on this index than any other country. Singapore's FDI-friendly policies – rating 7.9 in 2010 – have attracted disproportionately large amounts of FDI, captured in Figure 2.6 having received USD$55,076 million in 2010. This highlights the potential relationship between governing bodies, guidelines and regulations for attracting greater FDI. Of particular interest was that the most significant progress has been made by Lao PDR, moving from a 0.4 rating in 2005 to a 2.5 rating in 2010.

Another noticeable observation is across 2008 and 2009, during the global financial crisis, where, unsurprisingly, FDI attractiveness dropped for all ASEAN countries. Other than this dip, the quality of FDI- related policies has improved for many of the ASEAN countries, however, there has been a regression for Indonesia, the Philippines and Thailand during this period. FDI attractiveness has remained below average (below 1) for the Philippines and Indonesia since 2006.

Of all the countries, it is somewhat unexpected that Indonesia and Thailand are not making substantive progress, especially when considering their total FDI inflow size and rate of FDI inflow growth (refer to Figures 2.4 and 2.5) between 1990 and 2013. As noted earlier, Thailand and Indonesia were in the top four for attracting FDI with the former receiving USD$120,800 million and the latter USD$133,502 million. Indonesia was perceived to be more effective at attracting FDI (13 per cent compound annual growth rate compared to only

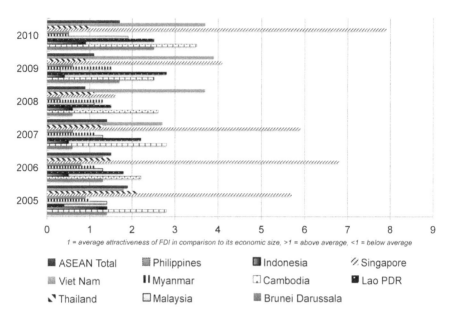

*Figure 2.8* Performance index for FDI attractiveness by ASEAN country [2005–2010]
Source: UNCTAD 2016.

7 per cent in Thailand). Thailand, from 2005 to 2010, experienced a period of political instability that could potentially relate to the country's poor outcomes relating to their FDI policy and regulation evaluation and may partly impact on the country's capacity to attract this investment.

## FDI inflow trends of ASEAN–10 countries

This next section looks at FDI in the ASEAN region. Figures 2.9 to 2.12 present two graphs to help capture the detail for each country as some results are quite extreme. Looking at the total FDI into ASEAN-10 countries (Figure 2.9), it is clearly evident that Singapore has received considerable investment between 1990 and 2013; disproportionately to other ASEAN-10 countries. Other than in the years of 1992, 1993 and 1998, Singapore has been the largest recipient of FDI in the ASEAN region. Malaysia, Indonesia and Thailand – the next of the largest FDI recipients – have experienced rapid fluctuations of inflow.

In a study conducted across Indonesia, Malaysia, the Philippines and Thailand this type of FDI inflow volatility was previously associated with poor economic outcomes of FDI inflow (see Choong, Liew, Chan and Ch'ng 2011). Between 1998 and 2003, repatriation of funds in Indonesia resulted in the only negative FDI figures, resulting in an FDI outflow of USD$4,550 million in 2000 and later climbing dramatically to USD$19,241 million in 2011.

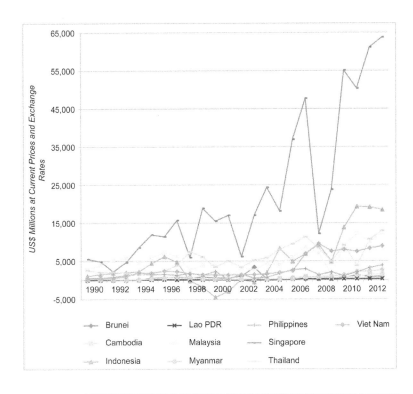

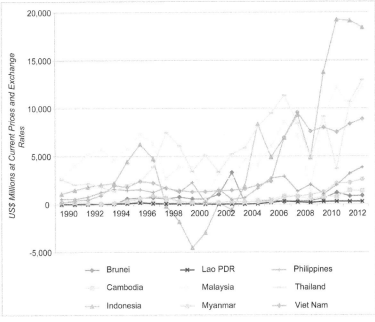

*Figure 2.9* FDI inflow into ASEAN-10 countries [1990–2013]
Source: UNCTAD 2016.

The Philippines and Viet Nam experienced generally consistent FDI inflows across this period; however, Viet Nam received a substantial increase from 2006 and caught up to Indonesia and Thailand during the GFC in 2008, to become the fifth largest recipient. In terms of total size of FDI inflow, Brunei follows the Philippines with steady investment over 1990 to 2012 and then Myanmar with rising FDI inflows.

Cambodia and Lao PDR both significantly lag behind their ASEAN neighbours with a comparatively low and flat trend-line. Although these countries receive significantly less FDI, they have had more predictable and stable inflows over this period. This suggests that in the ASEAN-10 larger recipients of FDI also experience greater year-to-year volatility in their inflows, and highlights a need for a more considered approach to addressing FDI-related policies that encourage stability, as well as an examination of institutional structures that ensure the directed use of resulting revenues (profit repatriation). The following figure (Figure 2.10) examines the FDI inflow from the perspective of per capita comparisons to account for population difference and impact.

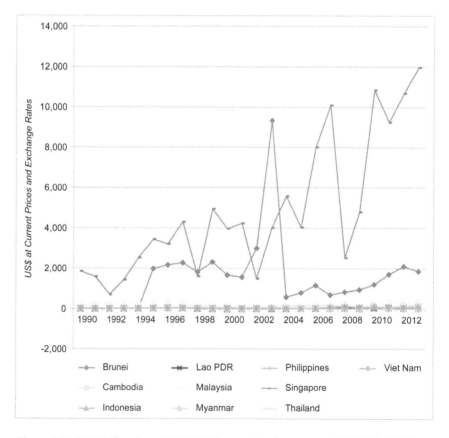

*Figure 2.10* FDI inflow into ASEAN-10 countries (as per capita) [1990–2013]
Source: UNCTAD 2016.

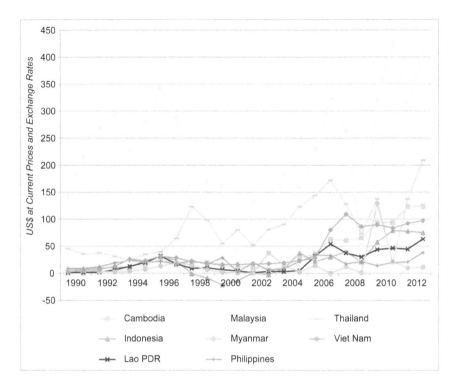

*Figure 2.10* (Continued)
Source: UNCTAD 2016.

The first key observation from Figure 2.10 is the disproportionate distribution of FDI inflows per capita for Singapore and Brunei compared to other ASEAN-10 countries between 1993 and 2013. Like previous figures focusing on FDI inflows, Singapore again has experienced substantial FDI investments, dipping sharply with the GFC of 2008 yet recovering quickly in 2010. Brunei's inflows peaked sharply in 2003 at USD$9,326 per capita and then fell dramatically in 2004 to USD$570.

Outside of these outliers, Malaysia is the stand-out recipient, averaging around USD$227 per capita, (after peaking around 2011 at USD$424). Thailand averages out around USD$85 per capita. Viet Nam and Cambodia then follow, at around USD$40 per capita for Viet Nam and USD$35 per capita. This means that, of the ASEAN-10, the most FDI inflow per-person living in these countries is Singapore, Brunei, Malaysia, Thailand, Viet Nam and Cambodia. Indonesia, Lao PDR, the Philippines and Myanmar's per capita inflows have remained relatively equal over this period, averaging around USD$20 per-person, although the year-to-year fluctuations between them have varied greatly.

The remaining observations from Figure 2.10 relate to the difference between the size of FDI inflow in Figure 2.9 and the size of FDI inflow per capita in

Figure 2.10. Clearly, the size of FDI inflow for Singapore still translates for this country as the largest recipient when considered on a per capita basis. Likewise, Malaysia is still considered one of the larger recipients of FDI inflows when factoring in their population. However, the biggest differences lie in looking at Brunei and Indonesia. First, on a per capita basis, Brunei figures particularly well in terms of FDI investments compared to overall size. On the other hand, Indonesia – a large recipient of total size of FDI inflow (Figure 2.9) – is perceived poorly for FDI investments when factoring in population.

This suggests two things. First, Brunei's FDI inflow has not been as insignificant as it appeared in Figure 2.9 but has rather been fairly well-proportioned to the number of people living there. This is a good sign, indicating that foreign investors are distributing their investments more evenly across these countries, rather than what it may seem in Figure 2.9. Second, the level of FDI inflows when accounting for size of population is disproportionately affected when considering Indonesia. Therefore this does not necessarily accurately reflect the comparative role of FDI in Indonesia.

Looking at the FDI inflow size into the ASEAN-10, by percentage of Gross Domestic Product (GDP) (Figure 2.11), it is evident that Singapore is the largest

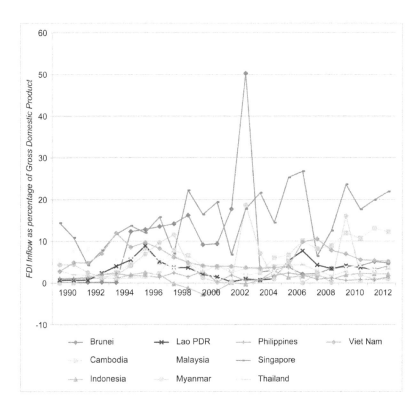

*Figure 2.11* FDI inflow into ASEAN-10 countries as percentage of Gross Domestic Product [1990–2013]

Source: UNCTAD 2016.

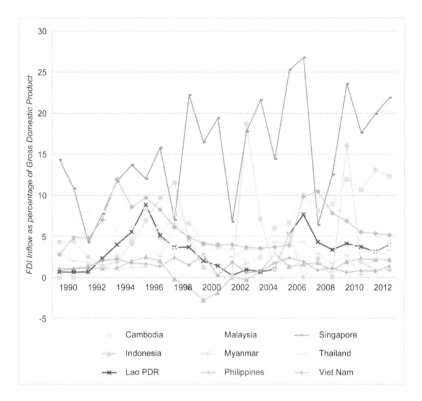

*Figure 2.11* (Continued)
Source: UNCTAD 2016.

recipient peaking at 27 per cent of GDP in 2007 and then levelling out at 22 per cent in 2013, after dropping to 6 per cent in 2008. Of particular interest in this figure is the pattern of FDI inflows by percentage of GDP for Brunei. Brunei experiences steady FDI inflow in comparison to the size of their economy from the mid-late 1990s (around the time of the Asian financial crisis) and then peaks at 50 per cent of GDP in 2003, only to fall to 3 per cent some 12 months later in 2004 where it remains relatively stable up until 2013.

It is immediately evident that unlike Figure 2.9 where Thailand and Indonesia experience significant amounts of FDI; in Figure 2.11 this seems to represent only a small percentage of their total GDP. Indonesia's peaked in 2009 reaching 3 per cent of their GDP and Thailand's peaked in 1998 at 6 per cent of their GDP. This does not compare to the peaks for Cambodia (13 per cent), Viet Nam (12 per cent), Myanmar (12 per cent) and Lao PDR (9 per cent), nor their averages throughout this period.

Accordingly, total FDI inflow size (Figure 2.11) does not capture the whole picture, as three of these economies are more likely to receive substantial economic impact from FDI (Viet Nam, Myanmar, Lao PDR), than the remaining three (Thailand, the Philippines, Indonesia). This means that as a percentage of all the goods and services produced, in Viet Nam, Myanmar and Lao PDR, FDI is responsible for the most of any other ASEAN-10 country.

Another interesting observation is that Thailand's FDI inflow per capita continued to increase after 1998 (Figure 2.10), while this inflow accounted for increasingly less of their GDP (Figure 2.11), hinting at possible economic growth effects stemming from FDI. This relationship is also apparent for Myanmar, where the FDI presented a peak of 12 per cent of their GDP in 1998 (Figure 2.11), and then continued to decrease to 4 per cent in 2013; corresponding to increases in FDI inflow per capita (Figure 2.10). This fluctuation may be accounted for with the political instability and difficult international relations the country had during this period.

Moving forward, Figure 2.12 illustrates that the dominance of FDI inflow on Gross Fixed Capital Formation (GFCF) has been much larger across all countries than it has been for GDP in Figure 2.11. The reliance of FDI for GFCF spiked to 170 per cent for Myanmar in 2003, 117 per cent for Singapore

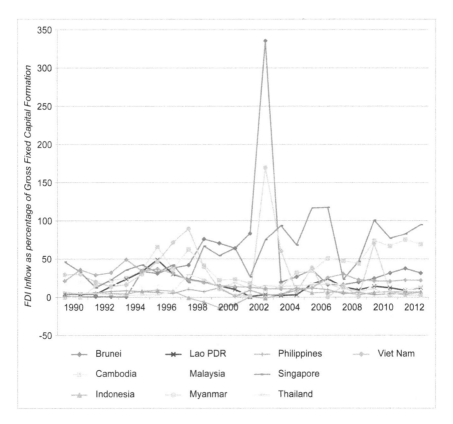

*Figure 2.12* FDI inflow into ASEAN-10 countries as percentage of Gross Fixed Capital Formation [1990–2012]

Source: UNCTAD 2016.

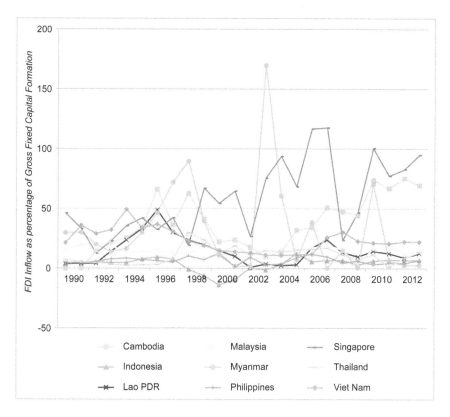

*Figure 2.12* (Continued)
Source: UNCTAD 2016.

in 2006/2007 and 75 per cent for Cambodia in 2012. The average reliance of FDI for GCFC and GDP over the 23-year period for all ASEAN-10 countries has been around 25 per cent for GCFC (Figure 2.12) compared to that of only 5 per cent for GDP (Figure 2.11). Accordingly, in the ASEAN-10 countries the effect of FDI is likely to be larger on GCFC than on GDP.

GCFC is a measure of *gross net investment* (acquisitions less disposals) in fixed capital assets by enterprises, government and households within the domestic economy. Based on Figure 2.12 this means that in Singapore, Brunei, Cambodia, Myanmar, Brunei, Viet Nam and Lao PDR between 1990 and 2013, FDI has been a highly important aspect of investment and development of fixed assets, such as property, plant and equipment.

In the Philippines and Indonesia, however, this does not appear to be the case. This suggests that future FDI inflow to the four countries that have received the least (see Figure 2.9) – Myanmar, Brunei, Cambodia and Lao PDR – may yield the largest potential for raising the development of fixed assets; helping to shape the path for future prosperity and human development in these under-invested and under-developed countries. Last, the observation that FDI has been accounting for less of the percentage of GCFC in most countries since 1996 to 1998 indicates that this was a key point in time where investment shifted away from fixed assets and toward higher yielding and riskier growth options.

## FDI and development trends for Thailand

Due to large differences in dollar amounts and units of measurement between the economic, social and environmental indicators throughout Figures 2.13–2.19, any potential trends or relationships between them are largely impercep-tible. Accordingly, to remedy this, the data in these figures has been indexed to allow for greater visibility of the way in which they are trending. The lines in these figures and their movement along the vertical axis should not be viewed as being representative of the size of FDI inflows or of any other indicators within the figures, but solely as the pattern by which they are trending. These figures demonstrate broad trends that can be examined currently, using acces-sible data, to highlight some potential relationships between the trends of FDI inflows and broader development indicators.

Looking first at the trends for the economic indicators within Thailand, Figure 2.13 demonstrates that between 1998 and the beginning of the global financial crisis (GFC) in 2008 that there was a gradual upwards trend for FDI inflow. However, after the crisis, FDI inflow appears to fluctuate rather sud-denly with peaks and troughs up until 2012 where it begins to align again with the rising trend of broader economic indicators. This pattern suggests that although the GFC had a significant impact on the flow of FDI into Thailand, it did not have a similar effect on the rest of Thailand's economy. Gross National Income, Gross Domestic Product and Gross Fixed Capital

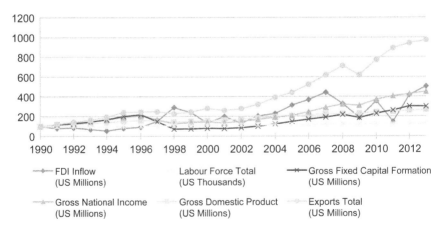

*Figure 2.13* Thailand: FDI inflow and economic indicators [1990–2013]
Source: UNCTAD 2016.

Formation all experienced steady growth post the crisis. Overall, this indicates that there may be a positive relationship between FDI inflow and broader economic trends.

Looking at Figure 2.14 below, enrolments into secondary and tertiary schools increased at a time of generally constant FDI inflows for Thailand. From 1995 to 2006, enrolments continued to rise with increasing FDI inflows, yet there was a marked increase in tertiary enrolments over this period. This is a likely trend, as you could expect growing numbers in secondary school to transfer across into higher, tertiary education. From 2006 to 2010, the amount of FDI inflows marginally decreased; yet, we still observe that enrolments for both secondary and tertiary continued to rise. It is difficult to draw conclusions from these trends. It is assumed that there would be some potential lag time between FDI investment and its translation to school enrolments; however, further examination is required. At best, we can suggest that some of the FDI inflow may have contributed to the improvement of school enrolments in Thailand, but regardless of this relationship, Thailand is mobilising towards having a more highly educated workforce; a workforce that can attract greater FDI inflows and apply these inflows to improving human development drivers.

Below, Figures 2.15 to 2.17 outline health and well-being indicators in Thailand, showing that FDI inflow per capita, although fluctuating over 1995 to 2011, is generally trending upwards with health expenditure, life expectancy and percentage of people with access to improved water sources and sanitation facilities. So, with the rise of FDI inflows and health expenditure, we are also seeing fewer infant and under-five deaths and improved adult mortality against a backdrop of improved sanitation facilities and improved access to water provisions. While some research indicates that the relationship between health and

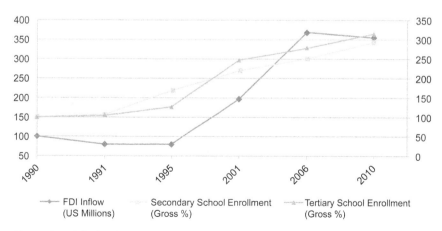

*Figure 2.14* Thailand: FDI inflow and education indicators [1991, 1995, 2001, 2006, 2010]

Source: The World Bank 2015a.

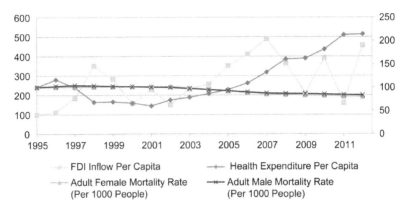

*Figure 2.15* Thailand: FDI inflow and health and well-being indicators one [1995–2012]

Source: The World Bank 2015b, 2015c, 2015d.

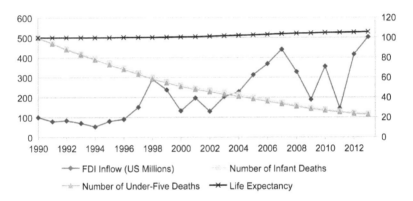

*Figure 2.16* Thailand: FDI inflow and health and well-being indicators two [1990–2013]

Source: The World Bank 2015e, 2015f, 2015g, 2015h.

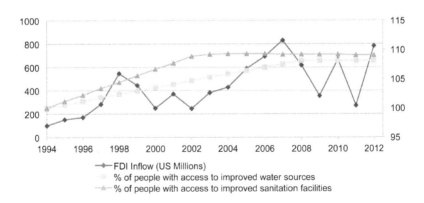

*Figure 2.17* Thailand: FDI inflow and health and well-being indicators three [1994–2012]

Source: The World Bank 2015e, 2015i, 2015j.

FDI may be non-linear as income increases, these general trends indicate improvements in health and well-being have generally paralleled increases in FDI into Thailand – although again, these are very tentative relationships not indicative of causal relations between these indicators.

Figure 2.18 provides details about some social progress indicators in Thailand. Between 1990 and 2013, the rising trend of FDI inflows was closely aligned with increasing numbers of telephone lines, scientific/technical journal articles and passengers carried by air transport. This alignment between FDI inflow and these social progress indicators has remained consistent throughout this 23-year period in Thailand, suggesting a potential association between the two.

Of particular interest was the decline in the number of telephone lines from 2008. Although this is different to the trend in Indonesia, Lao PDR and Myanmar, it could potentially be an indicator of increasing reliance on mobile-cellular and internet communication mediums. This explanation might further support the social progress of Thailand as it indicates the up-take of technological adoption and empowerment of its people.

Looking at the environmental indicators of Thailand, (Figure 2.19) the trend lines for $CO_2$ emissions and FDI inflow have both risen, with perhaps a very small to no alignment between the two. Any associations between the two, however, require further research to be conducted. The rising $CO_2$ emissions in Thailand represent a negative environmental footprint, which ought to be addressed in the coming decades by policy-makers and business operators. With regards to FDI inflow, the trend lines for forest area and electricity production from oil, gas and coal all have remained relatively flat throughout the period. Accordingly, it does not appear that changes in any of these could have an influence on each other.

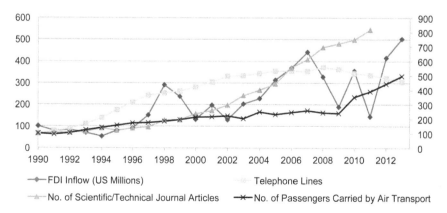

*Figure 2.18* Thailand: FDI inflow and social progress indicators [1990–2013]
Source: The World Bank 2015e, 2015k, 2015l, 2015m.

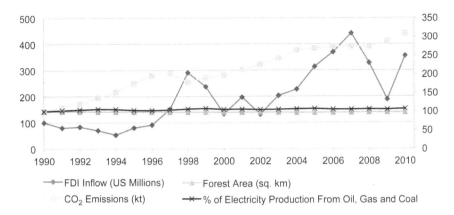

*Figure 2.19* Thailand: FDI inflow and environmental indicators [1990–2010]
Source: The World Bank 2015e, 2015n, 2015o, 2015p.

## Conclusion

This chapter has provided a review of existing and available panel data to understand the dynamics of FDI inflows within ASEAN and regions across the globe. Recent FDI inflows in developing economies and more specifically, in the ASEAN region over the last decade or more show promise as a region for investment. When examined on a per capita basis, it appears that there is more FDI flowing into the ASEAN per capita than all of the Developing Economies combined.

In terms of relative competitiveness of FDI inflows within ASEAN, Thailand performs strongly. Thailand rates in the top four ASEAN countries in terms of the total size of FDI inflow. The proportion of FDI flowing to specific ASEAN industries between 2005 and 2010 was of particular interest to this study, given our sample of organisations. Manufacturing experienced the strongest level of investment even during the financial crisis, which is perhaps a reflection of the stability of the industry in ASEAN. Our sample is largely representative of the Manufacturing sector, which further reinforces the attractiveness of Thailand for investment.

While the quality of FDI related policies had improved for many of the ASEAN countries, it was assumed to be poorer for Thailand despite the country's total FDI inflow size. Some of the statistics highlight Thailand's past political instability and whether it in fact is partly impacting on the country's capacity to attract this investment. Of further interest, was that Thailand, like some of the other larger recipients of FDI inflows, was found to experience rapid fluctuations of inflow. Fluctuations of this nature potentially highlight the requirement for a more considered approach that addresses FDI-related policies and encourages stability, plus an examination of institutional structures to ensure the directed use of resulting revenues (profit repatriation). FDI inflows only represented a small percentage of Thailand's total GDP. While Thailand's FDI inflow per capita continued to increase after 1998, these inflows accounted for increasingly less of their GDP (Figure 2.11), and therefore, hint at possible economic growth effects stemming from FDI.

A snapshot of possible trends between FDI inflows and broader development indicators concluded the chapter. A positive relationship was assumed to exist between FDI inflow and broader economic trends. Trends in higher education enrolments and improvements in health and well-being led to assumptions that FDI inflows may be associated with such indicators and social progress indicators (e.g. number of telephone lines); however, further research is required.

Likewise, $CO_2$ emissions were found to be rising in Thailand where the trend lines for forest area and electricity production from oil, gas and coal all remained relatively flat. These too were flagged for further examination to understand whether they need to be addressed in the coming decades by policy-makers and business operators. Despite these inconclusive relationships between FDI inflows and broader development indicators, the analysis presented within this chapter shows Thailand as an attractive, competitive country for investment with the potential for FDI inflows to impact positively upon their sustainable development.

The analysis also highlighted the difficult nature of determining the impact of FDI on the development progress of countries. This raises the ongoing question about whether FDI has the capacity to contribute towards the development progress of countries like Thailand. This research seeks to specifically engage in this ongoing debate, moving towards a better understanding of how large multinational organisations, as the key vehicles of FDI, address sustainability within their business activities. It is hoped through better understanding this process, that we can provide better tools and techniques for enhancing the positive impacts of FDI on development.

From this point, we now turn to conceptualising sustainability assessments from a private sector perspective. This provides the platform from which we analyse and present the results about the current techniques and tools being utilised by the private sector in engaging with sustainability and sustainable development within Thailand.

# References

ASEANstats 2016a. *Flows of inward direct investment to ASEAN by ASEAN's dialogue partners, 2000–2014 (in US$ million)* [Data file]. Available from http://aseanstats. asean.org/Selection.aspx?rxid=6e110de2-90e4-4ac7-b354-a3ac0fa9bdd2&px_ db=4-Foreign+Direct+Investment&px_type=PX&px_language=en&px_tableid=4- Foreign+Direct+Investment%5cFDIS003-FDI+flows+by+country+source+ 2000-2014.px

ASEANstats 2016b. *Flows of inward direct investment to ASEAN by host country, 2000–2014 (in US$ million)* [Data file]. Available from http://aseanstats.asean. org/Selection.aspx?rxid=6e110de2-90e4-4ac7-b354-a3ac0fa9bdd2&px_db=4- Foreign+Direct+Investment&px_type=PX&px_language=en&px_tableid=4- Foreign+Direct+Investment%5cFDIS001-FDI+flows+to+ASEAN+2000-2014.px

ASEANstats 2016c. *Flows of inward direct investment to ASEAN by economic sector, 2012–2014 (in US$ million)* [Data file]. Available from http://aseanstats.asean. org/Selection.aspx?rxid=6e110de2–90e4–4ac7-b354-a3ac0fa9bdd2&px_db=4-Foreign+Direct+Investment&px_type=PX&px_language=en&px_tableid=4-Foreign+Direct+Investment%5cFDIS005-FDI+Flows+to+ASEAN+by+Economic+Sectors+2012–2014.px

Choong, C. K., Liew, V. K. S., Chan, S. G., and Ch'ng, H. K. 2011. Foreign Direct Investment Volatility and Economic Growth in ASEAN-Five Countries. *International Journal of Academic Research*, 3(4), 221–224.

The World Bank, World Development Indicators 2015a. *Secondary education, pupils (SE.SEC.ENRL)* [Data file]. Available from http://databank.worldbank.org/data/reports.aspx?source=2&country=THA&series=&period=

The World Bank, World Development Indicators 2015b. *Health expenditure per capita (current US$) (SH.XPD.PCAP)* [Data file]. Available from http://databank.worldbank.org/data/reports.aspx?source=2&country=THA&series=&period=

The World Bank, World Development Indicators 2015c. *Mortality rate, adult, female (per 1,000 female adults) (SP.DYN.AMRT.FE)* [Data file]. Available from http://databank.worldbank.org/data/reports.aspx?source=2&country=THA&series=&period=

The World Bank, World Development Indicators 2015d. *Mortality rate, adult, male (per 1,000 male adults) (SP.DYN.AMRT.MA)* [Data file]. Available from http://databank.worldbank.org/data/reports.aspx?source=2&country=THA&series=&period=

The World Bank, World Development Indicators 2015e. *Foreign direct investment, net inflows (BoP, current US$) (BX.KLT.DINV.CD.WD)* [Data file]. Available from http://databank.worldbank.org/data/reports.aspx?source=2&country=THA&series=&period=

The World Bank, World Development Indicators 2015f. *Life expectancy at birth, total (years) (SP.DYN.LE00.IN)* [Data file]. Available from http://databank.worldbank.org/data/reports.aspx?source=2&country=THA&series=&period=

The World Bank, World Development Indicators 2015g. *Number of under-five deaths (SH.DTH.MORT)* [Data file]. Available from http://databank.worldbank.org/data/reports.aspx?source=2&country=THA&series=&period=

The World Bank, World Development Indicators 2015h. *Number of infant deaths (SH.DTH.IMRT)* [Data file]. Available from http://databank.worldbank.org/data/reports.aspx?source=2&country=THA&series=&period=

The World Bank, World Development Indicators 2015i. *Improved water source (% of population with access) (SH.H2O.SAFE.ZS)* [Data file]. Available from http://databank.worldbank.org/data/reports.aspx?source=2&country=THA&series=&period=

The World Bank, World Development Indicators 2015j. *Improved sanitation facilities (% of population with access) (SH.STA.ACSN)* [Data file]. Available from http://databank.worldbank.org/data/reports.aspx?source=2&country=THA&series=&period=

The World Bank, World Development Indicators 2015k. *Fixed telephone subscriptions (IT.MLT.MAIN)* [Data file]. Available from http://databank.worldbank.org/data/reports.aspx?source=2&country=THA&series=&period=

The World Bank, World Development Indicators 2015l. *Scientific and technical journal articles (IP.JRN.ARTC.SC)* [Data file]. Available from http://databank.worldbank.org/data/reports.aspx?source=2&country=THA&series=&period=

The World Bank, World Development Indicators 2015m. *Air transport, passengers carried (IS.AIR.PSGR)* [Data file]. Available from http://databank.worldbank. org/data/reports.aspx?source=2&country=THA&series=&period=

The World Bank, World Development Indicators 2015n. *CO2 emissions (kt) (EN. ATM.CO2E.KT)* [Data file]. Available from http://databank.worldbank.org/ data/reports.aspx?source=2&country=THA&series=&period=

The World Bank, World Development Indicators 2015o. *Forest area (sq. km) (AG. LND.FRST.K2)* [Data file]. Available from http://databank.worldbank.org/data/ reports.aspx?source=2&country=THA&series=&period=

The World Bank, World Development Indicators 2015p. *Electricity production from oil, gas and coal sources (% of total) (EG.ELC.FOSL.ZS)* [Data file]. Available from http://databank.worldbank.org/data/reports.aspx?source=2&country=THA& series=&period=

UNCTAD 2016. *Foreign direct investment: Inward and outward flows and stock, annual, 1980–2014* [Data file]. Available from http://unctadstat.unctad.org/wds/ TableViewer/tableView.aspx?ReportId=96740

# 3 The corporate sustainability assessment

*Hermann Lion, Cheree Topple
and Jerome D. Donovan*

This chapter reviews the existing research that has been undertaken on sustainability assessments. It involes a comprehensive literature review on how organisations integrate sustainability considerations into their business operations, specifically focusing within the impact assessment literature. This process led to the identification of a distinct cluster of research on horizontal impact assessments (sustainability assessments, integrated impact assessments, integrated assessments and integrated appraisals), which seeks to provide a multidimensional basis (environmental, economic and social) to planning tools used to assess the potential or actual impacts of a proposed intervention.

From the identification of this cluster of research on horizontal impact assessments, a conceptual framework has been developed. This led to the identification and development of seven steps that frame what we have labelled the 'corporate sustainability assessment'. A corporate sustainability assessment is a planning tool for the private sector on how to identify, assess and manage the impacts of their business operations across environmental, social and economic issues. Building from this point, the conceptual framework presents a basis for framing the research, as well as providing an informative chapter for practitioners on the state of the art in sustainability assessment knowledge. To conclude the chapter, an overview is provided of the methods used for this study as well as some more detailed information on the sample.

## Conceptualising the corporate sustainability assessment

As noted above, the following section of this chapter specifically engages and organises the extant literature related to horizontal impact assessments – including sustainability assessments, integrated impact assessments, integrated assessments and integrated appraisals. This focuses on establishing a clearer understanding of each of the seven steps we have identified and classified within the corporate sustainability assessment framework. We have presented below a basic visualisation of this framework, showing the flow between the different steps (please see Figure 3.1: Corporate sustainability assessment framework). We also draw upon empirical examples that support the further articulation of each step.

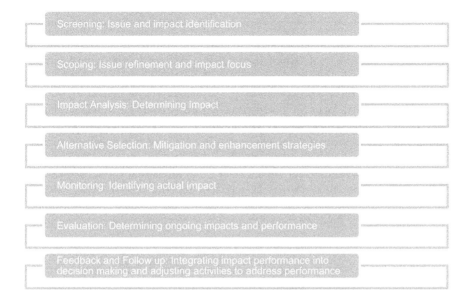

*Figure 3.1* Corporate sustainability assessment framework

Moving from this point, we now turn to examining each of the steps for the corporate sustainability assessment in a linear and sequential manner, following the framework illustrated above.

### Screening

Screening is the first step within our proposed corporate sustainability assessment, and is recognised as a salient step within impact assessments that is typically conducted across Health Impact Assessments (HIAs), Environmental Impact Assessments (EIAs) and Social Impact Assessments (SIAs), amongst others. Despite its commonality across impact assessments, screening can be difficult to clearly define simply because it is recognised as various other terms in the literature. Within the integrated assessment literature, screening is also known as 'problem identification', 'problem analysis', "the process of analysing the problem" (de Ridder et al. 2007, p.430) or "understand[ing] the issues" (Arce-Gomez, Donovan and Bedggood 2015, p.87).

According to Morrison-Saunders and Pope (2013), it is the screening step that determines whether a sustainability assessment should be conducted. Borrowing from the EIA literature, Weston (2000) broadly agrees that screening is the first step that determines whether an assessment should be carried out. At the project level, research is sparse; however, Eales et al. (2005) extends this focus of screening with reference to the 'Commission of the European

Communities'. Here, screening is defined by its capacity "to identify knowledge gaps and what further analysis and consultation are necessary to ensure a 'proportionate' level of impact assessment and mitigation" (Eales et al. 2005, p.116).

Rotmans and Van Asselt (1996, pp. 331–332) argue that at its core the impact identification stage (where the screening step resides) is about determining both, "what is possible and plausible?" and "what is desirable" in the context of the project? Gibson (2006, p.172) elaborates by suggesting that the process should first focus on "identifying appropriate purposes and options for new or continuing undertakings". While Eales et al. (2005) evaluated integrated appraisals that address sustainability considerations from a policy perspective they do, however, highlight some considerations that can be drawn to a project-level perspective. This includes initial stage of an integrated appraisal where it's advocated that potential impacts be screened across a mix of social, environmental and economic criteria. From a project-level perspective, one can make an intuitive jump about the importance of asking broad questions about the potential social, economic and environmental issues associated with the planned project.

Decision-makers need to set the assessment goals by asking the question, what should we achieve through this assessment? In the screening step, to properly identify sustainability issues, decision-makers should first define and determine the project's requirements (Bond, Morrison-Saunders and Howitt 2013). This allows decision-makers to frame the entire assessment process and determine the sustainability goals, principles and outcomes of the project (Bond and Morrison-Saunders 2011). At the project level, sustainability goals can be influenced by regulatory requirements, international industry guidelines and corporate policies. Furthermore, they can be determined from the involvement of key stakeholders (Pope, Annandale and Morrison-Saunders 2004).

Stakeholders can be external or internal to the organisation whom are impacted on by the proposed activity/ies (Orenstein et al. 2010). Engaging stakeholders early in the process of sustainability assessment enables the identification of a broad range of sustainability requirements that possibly would not have been considered by the project's proponents (Gibson 2006). An effective stakeholder engagement strategy ensures the credibility of the project and allows decision-makers to contextualise the sustainability requirements at the outset of the project. The inclusion and integration of stakeholders can also reduce the likelihood of trade-offs occurring during the assessment process (Gibson 2013; Morrison-Saunders and Pope 2013). It is critical that decision-makers engage with in-house as well as external experts and the main project stakeholders. However, within the literature it remains largely unknown how stakeholders should be engaged in the screening step.

*Empirical studies*

The use of project proponent led assessments has not been proposed in the horizontal impact assessment literature until recently (Bond, Morrison-Saunders and Howitt 2012); hence, empirical evidence of the screening step is difficult to locate. This section will focus on the following case examples: the Scarborough Field (Bond, Morrison-Saunders and Howitt 2013), the Northern Test Field (NFT) (Orenstein et al. 2010) and the Gorgon Gas Project (Pope, Annandale and Morrison-Saunders 2004; Pope, Morrison-Saunders and Annandale 2005).

SCARBOROUGH FIELD

The screening step has an objective of addressing sustainability at its core. And as part of this, it's necessary to achieve or address the three pillars of sustainability – environmental, economic and social. The onus is on the assessor or decision-maker to fully identify at the early stages of the sustainability assessment, the full breadth of sustainability considerations through engagement with in-house and/or external experts and main project stakeholders.

Scarborough Field, located some 250km off the north-west coast of Western Australia provides some insight into screening at this level, particularly at the internal level. In 2005, BHP Billiton voluntarily conducted an 'internal' sustainability assessment to identify a new site for a large liquefied natural gas (LNG) facility (Bond, Morrison-Saunders and Howitt 2013). Here, 'internal' means a sustainability assessment conducted by the proponent to inform their decision-making processes (Pope 2006).

Potential coastal sites within a 400km radius of the gas field were initially identified and then assessed against specific environmental, socio-economic and safety requirements (Bond, Morrison-Saunders and Howitt 2013). Community consultation and participation occurred throughout this step to facilitate transparency of the decision-making process (Bond, Morrison-Saunders and Howitt 2013). Engagement at this early stage of the sustainability assessment helps to identify a diverse range of sustainability requirements that perhaps could not be identified by just the project proponent.

Of the potential eight sites, BHP Billiton selected a favoured location and then conducted an engineering cost–benefit analysis of all possible sites – the organisation's favoured site presented the most cost-efficient solution. BHP Billiton then pursued with the formal EIA process for the establishment of the LNG facility at the favoured site. This case study highlights the role of stakeholder engagement early in the process to provide a set of diverse ecological, socio-economic and safety criteria for consideration. This process of stakeholder engagement is a more holistic experience of requirement identification that helps ensure a more seamless outcome for the delivery of sustainability assessment.

NORTHERN FIELD TEST

Orenstein et al. (2010) provide more detail about the integration of multidimensional teams to assist with decision-making in the screening step of assessment. Known as the Northern Field Test (NFT) project, this case study considers an integrated assessment undertaken by Royal Dutch Shell for a large 'heavy' oil pilot project located in Northern Alberta, Canada. The two primary objectives of the pilot project were "to assess the feasibility of a new heavy oil extraction technique" (Orenstein et al. 2010, p.150) and its economic viability for full-scale commercial development. To understand the impacts of the NFT project, Shell undertook a cross-disciplinary impact assessment that integrated dimensions from the environment, social, health and economic domains.

In order to achieve an integrated impact assessment approach, a multidisciplinary three-person team was assembled with representation from each discipline (the environment, social and health). In this particular case, the screening step commenced with exploratory discussion among the team leaders who screened the main sustainability considerations and potential impacts from their expert knowledge. These cross-disciplinary discussions in the screening step of the sustainability assessment, shows the mapping of the potential impact across the environmental, social and health disciplines, which resulted in a comprehensive list of sustainability concerns.

In addition, Shell created another structural team prior to commencing the IA – the Business Integration (BI) team that consisted of staff with knowledge in environment, social performance, regulatory affairs and communications (Orenstein et al. 2007, p.151). Although not directly engaged at the screening step, Shell's BI team was tasked with the creation of "non-technical values and beliefs that guided the development and implementation of specific strategies [and] the overall operating philosophy of the project" (Orenstein et al. 2007, p.151).

The benefits of this team were highly advantageous to the streamlining of different steps within the IA. For example, through its strong connections with local communities this team facilitated a two-way communication process between multiple stakeholder groups and the different team structures, which helped provide an "iterative and continuous integration of IA findings to the project decision-making process" (Orenstein et al. 2010, p.151).

GORGON GAS DEVELOPMENT

Presented from a slightly different lens, is a study of the Gorgon gas fields conducted by Pope, Morrison-Saunders and Annandale (2005). This example provides some detail about internal sustainability assessment and the setting of sustainability goals. Located off the North West Coast of Australia, it is one the nation's largest gas reservoirs discovered to date.

Under the Western Australian *Environmental Protection Act 1986*, Chevron–Texaco (the organisations undertaking the development) were required to complete a mandatory EIA. Of particular interest to this case, was that Chevron–Texaco completed an internal sustainability assessment concurrently with the

EIA requirement. The internal assessment, considered a rarity in practice, was to guide their decision-making process.

Pope, Morrison-Saunders and Annandale (2005) highlight the process-based nature and ambiguity of the criteria proposed by Chevron–Texaco, which could not be used to determine sustainability outcomes. For example, the organisation's principle of 'Social Equity and Community Well-being Enhancement' was met with the criterion of "community well-being will be sustained by effective identification and management of potential impacts on people's way of life, their culture or their communities" (Pope, Morrison-Saunders and Annandale 2005, p.300).

Likewise, there was a great discrepancy in the organisation's sustainability principles/criteria and the State of Western Australia. For example, the organisation's principle of 'Economic Benefit Delivery' had a criterion of profitability: "The Gorgon gas development will create profitable investment opportunities for the Gorgon Venture and for other industrial gas projects in Australia that depend on gas as a feedstock" (Pope, Morrison-Saunders and Annandale 2005, pp. 300–301). By comparison, the State's principle was for 'long-term economic health'.

This finding highlights the difference in sustainability interpretations for different entities and, as evidenced in this case, that the sustainability criteria proposed in an organisation's internal document could be considerably different to those outlined in a government decision-making tool (Pope, Morrison-Saunders and Annandale 2005). Furthermore, it highlights the limitations in this process with the potential for 'questionable' sustainability goals and considerations to emerge.

*Scoping*

Scoping adopts a similar form of process to that established in EIAs (Bond, Morrison-Saunders and Pope 2012). In the context of an EIA, Weston (2000, p.186) defines the scoping step as, "what environmental impacts need to be examined?" For the purposes of a sustainability assessment, the question then becomes, 'what are the economic, environmental and social impacts that need to be examined?' So, where the screening step focuses on identifying issues, scoping focuses on selecting those of merit for further investigation. As Canter and Ross (2014, p.21) suggest, current impact assessment practice seems to have an overwhelming focus on a multitude of requirements yet the success of scoping is to "focus on the issues of importance to the decision-maker and not try to do everything".

Morrison-Saunders et al. (2014b, p.5) argue for a "focused scoping process, which commences with the goal of sustainable development and then identifies which sustainability issues warrant further exploration in any given context, and therefore, which specialists should be involved". The scoping step is critical for establishing the sustainability objectives of a sustainability assessment. Earlier,

Morrison-Saunders and Pope (2013) asserted that decision-makers should strongly establish sustainability objectives, stemming from what was first formulated in the screening step. It is within the scoping step that decision-makers must contextualise and refine the sustainability objectives "derived from overarching sustainability principles which are highly integrated" (Morrison-Saunders and Pope 2013, p.38).

With the goal of establishing a refined list of issues that may arise from the planned activity, one of the concerns with this level of consolidation in the scoping step, is the likelihood of trade-offs between the sustainability dimensions as decision-makers prioritise the issues. In terms of managing the prioritisation of these issues with minimal trade-offs between dimensions, Bond, Morrison-Saunders and Howitt (2013, pp. 249–250) discourage the hierarchisation of dimensions and promote the embedding of the environmental, social and economic dimensions within each other "[. . .] a sustainability assessment might prove the incentive to introduce all pillars of sustainability into the planning process, which means socio-economic issues in environmental plans or environmental consideration in socio-economic plans." While this notion of embedding dimensions offers a frame for avoiding trade-offs it neglects to fully address the trade-off situation.

Further research suggests that trade-offs within the scoping step can be minimised through stakeholder involvement (Canter and Ross 2014; Gibson 2013; Morrison-Saunders and Pope 2013) and more specifically, if they are integrated within the process of setting sustainability goals of the planned activities (Pope, Annandale and Morrison-Saunders 2004). Gibson and Hassan (2005) strongly emphasise trade-offs be considered in an open process with the effective involvement of all stakeholders.

In addition to the selection of issues and impacts to investigate, the choice of tools and techniques are refined in the scoping step for deployment in the subsequent steps of the sustainability assessment.

## Empirical studies

This next section presents empirical findings that explore the scoping step at a project level for impact assessments related to sustainability. Only one study details the scoping step from an internal perspective (Orenstein et al. 2010), while the Basslink project (Duncan and Hay 2007) provides an external perspective (regulatory enforced) that aids a mechanical understanding of the scoping step.

BASSLINK PROJECT

It was within the scoping step of the Basslink project that researchers emphasised the environmental consequences of water-level changes for the Gordon River. Basslink – a major energy infrastructure development within the Tasmanian Wilderness World Heritage Area that covers about 20 per cent of the state's landmass (Duncan and Hay 2007). The Gordon River flows through this area. The two major structural features of the Basslink project include a power station and a 360km underwater power cable that connects Tasmania to the Australian-mainland power grid. This connection between the Gordon Power Station and the national grid requires a "higher volume and more variable [. . .] discharge from the Gordon Power Station down the Gordon River" (Duncan and Hay 2007, p.283). These discharges and changes to the overall volumes of water in the river were shown to potentially impact significantly upon the local eco-system particularly on river bank scour, vegetation and macro-invertebrate species.

Given that a dam disrupts the natural water flow for electricity production with the storage of large volumes of water during winter and the release of greater volumes during summer, environmental researchers questioned the minimal and maximal water levels required for maintaining river fauna. From a comprehensive multicriteria analysis (MCA), it quickly became apparent that there were economic implications from the water-flow restrictions (e.g., less water stored or released, less electricity can be produced and sold to the main grid). Consequently, the discharge of volumes of water were marked for further investigation as a result of the scoping step; however, the proponent was perceived to be more concerned about the cost implications of water release to the detriment of the river's ecosystem. Within this case, it appeared that there was an unequal consideration placed on sustainability dimensions within the scoping step, with the proponent giving priority to economic-based issues at the expense of the environmental issues.

NORTHERN FIELD TEST

While the integrated impact assessments conducted for the Northern Field Test project provide key insights for the screening step of the sustainability assessments, they shed equally powerful insights for scoping. In contrast to the Basslink project, Orenstein et al. (2010) highlights the process of stakeholder involvement in the scoping step for the Northern Field Test.

Shell assembled an external consultant team with expertise across the environmental, social and economic streams who conducted a technical scoping exercise of stakeholder concerns and issues. The consultant team held workshops with local stakeholder groups to identify and scope key issues, which were then refined for the IA. This type of stakeholder engagement enabled the decision-making team to formulate the sustainability objectives of the project that reflect a cross-section of their community stakeholders.

## Impact analysis

Where the scoping step prioritises sustainability issues for analysis, the impact analysis concerns itself with determining the potential or actual impacts of the planned activity/activities. Each identified issue prioritised in the scoping step is analysed to understand what effects or implications it will have for the business, the environment and the local community in which the activity pertains (Arce-Gomez, Donovan and Bedggood 2015). According to de Ridder et al. (2007, p.433), the analysis phase of a generic integrated assessment is "about characterising as far as possible the details of the plausible scenarios and policy interventions developed in [subsequent steps] with the final aim of selecting options for implementation". For efficiency, the analysis should only focus on the scoped sustainability objectives established in the previous step.

After four decades of research, practitioners have made significant progress in the various fields across ecological, social and health. However, few studies have looked at impact analysis from an integrated manner at the project level. A range of scholars have studied the integration of sustainability domains from a policy angle (Bond, Morrison-Saunders and Howitt 2012; Bond, Morrison-Saunders and Pope 2012; de Ridder et al. 2007; Hacking and Guthrie 2008), to extrapolate how these insights can be integrated within the impact analysis step at the project level.

Gibson (2006, p.174) has produced one of the seminal works in the field that addresses impact analysis from an integrative perspective. He proposes within the impact analysis step of the assessment, that decision-makers should be guided by eight considerations:

*   Long-term socio-ecological system integrity;
*   Livelihood sufficiency and opportunity for everyone;
*   Intra-generational equity;
*   Intergenerational equity;
*   Resource maintenance and efficiency;
*   Socio-ecological civility and democratic governance;
*   Precaution and adaption; and
*   Immediate and long-term integration.

The impact analysis step is considered one of the most technical and complex steps within broader impact assessments (Bond, Morrison- Saunders and Howitt 2012; Bond, Morrison-Saunders and Pope 2012; Pope, Morrison-Saunders and Annandale 2005). Decision-makers use a range of methods, tools and techniques to help effectively manage the analysis of the potential issues and impacts to inform organisational decision-making. For example, baseline studies have been used extensively in EIAs based on the enactment of The National Environmental Policy Act (NEPA) in 1970. At a general level, impact significance for baseline studies imply: "(a) measurement to test for change, (b) an adequate quantitative knowledge of conditions both before (the baseline) and after (the so-called monitoring) project initiation, and (c) the use of acceptable statistical procedures for data analysis" (Duinker and Beanlands 1986, pp. 4–5).

As mentioned previously, Bond, Morrison-Saunders and Pope (2012) have argued that sustainability assessments mimic the mechanism of EIAs and it is

therefore essential that such baseline studies are used for sustainability assessments. However, because the latter assessment is broader in its coverage, it is
essential that quantitative and qualitative analyses are performed to more accurately cover the gamut of environmental, social and economic impacts that are
likely to emerge as a focus of the assessment.

Within the impact analysis step, the decision-maker needs to determine the
acceptability or significance of an impact. Morrison-Saunders and Pope (2013,
p.57) suggests that "the notion of demarcating acceptable from unacceptable
impacts is core to sustainability assessment and to the effective management of
trade-offs." Understanding significance and acceptability of issues can be achieved
through a range of criteria or systems. Duinker and Beanlands (1986), for
example, discuss the use of categories ranging from major, moderate, minor
and negligible impacts to rate environmental impacts.

This process of impact determination as either 'critical' (Sadler 1996) or
'negotiable' (Sippe 1990) assists with the identification and enhancement of
preferred alternatives (Morrison-Saunders and Pope 2013). Furthermore, the
management of trade-offs can be more effective if the acceptability or significance
of impacts is compared against the overarching sustainability goals of the organisation set at the commencement of the sustainability assessment.

From this analysis, the outcomes are then used to inform either an alternative to be implemented (changes to business activities) or a mitigation strategy
to address these impacts (should it be negative). This raises the next step of
Alternative selection, which is discussed after the empirical cases of impact
analysis.

## Empirical studies

Various scholars have described the mechanics of the impact analysis step from
a policy perspective and few studies have been identified at the project level
(Dey 2001; Duncan and Hay 2007; Locher 2001; Pope, Annandale and Morrison-Saunders 2004). Demonstration of the impact analysis step extends upon
the empirical cases used to date, namely the Gorgon gas field, Basslink and the
Northern Field Test. Each of these empirical cases will highlight different aspects
of the impact analysis step.

GORGON GAS DEVELOPMENT

The Chevron–Texaco example mentioned earlier sheds light on the sustainability
assessment carried out in the Greater Gorgon gas fields. The location – Barrow
Island – was classified as a 'Class A Nature Reserve', with "unique and internationally significant conservation values" with some species of wildlife that
were endemic to the island and others that were extinct on mainland Australia
(Pope, Morrison-Saunders and Annandale 2005, p.294).

The assessment process for the Gorgon gas fields was unique. At the time,
there were no established processes for the review of development plans of

this nature in Western Australia. As such, the proponent prepared a triple bottom line (TBL) review document that was publicly reviewed. Despite this TBL approach, the social aspects associated with the project were not considered to be at the core of the assessment – there were no local community issues associated with the uninhabited island – and, therefore, the assessment focused heavily on evaluating the economic and environmental impacts of the proposal.

However, the approach to the sustainability assessment and important process trade-offs that occurred, resulted in an unsatisfactory sustainability outcome, with decision-makers – both at the organisational and at the legislative level (Western Australian State Government) – approving the development to be carried out in an environmentally sensitive zone despite the proposed impact analysis revealing the destruction of rare and sensitive fauna and flora. The initial baseline studies showed the threat to the environment and significance of the anthropogenic impacts. Additionally, the irreversibility of damage to the biosphere reinforced the 'unsustainability' outcome of this project.

Pope, Morrison-Saunders and Annandale (2005) argued that if the assessment would have been carried out within a classic EIA, the regulatory agency, in this case the Western Australian EPA, would never had allowed the approval of the proposal. However, as the proposal was reviewed within a broader sustainability assessment, the Western Australian State government approved the proposal based largely on economic outcomes. Unfortunately, further details about the methodology of the Gorgon Gas Project were not disclosed. This empirical example demonstrates that despite the undertaking of baseline studies and the predicted negative outcomes for the environment, decision-makers experienced trade-off challenges that compromised the impact analysis step and the sustainability outcomes of the project.

BASSLINK PROJECT

Likewise, the Basslink project in the Tasman, mentioned earlier in this chapter, is of considerable interest in relation to the step of impact analysis. This case study is a critical illustration of the technical details of impact analysis at the project level, where few empirical studies exist. As mentioned earlier, Basslink is a hydro-power generation project that connects the Tasmanian electricity system to mainland Australia's national electricity grid through an underwater power cable. The outcomes of such a project were predicted to have significant environmental and socio-economic impacts.

Through a predictive model, the Tasmanian Electric Market Simulation Model (TEMSIM), results of analysis undertaken showed that when simulating the operations in various conditions, the three power stations – the Gordon, Poatina and John Butters – all had significantly different patterns of operation with Basslink. The TEMSIM modeling showed potential impacts to water quality and fluvial geomorphology (which were considered relatively minor compared to the general environmental issues related to mining practices). While "the concentration of metal plumes originating from the mine lease site" and "mine tailing in river bed" (Locher 2001, p.256) were identified as potential issues that could emerge from more frequent use of the John Butters power station they were not considered significant enough to warrant the development of key mitigation measures.

NORTHERN FIELD TEST

The Northern Field Test project provides insightful detail about the integration of disciplines during the analysis step. In order to achieve an integrated impact assessment approach, a multidisciplinary three-person team was assembled with representation from each discipline (the environment, social and health). Exploratory discussions occurred within the teams where they screened the main potential impacts of operations for each specific discipline and then the impacts that overlapped when integrating the disciplines. These cross-disciplinary discussions in the screening step of the sustainability assessment show the mapping of the potential impact across the environmental, social and health disciplines, which resulted in a comprehensive list of sustainability concerns.

In this example, it became clear that the emissions from the NFT project had the potential to affect water quality. Examining this particular issue from each of the disciplines indicated that the poorer water quality could impact negatively on fish health and diversity and subsequently effect the traditional livelihoods and the health of the area's indigenous communities. Orenstein's et al. (2010) case study shows that integrative, cross-disciplinary teams with flat structures can provide holistic outcomes to the analysis step of the sustainability assessment that cannot be realised from single disciplinary analyses. This consultant team had a flat structure that facilitated open discussion and 'balanced' analysis from across the three areas.

## Alternative selection – mitigation and enhancement

Through the identification and measurement of impacts related to a business' activity/activities, the organisation is presented with a hierarchy of options for addressing impacts. These impacts are either addressed through mitigation – if they are negative impacts or through enhancement – if they are positive impacts (for more detail, see for example, sustainability-assessment.org 2016; João, Vanclay and den Broeder 2011). The alternative selection step examines the various technical possibilities to either reduce the potential negative impacts or optimise potential positive impacts of the sustainability assessment (Therivel 2004).

The sustainability objectives established in the earlier steps of the sustainability assessment effectively determine the broad alternatives considered within this step (Morrison-Saunders and Pope 2013). Closer inspection of the literature indicates that the objectives of the selected alternatives should be aligned with these sustainability objectives. Therivel (2004, p.168) identified the following mitigation strategies for use within projects. These measures include those that:

- Avoid impacts altogether,
- Reduce the magnitude and/or severity of impacts,
- 'Repair' impacts after they have occurred,
- Compensate for impacts (try to balance out negative impacts with other positive ones, but not necessarily in a like-for-like manner),
- Enhance already positive impacts.

Often described as a linear process in the literature, the selection of mitigation strategies appears to be more cyclical in practice. Newly proposed mitigation strategies should be re-evaluated against the sustainability objectives of the project and adjustments made where necessary.

## Empirical studies

This section will present few empirical studies that have been identified within the extant literature – the Northern Field Test and the City of South Perth. The first case is of significance to the step of alternative selection given its focus on the process of stakeholder engagement that helped shape the proposed mitigation and enhancement strategies. The second case also illustrates the benefits of effective stakeholder engagement but also shows the iterative process of aligning newly proposed mitigation strategies with the sustainability objectives of the project.

### NORTHERN FIELD TEST

Within the Northern Field Test in Alberta, a focus for Shell's IA was for the mitigation and management strategies to be integrated into their project planning process (Orenstein et al. 2010). This was achieved through two means, however, only the first technique has been discussed here as it is of interest to the mitigation and enhancement step.

First, feedback between the independent consultants and the Shell project team occurred on a continuous basis and involved multiple project stakeholders. Recommendations proposed by the consultants were shared with the project team throughout the report writing phase. This meant that the latter were part of the process and essentially co-creating recommendations so by the time the report was completed, the project team had "vetted" and "accepted" these recommendations. Through this iterative process of information flow between stakeholders:

- "An issue was raised by the community;
- The IA team would analyse the issue and find potential linkages;

- The IA team would suggest potential mitigation based on their understanding of the issue and the project;
- The mitigation action would then be brought to the project design team to see if this was feasible, practical, or if another solution existed; and
- This solution would then be tested with the IA team to see if it met the community's needs" (Orenstein et al. 2010, p.155).

The consultation and engagement with broad stakeholders provided an efficient process for the development of mitigation and enhancement strategies that built stakeholder trust by directly addressing their concerns. Community members expressed satisfaction and appreciation of Shell's openness and transparency to this process (Orenstein et al. 2010).

CITY OF SOUTH PERTH

Examples of decision-aiding tools like multicriteria decision analysis (MCDA) have been found in recent empirical studies. The City of South Perth, a local government in Western Australia (Pope and Klass 2010) is one such example of how the use of MCDA assisted in the identification of trade-offs and developing acceptable mitigation strategies (Morrison-Saunders and Pope 2013). Of interest was that the assessment was conducted internally and involved planting additional trees in the Sir James Mitchell Park, which was opposite the CBD of Perth.

Consultation with stakeholders at the outset of the assessment established sustainability criteria such as "enhancement of ecological integrity, maintenance of views, public safety, maintenance costs" (Morrison-Saunders and Pope 2004, p.58). Stakeholders also participated in addressing how the desired outcome could be met. Using a MCDA, five tree planting options were compared against each sustainability to provide an overall sustainability score.

Decision-makers were able to identify not just the highest scoring option but also where the selected option might need extra mitigation. For example, in this actual case, the highest scoring option overall performed weakly in comparison to other options for the criterion, "provision of suitable habitat for birds and other fauna" (Morrison-Saunders and Pope 2004, p.58). This allowed decision-makers to tailor specific mitigation strategies that could optimise the sustainability criteria by making changes to the option. For the City of South Perth this meant adding a number of specific tree species to the species mix to be planted in particular areas of the park (Morrison-Saunders and Pope 2013).

## *Monitoring*

Monitoring is one of the ex-post steps of the sustainability assessment where the focus is on capturing the ongoing impacts associated with the implemented activity/ies. McMullen (2010 cited in Bjorkland 2013, p.130) describes this step of monitoring as "a systematic method of collecting, analysing and integrating data and information about the conditions, components, and processes of an ecosystem".

Sustainability-assesments.org (2016) extend this understanding to emphasise the focus of monitoring on the organisation's performance "at a specific point in time". Detailing this further, they suggest that this step within the sustainability assessment should establish a clear basis for measuring the performance of the business not just for their activities but also for their impacts on surrounding communities. This can include the local community and government within the location of the operations, and how the direct and indirect activities of the organisations may be affecting changes (sustainability-assessments.org 2016).

The implementation of protocols and specific measures is essential to correctly monitor impacts across the key sustainability dimensions. There is a paucity of research in this area, particularly studies of an in-depth nature from the project perspective (Morrison-Saunders and Pope 2013; Morrison-Saunders et al. 2014a). Of those, Morrison-Saunders et al. (2014a) suggest that impacts of development across all three sustainability dimensions should be within acceptable limits and compared with the baseline. This implies that baseline studies should be used as points of reference, setting acceptable ranges for meeting sustainability measures. "When such limits are exceeded (or at risk of being exceeded), appropriate adaptive management action should be initiated, the results communicated and the new actions subject to ongoing follow-up" (Morrison-Saunders et al. 2014a, p.40).

As has been inferred from above, monitoring is a resource intensive stage that for maximum effect, should be fully integrated in the planning process. Despite this resource-intensiveness, organisations with sustainability assessments that overlook a strong monitoring component fear the risk of lacking credibility and long-term commitment to achieving sustainability outcomes (Bond, Morrison-Saunders and Pope 2012). Further effectiveness also hinges on the engagement of stakeholders within the local community: "Better management of the project in its local community, through better monitoring, is a particularly important objective and outcome for all the stakeholders involved" (Glasson 2005, p.225).

*Empirical studies*

No empirical study has been identified examining the use of monitoring measures within the sustainability assessment at a project level. Morrison-Saunders and Pope (2013) highlight a limited field of knowledge at this stage of the decision-making process. Related fields to sustainability assessment, such as EIA, HIA and SEAs have explored this step in greater depth and it is assumed that the practical knowledge gained from such studies can be extrapolated and applied at the project level for sustainability assessments.

One such study in socio-economic analysis was conducted by Akroyd (1999) who examined the monitoring and evaluation processes of a smallholder rice production process in Gambia yet, it has limited application. Given its focus on practices from the late 1970s to early 1990s, findings are difficult to extrapolate to a contemporary context. This is particularly prominent when we start to think about the advancements of computing over a potential 40 plus years and that practices dated back then perhaps did not involve the use of personal computers to help with data collection or analysis. Insights we have gained from this study highlight the significance of the early steps of the sustainability assessment at the outset of the assessment for effective monitoring and evaluation practices at the ex-post stage of the sustainability assessment.

*Evaluation*

While the monitoring step ensures the effective management of the implemented mitigation and enhancement strategies, decision-makers also need to evaluate these strategies. In its simplest form, evaluation is about "identify[ing] how things could be improved in the future (João, Vanclay and den Broeder 2011, p.177). Evaluation, like monitoring, is another ex-post step of the sustainability assessment, yet definitions of this step are difficult to locate within this field. Borrowing from socio-economic analysis, Akroyd (1999) makes reference to the International Fund for Agricultural Development's operational guidelines. Within, evaluation was defined "as the analysis of the information gathered during monitoring to determine the efficiency and effectiveness with which a project delivers its outputs and thus generates the expected impact" (Akroyd 1999, p.58). This definition of the evaluation step is appropriate for translation into the sustainability assessment literature given that it's not contained or specific to one or few sustainability definitions and therefore isn't context specific.

On the other hand, more recent project level work by researchers from sustainabilityasssessments.org (2016) provides an extensive definition of the evaluation step that is more specific to sustainability assessments. They describe the evaluation step as a "process, which aims to capture the ongoing impacts associated with the business activities. This enables a broader application of the impact analysis tools/methodologies to an ongoing process of investigating the success (or otherwise) of the strategies implemented by the organisation to manage their operations." The evaluation step can provide an important basis for adjusting or changing its operations to further mitigate or enhance their business impacts. The effectiveness of the evaluation step resides in whether "there are clear targets and objectives set across the different measurable areas, enabling the determination of organisational performance" (sustainability-assessments.org 2016).

*Empirical studies*

There are no empirical studies to our knowledge that provide key insights of the evaluation step of a sustainability assessment. What exists in the literature is a conceptual or theorised attempt to understand or foresee how practices should be conducted within projects. For example, within impact assessments more broadly, João, Vanclay and den Broeder (2011) provide IA practitioner's perceptions of the barriers to implementing enhancement in impact assessment practice. This is followed up with practitioner's suggestions of potential solutions to overcome these barriers. These findings are useful for understanding some of the requirements of the evaluation step however, little is known about this step from a more comprehensive, project perspective.

### Feedback and follow up

The final step of the sustainability assessment is feedback and follow up where decision-makers address mitigation and enhancement strategies to reinforce the overall sustainability outcome of the project. This step intends for the sustainability assessment to be seen as an iterative process where decision-makers re-analyse (step 3), re-mitigate and re-enhance (step 4) the project impacts. At the project level, decision-makers are constantly re-assessing the project's impacts against the sustainability goals and objectives. It is through this consistent process of feedback and follow up that "enables learning from experience to occur" (Marshall, Arts and Morrison-Saunders 2005, p.177).

Specific definitions of follow up for the sustainability assessment are difficult to locate. Borrowing from EIA, Morrison-Saunders and Arts (2004, p.4) describe follow up at the proposal level as "the monitoring and evaluation of the impacts of a project or plan (that has been subject to EIA) for management of, and communication about, the environmental performance of that project or plan".

Literature on the feedback and follow up step is sparse. Glasson (2005, p.225) goes as far to say that, "impact assessment follow up is still an Achilles' heel in contemporary practice." While some conceptual studies (Gibson 2013; Marshall, Arts and Morrison-Saunders 2005; Morrison-Saunders and Pope 2013; Morrison-Saunders et al. 2014b) argue that feedback and follow up is an essential step of assessments there is a paucity of literature within the sustainability area from the project perspective.

There are few empirical studies that identify the use of such mechanisms and implementation in practice for sustainability assessments. Lion, Donovan and Bedggood (2013) provid one of the first conceptualisations of loops and suggest that follow up loops exist when businesses apply EIAs at the project level. Further more, Lee (2006) argues that the depth and importance of such follow up loops would be directly correlate to the size and scope of the implemented project.

*Empirical studies*

To our knowledge, there are no empirical studies that investigate feedback and follow up within sustainability assessment. There are, however, some related fields, such as EIA, that provide some insights on how organisations manage such processes at the project level.

Zubair, Bowen and Elwin (2011) demonstrated in their article of environmental impact assessment in the Maldives the inadequacies that exist in the nation's EIA systems. Their research recommended the implementation of feedback loops that would enable "public participation at most stages of the process" (Zubair, Bowen and Elwin 2011, p.232) to improve the relations between the developer, the government and local community groups. The said proposed framework would "present an opportunity for the community to voice their concerns in a transparent manner, to address any grievance and potentially stop any irreversible action from happening" (Zubair, Bowen and Elwin 2011, p.232). However, the barriers of such implementation at the project level were yet to be realised.

This section of the chapter now concludes its focus on the leading research within the impact assessment field. It is clear from the review that there are specific gaps in the field: there are few empirical studies of multinational enterprises (MNEs) incorporating sustainability considerations into their business activities, specifically through a sustainability assessment framework. This provides a compelling basis from which to understand how the private sector might, and can, address sustainability in their business operations. The concluding section of this chapter will now provide an overview of the methods used in the study and more detailed information about its sample.

## Research methods and data collection

To address the objectives of our study, we conducted an exploratory, in-depth investigation of the sustainability practices of foreign multinational organisations. A case study research design was used that enabled us to consider the private sector experiences of sustainability practices across multiple organisations. The value of using case study for this research is that it enables us to "view and study something in its completeness, looking at it from many angles and attempting to understand the interconnectedness of the elements [that] comprise it" (Thomas and Myers 2015, p.15). Within this study, a case is broadly defined as a multinational organisation.

Several criteria were established to determine an organisation's eligibility for participation in the study (more information about the study's sample has been provided in the next section). Organisations had to be foreign multinationals, which for the purposes of this study meant they had to be headquartered in another country other than Thailand. Organisations had to be in manufacturing, services or mining sectors receiving foreign investment. And finally, they had to be either a small enterprise, defined by less than USD$10 million invested in Thailand;

a medium sized enterprise, with more than USD$10 million, but less than USD$100 million investment; or a large MNEs with over USD$100 million investment.

Qualitative methods including individual interviews and archival data were used in this study. Semi-structured interview schedules were used, which enabled flexibility for the interviewer to explore the professional experiences and insights of decision-makers within MNEs. The schedule was also balanced with more structured questions that reflected the objectives of the study. These interviews were conducted with managers at both the subsidiary and headquarter level of the participating organisations.

In addition to the interviews, archival data were collected for each organisation. These items were broad in scope and included a range of different organisational reports (e.g. Corporate Social Responsibility (CSR), sustainability and annual reports), organisational policies, procedures and other general information (e.g. vision statements, organisation's mission statement, and international commitments, etc.), plus publically available sources such as news reports.

Both the interview and archival data were used to provide a basis for the triangulation of data collection. Triangulation is the use of multiple methods, data sources, theories or researchers that are used as a means of corroborating evidence (Stake 1995). This was useful in cases where the occurrence of a phenomenon was identified and could then be corroborated with other data to determine its credibility.

The interviews were transcribed verbatim and after cleaning and blinding, were entered with the other data, into the qualitative data analysis software package, NVivo. The software enabled effective storage and organisation of a very large volume of data. These data were sorted in alignment with each organisation (assigned an organisational code and description of data source, i.e. subsidiary interview). All documents were coded in NVivo using general categories or 'open codes' (Ezzy 2002; Glaser 1978; Strauss and Corbin 1990).

Strauss and Corbin (1990, p.62) describe open coding as "the part of analysis that pertains specifically to the naming and categorising of phenomena through close examination of data". Through the process of coding themes started to emerge. With the emergence of themes, a case study template was developed that was used to record each theme and, in parallel, listed each step of the conceptual framework. This helped ensure that the empirical data addressed the steps identified in the conceptual framework. Where new information or interesting insights were provided, additional coding categories were developed to account for this information. These case study templates formed the basis for the thematic analysis in Chapter 4 though to 6.

## *Classifying sustainability practices*

Beyond the research methods, we developed a classification scheme to aid in the determination and differentiation of organisational performance across the seven steps. This involved four categories to describe the practices of each organisation – 1) World Class 2) International Practices, 3) Host Country Compliance and 4) Non-Disclosure. This enabled us to evaluate the relative performance of the organisations within the sample, as well as identifying types of practices for organisations across each of these four categories.

In terms of the categories, World Class represents the highest level performance of organisations across each step of the corporate sustainability assessment. In classifying organisations within this category, we were looking for organisations that went far beyond what was required by local regulations or basic international standards (such as ISOs). These organisations utilised some type of global guideline or standard to direct their practices, or activities that indicated a very comprehensive approach being adopted to their efforts to address sustainability across environmental, social and economic dimensions. We also utilised the well-established global guidelines, standards and principles to inform us on an initial judgement about classifying the organisation before exploring further their actual practices (and whether these guidelines, standards and principles in fact translated into activities). This included the Global Reporting Initiative (GRI) standards, the International Finance Corporation (IFC) sustainability principles, the Equator Principles, the United Nations Global Compact (UNGC) and the World Business Council for Sustainable Development.

The next category is referred to as International Practices, which was the second highest category in the classification scheme. This category indicated that the organisation is going beyond what is required by local laws and regulations, and engaging in the use of an international approach to their sustainability practices. In determining the classification of organisations within this category, we reviewed first whether the organisation had specific policies or procedures in place to address sustainability within their business operations. This included corporate policies for environmental management, social inclusion, health and safety, community engagement or economic empowerment. There were several common bases that were initially identified and later refined as we began the classification of these organisations within this category. This included the MNEs home country regulations (if this exceeded expectations within Thailand), international standards (i.e. ISO 14000, ISO 9000, ISO 50001, ISO 26000) that were not required through local regulations, or industry specific sustainability policies that were set through an international body. In general, we were looking for differences in the types of practices that indicated these corporate policies and procedures, or commitments to different international standards, showed that the organisation was going beyond requirements set within Thailand.

We also decided to differentiate organisations between World Class practices and International Practices based on the degree to which they implemented global guidelines or standards. Where organisations indicated some alignment or potential commitment towards achieving the requirements of the GRI standards, UNGC principles or other global guidelines/standards, we sought to determine how much this translated into actual practices of these organisations within Thailand. Thus, some organisations were classified within this category if we could not determine how these global guidelines/standards actually informed and directed the types of activities these organisations put in place. Our interviews, in particular, were aimed at determining the sequence between the organisational commitments to these global guidelines/standards, and how this was implemented in their operations within Thailand. Archival data also were useful in this classification, with reporting processes often indicating how far practices associated with our corporate sustainability assessment framework were being implemented. For instance, organisations utilising the GRI reporting guidelines often indicated within their sustainability reports the extent to which different data were collected, the breadth of their materiality assessment adopted and where and to what extent mitigation or enhancement strategies were being implemented.

The third category is referred to as Host Country Compliance (or Host Country practices), and indicated that the organisation specifically referred to local laws directing their practices. In this category, we looked to see whether the organisation sought to go beyond local laws and regulations (and was therefore potentially within the International Practices category), or whether they expressed the importance of explicitly complying to local regulatory requirements associated with sustainability in their business operations. These local regulations may relate to different requirements under the investment, environmental, social, enterprise or employment laws. We were also able to differentiate this classification between organisations within the International Practices category through statements made by organisations about activities taken beyond regulation, such as adopting certain corporate policies around environmental management.

The final classification we utilised was Non-Disclosure, which was our lowest classification relating to the sustainability practices. This classification indicated that we were unable to determine the extent of the MNE's sustainability practices; this includes even meeting basic local regulatory requirements. We included organisations in this category if we were unable to see evidence or have explicit examples of what sustainability practices organisations were putting in place, even if respondents in the interviews made statements regarding global, international or host country practices. We sought to find specific examples of their practices to demonstrate broad statements, so it was not uncommon for organisations in this classification to state how they adopt all local laws for sustainability or environmental protection, but when asked to elaborate on how this occurred, which law they were following and how this was demonstrated by substantive activities of the organisation (including through our field visits to their operational location), the respondents were unable to demonstrate the substance of their statements.

It should also be noted that some organisations were put into this classification due to the inability to get sufficient information to classify their practices – this was particularly experienced through organisations from North East Asia, who often demonstrated significant reluctance to respond to questions or to requests for further interviews. Of course, this might not mean that they are not adopting any practices, and may just relate to a transparency, language or corporate communication approach; it, nevertheless, translated into our classification of these organisations within this classification.

Moving beyond this classification scheme adopted as part of this research, the next section concludes this chapter with an overview of the data sample utilised. This includes identifying most broadly where these multinational enterprises have their headquarters located (region), the size of their investment and the sector that they operate within. While over 46 organisations were initially interviewed in the broader sample of multinational enterprises for Thailand, our sample was reviewed and refined during the process of interviewing due to limitations on organisation involvement, availability of respondents and willingness of the organisations to be involved in follow up interviews for further information. The final sample of organisations was 29, although our study here only includes 23 organisations, as a further six organisations were removed due to the inability to triangulate the data collected, limitations in the amount of data detailing their practices, or limitations on the use of the data collected (due to respondent preferences on reporting – with this research utilising rigorous research protocols based on Australian research standards that direct the handling of data and respondent preferences for reporting).

### Thailand sample

An overview is visually presented of the data collected for examining MNEs operating in Thailand, contextualising this within the broader context of investment entering the region. As noted above, the Thailand sample of MNEs that forms the basis for the evaluation of sustainability practices is comprised of 23 organisations. Of these, 74 per cent are considered large by international standards, with over USD$100 million invested in Thailand. The remaining 26 per cent are considered within the Small to Medium Enterprise (SME) category, with roughly half of these being small (below USD$10 million investment).

The world map below indicates the percentage of firms from different regional locations, with 30 per cent from North East Asia and Australasia, 13 per cent from North America, 17 per cent from Europe and 8 per cent from South Asia and ASEAN. This largely reflects the dominance of these countries within the top investment sources for FDI in the region (with the darker blue colour on the map indicating the significance of investment from these locations for the overall region, with the EU and Japan dominating). The sample does have a larger representation from of MNEs from Australasia than what is reflected within regional dynamics.

The sector breakdown also indicates a dominance of manufacturing firms in the sample (70 per cent), which also reflects current patterns of FDI entering into Thailand. A smaller percentage of services and mining organisations were also captured as part of the sample to illustrate some initial insights into other sectors.

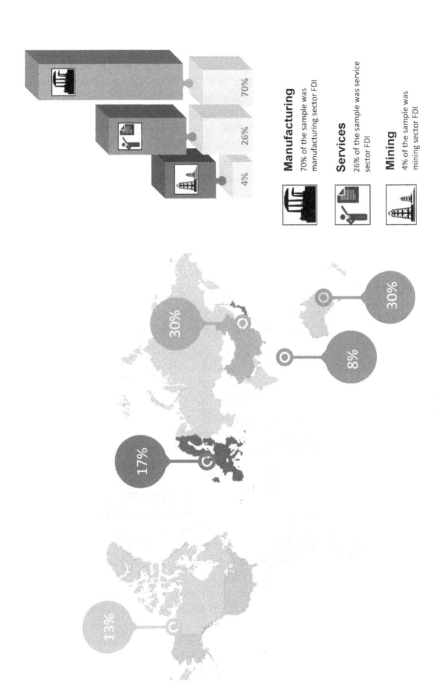

**Manufacturing**
70% of the sample was manufacturing sector FDI

**Services**
26% of the sample was service sector FDI

**Mining**
4% of the sample was mining sector FDI

70%

26%

4%

30%

8%

30%

17%

13%

*Figure 3.2* Investment sources and sectors for Thailand

*Table 3.1* Overview of sample

| Organisation Code | Sector | Size | Home Country Region |
|---|---|---|---|
| TH01 | Manufacturing | Large | North East Asia |
| TH02 | Manufacturing | Large | North East Asia |
| TH03 | Manufacturing | Large | North East Asia |
| TH04 | Manufacturing | Large | Europe |
| TH05 | Manufacturing | Large | South Asia |
| TH06 | Manufacturing | Large | North East Asia |
| TH07 | Manufacturing | Large | North East Asia |
| TH08 | Manufacturing | Large | North America |
| TH09 | Manufacturing | Small | Australasia |
| TH10 | Manufacturing | Large | Europe |
| TH11 | Manufacturing | Large | Europe |
| TH12 | Manufacturing | Large | North America |
| TH13 | Manufacturing | Large | North East Asia |
| TH14 | Manufacturing | Large | North East Asia |
| TH15 | Mining | Large | Australasia |
| TH16 | Services | Medium | Australasia |
| TH17 | Services | Small | Australasia |
| TH18 | Manufacturing | Large | Australasia |
| TH19 | Services | Small | Australasia |
| TH20 | Services | Large | Australasia |
| TH21 | Manufacturing | Medium | Europe |
| TH22 | Services | Small | North America |
| TH23 | Services | Large | ASEAN |

Table 3.1 provides a more detailed breakdown of the organisations with the sample, including the organisational code, sector, size and home country region. The organisation code has been utilised to de-identify all organisations within the sample. This protects the confidentiality and anonymity preferences of respondents, with the majority of the organisations having at least one respondent requesting anonymity for their involvement in the project. We therefore removed all identifying features that would enable the identification of respondents to protect their preferences.

## Conclusion

This review of the sustainability assessment literature both highlights the specific gaps in the impact assessment field and the emergence of a conceptual framework for use in this study. Our conceptual framework presents seven key steps that address issues and impacts associated with business activities. It is worth noting, that while the steps have been defined as separate procedural steps, we do acknowledge that there is some blurring between them and that in reality, they may not be as distinct as this framework illustrates. Nonetheless, we have tried to provide a framework that is readily accessible despite it not being a linear process in actual practice. To close this chapter, we provide a brief summary of the framework's seven steps before moving to Chapter 4, which will provide a brief overview of the sustainability performance of the multinational enterprises within the sample.

In summary, the steps of the conceptual framework consist of the following:

1   **Screening** seeks to identify issues and impact areas associated with both the direct and indirect aspects of the organisation's business operations.
2   **Scoping** is where the sustainability goals are refined and from here, the issues identified in the screening step are prioritised for further exploration in the assessment.
3   **Impact analysis** is where each issue identified and prioritised in the scoping step is analysed to understand the effects and/or implications it will have for the business, the environment and the local community in which the activity is located.
4   **Alternative selection** is about how to deal with different types of impact – be it negative (through mitigation) or positive (through enhancement) impacts.
5   **Monitoring** aims to capture the impacts of the mitigation and enhancement strategies of the business activity on an ongoing basis through measurable methods.
6   **Evaluation** of impacts occurs through the monitoring of the implemented mitigation and enhancement strategies related to the business' activity.
7   **Feedback and follow up** is the final step of the sustainability assessment where organisations integrate their performance data to inform their decision-making processes once again, and address their impacts potentially through adjusting their mitigation and enhancement strategies.

## References

Akroyd, D. 1999, 'Logical framework approach to project planning, socio-economic analysis and to monitoring and evaluation services: A smallholder rice project', *Impact Assessment and Project Appraisal*, vol. 17, no. 1, pp. 54–66.

Arce-Gomez, A., Donovan, J.D. and Bedggood, R.E. 2015, 'Social impact assessments: Developing a consolidated conceptual framework', *Environmental Impact Assessment Review*, vol. 50, pp. 85–94.

Bjorkland, R. 2013, 'Monitoring: The missing piece: A critique of NEPA monitoring', *Environmental Impact Assessment Review*, vol. 43, pp. 129–134.

Bond, A.J. and Morrison-Saunders, A. 2011, 'Re-evaluating sustainability assessment: Aligning the vision and the practice', *Environmental Impact Assessment Review*, vol. 31, no. 1, pp. 1–7.

Bond, A.J., Morrison-Saunders, A. and Howitt, R. 2012, *Sustainability assessment: Pluralism, practice and progress*, London: Routledge.

Bond, A.J., Morrison-Saunders, A. and Howitt, R. 2013, *Sustainability assessment: Pluralism, practice and progress*, London: Routledge.

Bond, A.J., Morrison-Saunders, A. and Pope, J. 2012, 'Sustainability assessment: The state of the art', *Impact Assessment and Project Appraisal*, vol. 30, no. 1, pp. 53–62.

Canter, L. and Ross, B. 2014, 'A basic need for integration – bringing focus to the scoping process', *Impact Assessment and Project Appraisal*, vol. 32, no. 1, pp. 21–22.

de Ridder, W., Turnpenny, J., Nilsson, M. and Von Raggamby, A. 2007, 'A framework for tool selection and use in integrated assessment for sustainable development', *Journal of Environmental Assessment Policy and Management*, vol. 9, no. 4, pp. 423–441.

Dey, P.K. 2001, 'Integrated approach to project feasibility analysis: A case study', *Impact Assessment and Project Appraisal*, vol. 19, no. 3, pp. 235–245.

Duinker, P. and Beanlands, G. 1986, 'The significance of environmental impacts: An exploration of the concept', *Environmental Management*, vol. 10, no. 1, pp. 1–10.

Duncan, R. and Hay, P. 2007, 'A question of balance in integrated impact assessment: Negotiating away the environmental interest in Australia's Basslink project', *Journal of Environmental Assessment Policy and Management*, vol. 9, no. 3, pp. 273–297.

Eales, R., Smith, S., Twigger-Ross, C., Sheate, W., Özdemiroglu, E., Fry, C., Tomlinson, P. and Foan, C. 2005, 'Emerging approaches to integrated appraisal in the UK', *Impact Assessment and Project Appraisal*, vol. 23, no. 2, pp. 113–123.

Ezzy, D. 2002, *Qualitative analysis: Practice and innovation*, Allen & Unwin, Crows Nest.

Gibson, R.B. 2006, 'Sustainability assessment: Basic components of a practical approach', *Impact Assessment and Project Appraisal*, vol. 24, no. 3, pp. 170–182.

Gibson, R.B. 2013, 'Avoiding sustainability trade-offs in environmental assessment', *Impact Assessment and Project Appraisal*, vol. 31, no. 1, pp. 2–12.

Gibson, R.B., Hassan, S., Holtz, S., Tansey, J., and Whitelaw, G. 2005, *Sustainability assessment: Criteria and processes*, Earthscan, London.

Glaser, B.G. 1978, *Theoretical sensitivity: Advances in the methodology of grounded theory*, Sociology Press, Mill Valley.

Glasson, J. 2005, 'Better monitoring for better impact management: The local socio-economic impacts of constructing sizewell B nuclear power station', *Impact Assessment and Project Appraisal*, vol. 23, no. 3, pp. 215–226.

Hacking, T. and Guthrie, P. 2008, 'A framework for clarifying the meaning of triple bottom-line, Integrated, and sustainability assessment', *Environmental Impact Assessment Review*, vol. 28, no. 2, pp. 73–89.

João, E., Vanclay, F. and den Broeder, L. 2011, 'Emphasising enhancement in all forms of impact assessment: Introduction to a special issue', *Impact Assessment and Project Appraisal*, vol. 29, no. 3, pp. 170–180.

Lee, N. 2006, 'Bridging the gap between theory and practice in integrated assessment', *Environmental Impact Assessment Review*, vol. 26, no. 1, pp. 57–78.

Lion, H., Donovan, J.D. and Bedggood, R.E. 2013, 'Environmental impact assessments from a business perspective: Extending knowledge and guiding business practice', *Journal of Business Ethics*, vol. 117, no. 4, pp. 789–805.

Locher, H. 2001, *Summary Report. Basslink Integrated Impact Assessment Statement: Potential effects of changes to hydro power generation, prepared for* Hydro Tasmania, Hobart.

Marshall, R., Arts, J. and Morrison-Saunders, A. 2005, 'International principles for best practice EIA follow-up', *Impact Assessment and Project Appraisal*, vol. 23, no. 3, pp. 175–181.

Morrison-Saunders, A. and Pope, J. 2013, 'Conceptualising and managing trade-offs in sustainability assessment', *Environmental Impact Assessment Review*, vol. 38, pp. 54–63.

Morrison-Saunders, A., Pope, J., Bond, A. and Retief, F. 2014a, 'Towards sustainability assessment follow-up', *Environmental Impact Assessment Review*, vol. 45, pp. 38–45.

Morrison-Saunders, A., Pope, J., Gunn, J., Bond, A. and Retief, F. 2014b, 'Strengthening impact assessment: A call for integration and focus', *Impact Assessment and Project Appraisal*, vol. 1, no. 32, pp. 2–8.

Orenstein, M., Fossgard-Moser, T., Hindmarch, T., Dowse, S., Kuschminder, J., McCloskey, P. and Mugo, R.K. 2010, 'Case study of an integrated assessment: Shell's north field test in Alberta, Canada', *Impact Assessment and Project Appraisal*, vol. 28, no. 2, pp. 147–157.

Pope, J. 2006, 'Editorial: What's so special about sustainability assessment?', *Journal of Environmental Assessment, Policy and Management*, vol. 8, no. 3, pp. v–ix.

Pope, J., Annandale, D. and Morrison-Saunders, A. 2004, 'Conceptualising sustainability assessment', *Environmental Impact Assessment Review*, vol. 24, no. 6, pp. 595–616.

Pope, J. and Klass, D. 2010, 'Decision quality for sustainability assessment', *Conference Proceedings of the 30th Annual Conference of the International Association for Impact Assessment: Transitioning to the Green Economy, Held Geneva, Switzerland*.

Pope, J., Morrison-Saunders, A. and Annandale, D. 2005, 'Applying sustainability assessment models', *Impact Assessment and Project Appraisal*, vol. 23, no. 4, pp. 293–302.

Rotmans, J. and Van Asselt, M. 1996, 'Integrated assessment: A growing child on its way to maturity', *Climatic Change*, vol. 34, no. 3–4, pp. 327–336.

Sadler, B. 1996, 'International study of the effectiveness of environmental assessment, final report', *Environmental Assessment in a Changing World: Evaluating Practice to Improve Performance' Canadian Environmental Assessment Agency and the International Association for Impact Assessment, Minister of Supply and Services, Canada*.

Sippe, R. 1990, 'Power and accountability: The contribution of environmental impact assessment to sustainable development in Western Australia', *Conference Proceedings of the Science, Assessment and Sustainability Conference, International Association for Impact Assessment Held in Vancouver, Canada*.

Stake, R.E. 1995, *The art of case study research*, SAGE, Thousand Oaks.

Strauss, A.L. and Corbin, J.M. 1990, *Basics of qualitative research: Grounded theory procedures and techniques*, SAGE, Newbury Park.

sustainability-assessment.org 2015, *Corporate Sustainability Practices*, Sustainability Assessment, viewed 9th December 2015, http://www.sustainability-assessment.org/

Therivel, R. 2004, *Strategic environmental assessment in action*, Earthscan, United Kingdom.

Thomas, G. and Myers, K. 2015, *The anatomy of the case study*, SAGE Publications, London.

Weston, J. 2000, 'EIA decision-making theory and screening and scoping in UK practice', *Journal of Planning and Environmental Management*, vol. 45, no.2, pp.185-204.

Zubair, S., Bowen, D., & Elwin, J. 2011, 'Not quite paradise: inadequacies of environmental impact assessment in the Maldives', *Tourism Management*, vol. 32, no. 2, pp. 225–234

# 4   Sustainability practices in Thailand

*Jerome D. Donovan, Eryadi K. Masli, Cheree Topple, Masayoshi Ike, Thomas Borgert, Teerin Vanichseni, Laddawan Lekmat, Lalita Hongratanawong and Jirapan Kunthawangso*

Having provided a detailed account of the theoretical framework, research methods and sample in Chapter 3, we now turn to exploring some of the initial findings. This chapter serves to provide a high-level overview of the results, illustrating the percentage of organisations classified within different categories of performance for their sustainability practices. Ranging from World Class to Non-disclosure, this chapter also elaborates upon the types of practices seen across these different levels of performance. This will serve as a useful anchor point for the sustainability practices of multinationals within Thailand, before the subsequent chapters review more specific results and examples from organisations within both the manufacturing and service sectors.

The analysis in this chapter will follow the seven steps of the corporate sustainability assessment established in Chapter 3. In utilising this approach, this chapter is able to provide a gauge as to the overall performance of the foreign multinationals within the sample, before examining the comparative performance of the service and manufacturing sectors. This will also provide a succinct contribution to existing knowledge of the sustainability practices of multinationals, which has received relatively little attention in the extant literature. This, to our knowledge, will be the first larger scale study to provide empirical support to the conceptual and theoretical work that has been previously undertaken by scholars in the discipline.

Launching from here, this chapter will now provide a high-level snapshot of the overall performance of multinationals within the sample across the seven steps. Subsequent to this, the chapter will then turn to examining the performance across each of the seven steps.

## Overview of MNE sustainability practices

Most broadly, the following figure (Figure 4.1) demonstrates the performance of MNEs in Thailand across the seven sustainability steps and the four categories of classification. The radar chart is indexed with the percentage of MNEs at each step within our corporate sustainability framework within each of the four categories.

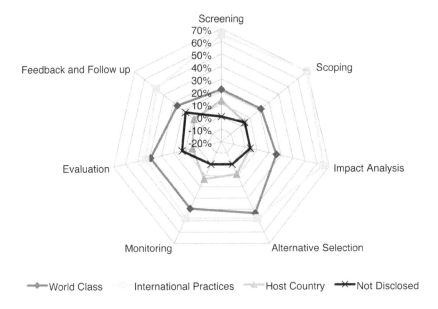

*Figure 4.1* Sustainability practices of MNEs in Thailand

It is quite clear from examining this figure that there is a dominance of MNEs adopting International Practices. This is consistent right across the seven steps of the corporate sustainability assessment. The next most prominent category is World Class performance. The Host Country and Non-disclosure categories do not figure highly when reviewing this figure. While a dominance of MNEs operating at the level of International Practices is not overly positive when looking from the perspective of MNEs and the role of foreign direct investment in the development progress of Thailand, it does nevertheless indicate a tendency to go beyond the local regulations when addressing sustainability.

Indeed, the higher level of International Practices being implemented across the sample indicates that these organisations are attempting to address sustainability beyond the regulatory requirements. This also indicates the potential of these organisations continuing to develop their practices further, shifting towards adopting World Class practices, through a voluntary approach. The low level of Non-disclosure across the sample also indicates a general engagement of MNEs in being transparent in their practices for sustainability.

Obviously for both the host country government and society, the desire would be to see these organisations adopting practices at the World Class level. This would see an increasing emphasis on the use of guidelines that holistically address sustainability across environmental, social and economic dimensions. Moreover, it might translate into the further use of globally accepted standards or guidelines developed by the Global Reporting Initiative (GRI), the World Business Council for Sustainable Development, the United Nations Global Compact (UNGC), amongst many others, which would see the implementation of proactive policies by MNEs in engaging sustainability across their business activities.

Moving beyond this high-level overview of the overall practices, we now turn to examining the individual steps of the corporate sustainability assessment framework. With this examination, we will present some general findings from across the framework that will highlight differences in the practices of the MNEs that are associated with each of the four performance categories.

## Screening

Turning first and foremost to the screening step, our understanding of screening has been informed from the descriptions of Gibson (2006), Bond, Morrison-Saunders and Howitt (2013) and, Bond and Morrison-Saunders (2011). Screening essentially is about identifying the appropriate issues that emerge for a new or continuing project. This process of effective identification comes from defining and determining the project's sustainability requirements. This can be influenced by regulatory requirements, international industry guidelines and corporate policies of the decision-maker, and from key stakeholder groups.

Results indicate 22 per cent of MNEs operating in Thailand are adopting World Class practices (see Figure 4.2, Screening practices of MNEs in Thailand). It was evident in a range of these organisations that different global initiatives were being integrated, such as the GRI, UNGC, Carbon Disclosure Project (CDP) and a range of international standards (ISOs 22000, 26000 and OHSAS 18000). These organisations were clearly attempting to go beyond the financial bottom line to include sustainability considerations across environmental, economic and social dimensions of the local community into their business activities.

By far the most prevalent category is International Practices, with 65 per cent of the sample classified within this category. Organisations within this category had a significant tendency towards concentrating on environmental management and mitigation, often adopting CDP and a range of ISOs including 50001', 9000, 14000 (or in some cases, particularly for organisations from North East Asia, reference was made to home country environmental laws) and were also accounting for significant reporting around their carbon footprint (often linked with the CDP). This included within the manufacturing sector, where it was quite

*Figure 4.2* Screening practices of MNEs in Thailand

common to see full life-cycle assessments conducted on their environmental impact and mitigation strategies. These organisations also tended to have a more ad-hoc approach to addressing socio-economic issues within their operations, typified by a focus on health and safety initiatives and corporate social responsibility programs that did not appear to be very systematic nor actually address issues and impacts from their business activities.

The final category was organisations within the Host Country Compliance category, with 13 per cent of MNEs operating at this level. These organisations made specific comments around the local regulatory context, and specific reference to conforming with all the local legal and regulatory requirements for foreign investors. Here, organisations also drew on ex-ante requirements (particularly for environmental impact assessments) that influenced their investment decisions and their legal requirements for operating within Thailand. This was particularly in the form of environmental protection, where organisations made specific reference to the range of different issues and indicators that needed to be considered.

Attention now turns to looking more closely at the issue and impact identification (screening) practices adopted by foreign multinationals operating within Thailand. As discussed earlier, this step within the sustainability assessment framework is particularly important for enabling organisations to identify and specify the broad range of potential and actual issues and impacts associated with their business activities within the local community of the proposed project.

In Thailand, it was apparent that this step was much more complex than implied by the extant literature and conceptual work previously discussed in Chapter 3. It appears that the headquarter operations, the organisation's strategy and the international commitments of the organisation to different global sustainability standards and guidelines are all critical factors in determining the approach implemented to screening.

In particular, the majority of organisations make it clear that basic business acumen still drives all decisions before considering sustainability. It was commonly noted by different respondents across the cases that the investment in Thailand must first address the organisation's financial bottom line – it must be profitable. Once the organisation was able to determine this, they started to extend their analysis into other factors affecting their operations, such as ability to implement the corporate strategy, local laws, human resource availability, location and position within the region, type of operations, amongst other factors.

With investment in Thailand deemed financially viable, then MNEs' attention then focused on addressing the sustainability agenda. This generally began with the organisations explicitly adopting the policies and procedures of their headquarter operations, and in the case of sustainability, the strategy, policies and procedures to address sustainability. It was very clear that the headquarter operations had a decisive role in whether the subsidiary/operations in Thailand was going to address sustainability and to what extent. Organisations that did not have a comprehensive corporate strategy, or international commitments and guidelines at the headquarter level, tended to adopt lower-level practices to address sustainability and be more compliance driven or conform to very basic international standards.

For higher-level practices being implemented within Thailand, it was clear that the headquarter approach to sustainability was critical. Where they had commitments to the GRI, UNGC, amongst others, it was much more likely that at this step they would have multiple levels of issue identification and selection. Starting with a core set of issues/indicators aligned with their international commitments, consistently applied across their international operations. This is where standards like that of GRI were important, identifying a range of core issues that should be considered in all contexts.

The next element of screening for these organisations was through the consideration of locally relevant issues, including looking at local problems/issues/ challenges that need consideration, or differences in regulatory requirements that could also be addressed. Finally, it was evident that organisations in this category also had global agendas for what they wanted to cover from a corporate perspective, which would also direct the subsidiary to consider these issues. This could include engagement with local businesses and supply chain integration, education policies or initiatives, or contributing towards certain types of social issues, like HIV prevention.

These organisations tended to have specific processes that allowed the clear specification of the types of issues and impacts that they could face when operating in Thailand. These were both specific and direct business activities, like environmental management systems for potential pollution from facilities or electricity and water consumption for production, amongst others. They could be broad with indirect impacts associated with operations within a specified location. For example, the movement of labour to a location to provide a workforce for operations; pressure on local infrastructure to provide facilities for a migrant workforce; or, an ability to engage local workforce mobilisation through improved training facilities for the local community.

These organisations clearly went beyond the simple 'bottom line' approach of financial analysis, return on investment, operational costs, risks and potential uncertainties. Broadening the consideration of issues and impacts for inclusion in the business plan, engaging with the external community including the government, local community leaders, minorities and disadvantaged groups, and non-governmental organisations (NGOs). These stakeholder groups provide invaluable insights that extend far beyond the traditional business focus of organisational decision-making, and allow the local context to be considered.

## Scoping: issue refinement and impact focus

Within the literature, the scoping step is closely linked with the screening process. The scoping step commences with the refinement of the sustainability goals that were established in the screening step and from here, the issues identified in the screening step are prioritised for further exploration in the assessment. Like screening, scoping also requires the integration of stakeholders in this process to assist with scoping key issues from a community perspective, and thus the refinement of these key issues.

Results indicate that 22 per cent of MNEs operating in Thailand are adopting World Class practices (see Figure 4.3, Scoping practices of MNEs in Thailand) for the scoping step. Global guidelines again played an important role here, particularly through the GRI Organization and the use of materiality assessments. Organisations within this category utilised the materiality assessment procedures to engage with local stakeholders (with some links with screening for issues) to determine which issues and impacts were most important, in addition to the issues and impacts identified in the previous step. This resulted in a localisation and stakeholder perspective being incorporated into their activities to address sustainability.

The prevalence of International Practices was again evident in this step, with 70 per cent of MNEs classified within this category. International Practices reflect a tendency of MNEs in Thailand to use a technical approach with pre-established lists of considerations. This includes the use of discipline, industry or organisational specific standards (such as the CDP; Environmental, Health or Safety Systems), that may not offer an entire coverage of relevant local issues/impacts or a methodology to include impacts that are most significant for the local community. There was also a tendency within the manufacturing sector to only consider the locally relevant issues and impacts for environmental issues, albeit, in a very comprehensive manner (through a life-cycle assessment).

The final two categories, Host Country Compliance and Non-disclosure, only had a very small percentage of the sample in each – with 4 per cent of organisations, or 1/23, being classified in both of these categories. Both of which were service organisations. For the Host Country category, it was evident that the localisation of issues and impacts considered, and stakeholder involvement, was through the local contextualisation of environmental and social laws that adapted the practices of the organisation to suit the local context. The organisation within the Non-disclosure category did not reveal any information to indicate any localisation or refinement of issues was being undertaken.

Figure 4.3 Scoping practices of MNEs in Thailand

As detailed above, our review of the extant literature indicated that scoping allows organisations to focus on the type of locally relevant issues and impacts that they need to measure, monitor, evaluate and report on. This literature implies that this process refines all of those issues and impacts identified within the screening step, and then focuses the organisation on what is most important within the context of the specific project.

In doing so, this step is thought to also be contingent on the earlier screening step, as without appropriate breadth and depth to the issues and impacts identified, the scoping of these issues and impacts will be irrelevant. That is to say, at the core of the screening step, a foundation of issues and impacts must be identified, with additional issues and impacts that are relevant for the local community and broader stakeholder groups. Without the identification of locally relevant issues and impacts, this step will essentially entail prioritising generic issues and impacts that may or may not be relevant for the local community.

What we actually found from examining the data was that this step was split between two key approaches. First, a group of organisations appear to have utilised an established list of issues from the screening step (be it from a broad sustainability perspective, or a narrow single dimension perspective, such as environmental standards) and changed this very little in scoping, with some minor embellishments through stakeholder engagement. Or second, they utilised these issues identified in screening and actively engaged with stakeholders to determine which should be prioritised and focused upon. The majority of organisations tend to retain all the key issues identified through established lists within the screening step, and this may be directed through international commitments to global guidelines or international standards, or even local regulatory requirements.

It was at the World Class category where we saw the second perspective emerge. Organisations that were within this category tended to move beyond the core set of indicators derived from global guidelines or international standards that they were committed to. The majority of the MNEs that were classified within this category utilised a materiality assessment to differentiate the issues and impacts they focused on, and engage with external stakeholders, and particularly the local communities in which they operated. While we will explore the materiality assessment more through practical examples in the following chapters, it is worth noting here that this is a tool that seeks to identify and prioritise issues and impacts from both an internal and external perspective. Essentially organisations using a materiality assessment identify a range of stakeholders to ask what is most important to them, and they weigh this against the priorities of the organisation. From this, organisations are able to identify and focus on particular issues that are of most importance or impact to both their stakeholders and the organisation.

The issues and impacts that were identified through the materiality assessment were often integrated on top of the existing core issues and impacts already identified by the organisation through the screening step. This did not result in a narrower perspective of what was analysed, but rather extended the core areas covered with specific issues and impacts that reflected the perspective of external stakeholders. So scoping in the context of our sample of MNEs actually reflects a different scenario than what was expected from extant literature. Rather than being a process to refine issues and impacts for the organisation, it was actually a process – through a materiality assessment – to bring in the external perspective through stakeholder engagement to identify meaningful issues and impacts that the organisation should also consider in their operations.

## Impact analysis: determining the impact of business activities

In impact analysis, each issue identified and prioritised in the scoping step is analysed to understand the effects and/or implications it will have for the business, the environment and the local community in which the activity is located. Organisational decision-making is informed by the use of various methods, tools and techniques, and with the mimicking of mechanisms from EIAs for sustainability assessment, baseline studies are considered essential for impact analysis. Both quantitative and qualitative analyses are expected to be used in this step, particularly with the diversity of measures likely to emerge from a broad focus on environmental, social and economic impacts.

With regards to the impact analysis step, the results indicate an increase in the number of organisations adopting World Class practices – with 26 per cent in this category, versus 22 per cent in screening and scoping (see Figure 4.4, Impact analysis practices of MNEs in Thailand). These organisations are adopting comprehensive practices to measure their issues and impacts across environmental, economic and social dimensions. Two particular international guidelines played an important role in these organisations: the GRI and the UNGC. It was clear from the organisations in this category that many utilised these two sources of international guidance to direct how and what issues and indicators were utilised to determine their impact.

Turning to International Practices, the ongoing high level of organisations classified within this category is again evident with 65 per cent of MNEs adopting International Practices. This reflects the tendency of the impact analysis

*Figure 4.4* Impact analysis practices of MNEs in Thailand

techniques of MNEs in Thailand to focus largely on environmental issues and impacts – with a limited account of social, economic and community-based indicators. This was particularly linked with the adoption of international standards by the manufacturing sector, such as through the CDP, which offers an excellent basis for determining and reporting $CO^2$ emissions, but was not designed to integrate other non-environmental impacts. While these organisations were clearly going above local requirements, they still have some progress needed to more fully account for social and economic indicators beyond the financial bottom line.

In the final two categories, Host Country Compliance and Non-disclosure, again only one organisation was classified in each category, reflecting a similar result as scoping. For the Host Country category, it was clear that the service organisation classified in this category was focusing on measuring only those issues that were required by the local government. For the service organisation in the Non-disclosure category, we were unable to determine whether they were utilising any methods to determine their impact.

Looking more closely at the results, it was clear to see the progression of practices in the screening and scoping steps into the impact analysis. Both organisations in the bottom two categories remained in these bottom two categories. At the Host Country level, the organisation focused on the areas specifically required by the government. For the Non-disclosure category, it was unclear whether the organisation was actually attempting to analyse any impacts other than the financial perspective orientated around the profitability of the organisation's operations in Thailand. Organisations in the World Class and International Practices categories tended to conform to the level of practices implemented in the first two steps, focusing on the scope of issues and impacts already identified and aligning this with their measurement approach.

For organisations that were adopting International Practices, it was evident that they tended to be drawing on a range of international standards and guidelines with limited stakeholder engagement and localisation, and subsequently followed these practices when implementing their impact analysis. These organisations did not seek to go beyond the areas already identified in screening and scoping, and did not seek to extend the analysis beyond identifying measurement tools and methods associated with these issues. There was also a tendency for these organisations to adopt technical-based approaches, with a focus on environmental issues and indicators. A more limited account was given to social and economic indicators when determining their impact and identifying tools and techniques for measuring these.

With regards to the World Class category, the link with earlier practices was again evident, with these organisations largely adopting similar-level practices in screening and scoping. From the identified issues, drawn from the core sustainability issues required through their international commitments and guidelines as well as the localised or externally identified issues, they proceeded to identify different methods for capturing data on these issues. It was quite apparent across the organisations within this category that the corporate or headquarter strategy was critical in directing the subsidiary activities around the methods and systems put in place for their impact analysis.

The corporate or headquarter strategy for impact analysis was also very much informed by the international or global guidelines that these organisations used. Many of the impact analysis approaches or issues areas covered were linked back to requirements for their international or global compliance mechanisms. This even informed the methods implemented and type of data that the organisations sought to collect, with the GRI, for example, identifying a range of different reporting requirements that were linked with how these organisations would conduct the impact analysis. This was also evident across the impact analysis areas covered in the UNGC Principles and different industry or issue standards such as the CDP.

Baseline points were also identified by these organisations, demonstrating that these organisations planned to establish longitudinal monitoring for their activities through their impact analysis approach. The baseline usually offered an anchor point for ongoing impact analysis of key issues, capturing an early point of impact analysis with data, and then measuring later performance data against these. This was not consistently applied across all their issue areas, with some MNEs showing a tendency to regularly update their impact analysis through new issues and impacts identified in their materiality assessment.

It is also worth noting that many of the organisations within the World Class category were adopting multidisciplinary tools trying to capture their different impacts, not just solely focusing on scientific methods for determining impacts. This ranged from very technical and quantitative methods, through to qualitative and more discrete approaches to determining impact through participatory methods (such as focus groups, interviews and observation). There was a heavier reliance though on quantitative methodologies, which allowed for easier impact analysis and determination of performance across the different issue and impact areas.

## Alternative selection

From the analysis of impacts and issues related to the business activity, the decision-maker determines whether: an alternative is to be implemented and therefore, change the business activity; or, a mitigation strategy is needed to address the impact, should it be negative; or, provide a level of enhancement, if the impact is positive. Furthermore, there is an iterative process within this step, where any newly proposed mitigation or enhancement strategies are examined for alignment with the sustainability objectives of the project to ensure the sustainability outcomes set at the beginning of the assessment are likely to be fulfilled. As has been seen in the previous steps of the conceptual framework, effective stakeholder engagement is paramount to the process, and within this step, is critical for the shaping of the mitigation and enhancement strategies.

Results for alternative selection see a dramatic change from what was evident in earlier steps of the corporate sustainability assessment with some 43 per cent of organisations operating within Thailand classified at the World Class level. This is significantly higher than the first three steps. Again, global guidelines played an important role here, flowing from the impact analysis undertaken. But, it was also evident that organisations focused on adopting ISOs, and in particular, ISO 26000, were also undertaking a comprehensive approach to implementing strategies for both mitigation and enhancement for the issues that they had identified. This was consistently seen across all sustainability dimensions, although the manufacturing sector had a significant focus on undertaking a life-cycle analysis and identifying ways to address their environmental footprint right across their direct and indirect issues/impacts.

For International Practices, while there was a significant percentage of the sample in this category, it saw a large decrease from the previous steps resulting from the increase seen in the World Class category. In total, 48 per cent of organisations were classified in the International Practices category. These MNEs tended to have a more significant focus on environmental strategies, again driven by the larger percentage of manufacturing organisations in the sample. A major point of differentiation for the practices here was the scope of the focus on socio-economic strategies being implemented beyond basic human resource strategies (including health and safety, training and development, amongst others) and corporate social responsibility programs, including through donations, community activities and sponsorships.

As can be seen in Figure 4.5, the remaining 9 per cent or 2/23 organisations in the sample were classified in the Host Country Compliance category, with no organisations in the Non-disclosure category. Both of these organisations were in the service sector and emphasised the importance of local regulations and laws in directing changes that they made to their operations when entering into Thailand.

When examining these results more closely, it is clear that organisations are broadly engaging with the need to adjust their practices in response to sustainability issues. It could be seen from the Host Country Compliance category through to the World Class category, with practices becoming more comprehensive and more broadly addressing the sustainability dimensions as they move towards the World Class category. At both the Host Country and International

*Figure 4.5* Alternative selection practices of MNEs in Thailand

Practices category, organisations have a heavy focus on addressing and changing their practices for environmental protection, driven at the most basic level by local laws and regulations. This becomes more comprehensive moving into the International Practices category, with different discipline specific standards, ISOs and home country regulations influencing the scope of alternatives being implemented.

It is worth noting that for International Practices, the majority of these MNEs were adopting comprehensive mitigation strategies for environmental issues. This, particularly for the manufacturing sector, was directed through life-cycle assessments capturing a broad scope of both direct and indirect environmental impacts that would be created by organisations. This was a very interesting insight into organisational practice, with organisations in this category taking into account the environmental impact of the full range of value chain activities, including consumption of their products. This did not appear directed by any specific international standards or global guidelines, but rather was very typical for manufacturing organisations.

For those MNEs within the World Class category, there was a strong correlation with the commitment to global guidelines or international standards in both the comprehensive nature of their alternative selection, and the reporting of these activities. Both the Global Reporting Initiative and UNGC again figured prominently, but it was also apparent for several organisations from North East Asia that ISOs also played a role. This was particularly in regards to ISO 26000, with these organisations not only addressing comprehensive environmental mapping of their impact and strategies, but also actively engaging with the social and economic dimensions of their business operations.

It should be noted for all these organisations with the World Class category, it was not clear that they were implementing alternatives for all issues and impacts, but rather it appeared to be more selective to address major indices and issue areas that were prioritised. For environmental issues and impacts, it appeared to be much more comprehensive, covering major issue areas like pollution, recycling, carbon emissions, water use and electricity consumption. These were linked with reporting requirements such as through the GRI and the CDP. For social and economic issues, this appeared to be much broader, and although this was again linked with international standards and global guidelines, it appeared to be narrow in the scope of strategies being implemented to address impacts. Major categories tended to be linked with occupational health and safety, community engagement, training and development and equity and diversity within their operations.

It was clear, however, that these organisations were indeed engaging with key areas and were seeking to implement either mitigation or enhancement strategies. Mitigation strategies were prevalent in the environmental dimension, with organisations seeking to lower their impact by identifying a range of different initiatives to do this. For the social and economic dimensions, it was clear that organisations were generally working towards enhancement strategies, such as increasing the level of training hours, increasing the community engagement and local programs, increasing the level of minorities or disadvantaged groups employed and similar activities. Very few areas within the social or economic areas were dealt with as mitigation strategies, except for issues like safety levels, injuries or deaths.

## Monitoring

The monitoring step of the corporate sustainability assessment is about capturing the impacts of the mitigation and enhancement strategies of the business activity on an ongoing basis. This will include measuring the performance of the business' activities and also the impacts of the business on its surrounding communities. Furthermore, this monitoring of performance can be communicated to broader stakeholder groups, like the local community or government organisation. This can be achieved through sustainability reporting or compliance reports set by regulatory agencies and is effective for promoting transparent processes.

In terms of the monitoring step, results indicate again a very high level of organisations classified in either World Class or International Practices categories (please see Figure 4.6 Monitoring practices of MNEs in Thailand). Thirty nine per cent of the organisations in the sample were classified in the World Class category, and while a drop from the previous step, it is nevertheless indicative of organisations adopting a broad based monitoring program within Thailand. While some MNEs in this category appear to be adopting more CSR directed programs for socio-economic monitoring, it was evident across many of them that the reporting requirements of global standards and guidelines – including again both the GRI and UNGC – had an important influence on the scope and coverage of issue areas and indicators capturing data on their relative sustainability performance. It is also worth noting the influence of the headquarter reporting requirements, as many MNEs collected monitoring data for Thailand, but often aggregated the reporting of this through their sustainability reporting.

Forty-eight per cent of the MNEs within the sample were classified within the International Practices category. This, like the earlier steps, reflects a large

World Class    International    Host Country    Non-Disclosure
               Practices

*Figure 4.6* Monitoring practices of MNEs in Thailand

number of organisations that tend to focus more on capturing monitoring data around their environmental performance (albeit in a very comprehensive manner) directed through life-cycle assessment methodologies. Many of them often link their activities to international standards and guidelines such as the CDP, ISOs or home country regulations. Organisations were also classified in this category if they had limited socio-economic indicators for monitoring, with many organisations only covering very high-level health and safety or training indicators for the social aspect, and some basic information on the economic contributions of the organisation to the local community through employment creation and taxes.

In terms of the Host Country Compliance category, the remaining 13 per cent of organisations within the sample were classified within this category. No organisations were classified within the Non-disclosure category. For the Host Country Compliance category, it was evident that organisations prescribed to local requirements for reporting of data, and that this directly influenced the type of monitoring behaviour they implemented. Reference was drawn to local laws, such as for environmental protection, taxation, human resource reporting (health and safety), that formed the basis of the regular monitoring these organisations had to undertake.

As noted above, no organisations were classified in the Non-disclosure category. However, three organisations in the service sector were focused specifically on collecting monitoring data only as required by local regulations. In examining the higher-level practices of organisations when addressing the monitoring step, we specifically focused on whether these organisations were collecting data consistently across environmental, economic and social dimensions, and also whether it was a longitudinal data collection process. The longitudinal perspective was demonstrated with the organisation capturing monitoring data across an extended timeframe, rather than just a snapshot at one point in time. This is particularly important in how the organisation can then use this information to frame the evaluation processes in the following step and determining their performance.

Organisations within the International Practices category often demonstrated that a systematic and well-grounded monitoring system was in place for their activities in Thailand, particularly when examining headquarter operational requirements and how this influenced their local activities. This includes an alignment with a range of ISOs and home country regulation requirements, which directed organisations towards collecting and reporting on certain key issues and impacts. The key point of differentiation we made in classifying organisations within this category was the scope of the coverage for socio-economic issues, with organisations in this category tending to have a more limited focus beyond environmental issues. This was particularly prevalent in the manufacturing sector, where organisations conducted very comprehensive environmental monitoring with a breadth of different indicators associated with environment-related issues and impacts. Despite this, the socio-economic indicators that we identified tended to be a lot narrower.

Within the World Class category, it was clear in the majority of these organisations that the headquarter operations had an important role in the type and extent of the monitoring being implemented. Across these organisations, the headquarter operations would implement the systems for collecting and analysing the information required for monitoring. This was often aggregated at the regional or international level in the reporting methods implemented by the headquarter operations. Driving the approach behind this was a clear alignment with different international standards and global guidelines that these organisations were part of. This includes many organisations organising and presenting their monitoring data in accordance with the GRI standards, including through dedicated sustainability reports.

These organisations largely utilised external auditing mechanisms for the monitoring of data they collected. This data tended to be collected on an annual basis, and presented through the organisation's external reporting mechanisms including sustainability, CSR and annual reports. Some organisations also provided interactive online platforms for the communication of these data, enabling interested stakeholders to be presented with the results of their monitoring activities. One limitation of the reporting on monitoring data was the aggregation of cross-country and regional data. This prevented MNEs seeing changes in the monitoring data for their operations in Thailand.

Building from the early steps, the monitoring step provides the method for capturing specific data around how the organisation is performing relative to its different issue and impact areas. As detailed earlier, issue and impact categories and areas should translate down into specific indicators or methods for measuring the performance of the organisation against its sustainability activities. Through the monitoring step it was evident that a link exists between earlier steps, such as screening, scoping and impact analysis, and the indicators and measurable areas reported on by organisations in their different reporting methods. This was largely conducted through quantifiable measures, capturing very specific figures related to the particular issue or impact (i.e. level of carbon emissions, or amount of recycling).

The use of qualitative tools or techniques to capture more difficult-to-quantify impacts was not widely evident, such as social or cultural change to local communities. This would have required the use of tools such as focus groups, interviews or observation. It appears organisations at all levels of performance, including Host Country Compliance, International Practices and World Class, had a distinct preference towards the reporting of easily quantifiable data for their monitoring. We could see the widespread use of technical and scientific methods throughout our analysis, with participatory tools much less evident for monitoring activities.

## Evaluation

It is through the monitoring of the implemented mitigation and enhancement strategies related to a business' activity that enables the organisation to evaluate its impacts. The effectiveness of this step is largely determined by the quality of the targets and objectives set across the different measurable areas, which then enable the organisation to determine its level of organisational performance (see for more details, www.sustainability-assessments.org). Various impact analysis tools and methodologies are used to investigate performance measures of the business and it is through the process of evaluation that the business can adjust or change its practices to further mitigate or enhance their impacts.

In regard to Figure 4.7, evidence indicates some 82 per cent of organisations are integrating an evaluative function into their monitoring activities at either the World Class (39 per cent) or International Practice (43 per cent) levels. This step shows that MNEs adopting World Class practices in monitoring are also doing so in the evaluation step – this is a consistent pattern for both the manufacturing and service sectors. This is a positive sign that these organisations are not only collecting data on their performance, but are tracking this, and evaluating their performance across a longitudinal perspective. It is again evident that these organisations within the World Class category are often adopting the GRI standards and the UNGC principles. As part of this, the organisations have obviously committed to reporting on their performance. While several organisations were adopting more CSR based style reporting, they nevertheless were classified in this category due to the more expansive coverage of issues and impacts across environmental, social and economic dimensions.

Moving to those organisations within the International Practices category, some 43 per cent of MNEs were considered at this level. Organisations within this category again tended to have a focus on their commitment to international standards and guidelines such as through the CDP, ISOs or home country regulation, when reflecting on the types of practices they were adopting within Thailand. Again, as was evident in the monitoring step, these organisations had a particular focus on the environmental dimension, although they were also consistently going beyond the local regulatory requirements in socio-economic evaluation techniques. Despite going beyond local regulatory requirements, it is clear that the socio-economic perspective is quite limited within their operational activities within Thailand, and tended to be constrained to general workforce issues, local community based programs (like sponsorships and donations), and some general economic indicators such as employment creation, level of local economic contribution through taxation and in some cases supply chain integration.

In terms of the Host Country Compliance and Non-disclosure categories, it was evident that a shift had occurred from the monitoring step. While there was only one organisation in the Host Country Compliance category, three organisations from the sample were classified in the Non-disclosure category, seeing the most significant increase across the steps for Non-disclosure. When examining this result closer, it is evident across the two categories that all four organisations are service-based organisations. This result also indicates that while these organisations may collect data to conform to international or host country

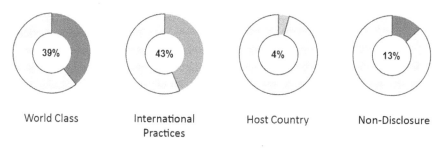

*Figure 4.7* Evaluation practices of MNEs in Thailand

requirements, they do not (or at least it is not evident to us) utilise these data to determine their performance from year to year, nor do they consider whether their sustainability performance is improving.

Closer examination of these results suggest that the organisations in the Non-disclosure category were not conducting any form of evaluation on the data that they were collecting, with two of these organisations clearly adopting a Host Country Compliance process for collecting and monitoring sustainability issues. The other organisation in the Non-disclosure category shifted from adopting International Practices for their monitoring, with no evidence that they were utilising the information they collected to evaluate their performance. With the one organisation in the Host Country Compliance category for evaluation, it was clear that they only sought to meet the local regulatory requirements, particularly with regards to environmental issues.

For both the International Practices and World Class category, our analysis showed a clear sequence from issues in screening and scoping, to impact analysis, into monitoring and evaluation processes. A key point of differentiation in these organisations was around the scope of issue coverage beyond the environmental perspective. Organisations within the International Practices went above and beyond requirements of the local regulatory context, but it was clear that they had a focus on looking at the environmental issues affected by their operations. Nevertheless, the underlying factors and processes for evaluation were similar for both these categories, with those organisations in the World Class category moving beyond a focus on environmental issues and more commonly referring to global guidelines and particularly the GRI and the UNGC when doing so.

Looking most broadly at these organisations, it was clear that the headquarter operations are critical for determining type of practices these organisations are adopting. For the International Practices category, this was also linked inherently with the international commitments that the headquarter operations aligned with, including a focus on different international standards such as ISO 50001, ISO 9000 and ISO 14000. The majority of these organisations were also adopting the CDP requirements around capturing $CO_2$ emissions, and this was largely linked with the fact that all but one of these organisations was in the manufacturing sector (the other organisation was in the mining sector). For the World Class practices, as noted above, the headquarter commitments to global guidelines were clearly influential in the types of systems and practices that they implemented in the subsidiary operations within Thailand.

Moving beyond the influence of the headquarter operations and their commitments to either International Practices or standards, and global guidelines or principles, there was a clear identification by these organisations of the sustainability areas they were covering, which linked with the earlier steps of the sustainability assessment, through to the monitoring data they were collecting. Where organisations were adopting a more comprehensive approach across the main sustainability dimensions, this was translated through into the monitoring and evaluation practices, with clear indicators attached to issue areas, longitudinal data collected, and measured against baseline measures to demonstrate the performance of the organisation over a specified period of time. As part of these, organisations often showed different points in time on their relative performance, and tagged this against targets they had set – sometimes directed through international commitments – on the type of performance outcomes they were looking for.

One final common issue we experienced in examining the evaluation practices of these organisations was the tendency for a top-down approach to be implemented through the headquarters. This was particularly apparent in the case of their monitoring and evaluation practices, with a tendency for the headquarters to implement global systems, processes and procedures for their sustainability practices, but then report on this through an aggregated manner. This resulted in a distinct difficulty in determining the individual performance of different operations around the world, including in Thailand where we focused on the specific performance and activities that were implemented to address their performance. While it was evident from both the comments of respondents and the reporting mechanisms of these organisations that they were indeed putting in comprehensive evaluation mechanisms, the process of reporting on a global basis obfuscated the ability to analyse the individual country activities in Thailand.

## Feedback and follow up

The final step – feedback and follow up – is described as an essential step of an assessment yet there remains a void in the sustainability assessment literature about its practice from the project perspective. Within this step, organisations integrate their performance data to inform their decision-making processes and address their impacts potentially through adjusting their mitigation and enhancement strategies. This is thought of as an iterative process of feedback and follow up that reinforces the overall sustainability objectives of the project.

In this step as illustrated in Figure 4.8, the level of organisations classified within the World Class category dropped dramatically to 26 per cent. This is a 13 per cent decrease from the evaluation step, and shows that a more limited selection of organisations are seeking to reintegrate information about their performance (from the evaluation) to inform their decision-making and then adjust their activities. Those organisations that are undertaking World Class practices within their feedback and follow up step are actively implementing new mitigation and enhancement strategies to address different issues and impacts as they emerge, and adjusting existing strategies based on their performance outcomes from evaluation. Again, the commitment to the GRI and UNGC appear to be directly related to the types of activities implemented by these organisations, with the reporting mechanism of the former in particular, enabling us to ascertain how MNEs are addressing issues and impacts across the range of dimensions and adjusting their activities.

A higher level of International Practices was evident in this step, with some 47 per cent of organisations classified within this category. As recognised in earlier steps, this category was dominated by MNEs that were clearly implementing comprehensive activities for their environmental management, adjusting or implementing new mitigation strategies to address issues and impacts. It was the limited socio-economic engagement that resulted in the majority of these organisations remaining in this classification, despite having committed to a range of international guidelines and standards. It continues to show a major limitation in a more holistic engagement with sustainability and sustainable development through social and economic activities.

While two organisations were classified in the Host Country Compliance category, focusing on compliance with the laws and regulations, it was the Non-disclosure category that saw the greatest increase in numbers. With 17 per cent, or four organisations within the sample, not clearly demonstrating activities to integrate ongoing performance outcomes to improve or adjust their operational activities. This was obviously also linked with a lack of evaluation evident in the previous step, which inhibits the organisation's ability to identify areas where to change or improve performance. One organisation in this category, however, was collecting data on sustainability and evaluating their performance, but failed to show any evidence that they were responding to their performance. This was also reflected in the archival data collected, which demonstrated that this organisation had a negative impact on the local community – through their environmental impact – but was failing to take any action to rectify this issue.

World Class    International Practices    Host Country    Non-Disclosure

*Figure 4.8* Feedback and follow up practices of MNEs in Thailand

Feedback and follow up was perhaps the most difficult step to determine the practices of organisations within this study, with the need to demonstrate the cyclical and integrative approach to evaluating performance and making changes to operations in response to their performance outcomes. This is perhaps part of the reason for seeing the highest level of non-disclosure out of all the steps of the corporate sustainability assessment. With four organisations, or 17 per cent, of the sample within the Non-disclosure category, we found no evidence to reflect these types of practices being implemented. This was in part also explained by the fact that these organisations had lower overall performance across the majority of the earlier steps, inhibiting their ability to determine their sustainability performance and effect change as a result of this. One organisation in this category, however, had been performing quite consistently within the International Practices category until it came to this step. Here it was evident that the organisation focused more on addressing the reporting requirements of their international commitments – particularly for the ISOs they were committed to for environmental management systems and electricity consumption – than aiming to improve their performance progressively as part of determining their performance.

For the Host Country Compliance category, it was evident that the two organisations within this category were only focused on making changes to their practices depending on the outcomes of performance evaluations by government regulators. This was not aimed at making ongoing improvements, nor was it a voluntary initiative to demonstrate their engagement in addressing sustainability. It was rather quite clear that this was a compliance seeking approach to meet the expectations of the government – should they need to do so.

However, when we look at both the International Practices and World Class category we see a very different approach being taken by the organisations in the sample. It was again evident that the main differentiator between these two categories was the scope of coverage in the sustainability issues covered by these organisations, with organisations in the International Practices category having a greater tendency to focus on environment related issues and to progressively address this. The 26 per cent of the organisations within the World Class category were clearly attempting to put more proactive practices in place to not only address social, economic and environmental issues associated with their operations, but also to actively change their practices depending on their performance.

For both these categories, it was clear that the headquarter operations had an ongoing role in determining the types of activities being implemented by these organisations in Thailand. This is linked with both the international commitments and global guidelines being used by these organisations, with a clear global approach being adopted quite consistently across the firms in both categories. Life-cycle based assessments were also prevalent in the sample, particularly across the mapping of environmental issues and how changes were being implemented to improve performance and mitigate impacts.

While it was evident that organisations were progressively implementing changes to how they addressed their impacts, it was not known whether these were being adjusted as a response to performance outcome. Rather, it appeared many organisations had core initiatives framing their alternative selection, for instance in implementing new technology for recycling, which would be implemented across all their operations. So while it was clear that organisations were linking in new mitigation or enhancement strategies to improve their sustainability performance, it was unclear if this was just due to new corporate initiatives or if it was specifically related to their performance. It was nevertheless evident that these initiatives, when implemented, could be linked back to their sustainability performance.

A final common situation we found was the difficulty in determining whether there were a range of initiatives that were just targeted for organisational activities in Thailand. Global initiatives to improve sustainability performance were abundant, but specific cases of adjusting mitigation or enhancement strategies was often more linked with ad-hoc CSR activities to promote certain social engagement programs being used by the organisations. With this observation appearing a common practice across the organisations, it seems that further effort is needed – particularly in reporting – to delineate sustainability activities for all operations, rather than relying on an aggregated global approach. This would increase transparency and accountability in the activities of these organisations.

## Concluding comments on performance of MNEs in Thailand

Given this broad overview on the outcomes of our data analysis, we have established a significant percentage of our sample organisations are adopting sustainability standards that go beyond the regulatory requirements of the Thailand government. This is a positive outcome highlighting the voluntary adoption of standards and guidelines that seek to address social, economic and environmental issues and impacts created by these organisations' business activities. Here, we also see the importance of the global approach adopted by these multinationals, particularly when it comes to implementing comprehensive sustainability practices throughout their international operations.

We now move to building from this sample overview into examining the sustainability practices of these organisations in more detail, with a specific focus on elaborating upon industry specific examples across the practices of the manufacturing and service sectors. We do not provide any detail on the mining sector organisation within our sample due to confidentiality and anonymity – given the greater likelihood of identifying the organisation through providing detailed examples across the sustainability practices it adopts. We have, however, kept this in the broader statistics to give a gauge of the overall sample performance. The next chapter focuses specifically in on the manufacturing sector, which forms the most detailed and largest component of our sample.

# 5 Sustainability practices of manufacturing MNEs

*Jerome D. Donovan, Cheree Topple,
Eryadi K. Masli, Thomas Borgert,
Masayoshi Ike, Monica Van Wynen,
Teerin Vanichseni, Laddawan Lekmat,
Lalita Hongratanawong
and Jirapan Kunthawangso*

This chapter provides a detailed analysis of the sample of foreign multinationals operating in the manufacturing sector in Thailand. In doing so, this chapter seeks to first and foremost elaborate upon the common sustainability practices being adopted by these organisations when operating in Thailand. This follows a similar pattern of evaluation as the preceding chapter, and is bound by the conceptual framework developed in Chapter 3. In utilising this approach, this chapter is able to provide a measure to the relative performance of foreign multinationals operating within the manufacturing sector. This chapter also looks at the comparative performance against the broader sample of foreign multinationals operating within Thailand. This will in turn enable the determination of important differences evident in how manufacturing organisations are performing, and their relative practices across the sustainability assessment framework.

Furthermore, this chapter provides a detailed analysis of the specific practices being adopted by the manufacturing sector in addressing sustainability. This includes the detailed management decision-making processes, the tools and techniques used, and the specific focus within this sector when addressing sustainability. Through the articulation of these relative practices within the manufacturing sector, it provides an important basis for greater understanding of how sustainability is integrated into manufacturing organisations strategic and tactical and operational decision-making. More importantly it also provides a platform from which other organisations can gain insight and learn to adapt their own practices to reflect the leading approaches identified within this research.

Building from this point, this chapter will now turn to the examination of the broader classifications of the performance across the seven sustainability practices, measuring the manufacturing sector against the country averages. At each of the seven sustainability practices, examples will be provided of the specific practices being adopted at each level – World Class, International Practices, Host Country Compliance and Non-disclosure.

## Manufacturing MNEs in Thailand

When examining the manufacturing sample there was a dominance of large MNEs (with 87 per cent above USD$100 million of investment) from North East Asia (44 per cent) and Europe (25 per cent). A closer look at the size differences within the sample shows that approximately 13 per cent (2/16) of manufacturing organisations are classified as small to medium sized enterprises. The remaining 87 per cent (14/16) of organisations in the manufacturing sample were classified as being large organisations.

With regards to their home country origin, 44 per cent (7/16) of the sample of manufacturing organisations had headquarter operations in North East Asia. About 25 per cent (4/16) of the manufacturing MNEs had their home country location situated within Europe, with a smaller percentage of organisations' home locations across North America, Australasia and South Asia (5/16, 32 per cent).

Table 5.1 illustrates the size and home country differences across the manufacturing sample. It also includes the organisation code used as part of the de-identification process for all organisations involved in the sample.

With this broad classification of the manufacturing sample in mind, the chapter will now turn to examining the practices of these organisations across the individual steps of the sustainability assessment. This will begin with screening practices, elaborating first on the overall results from the sample across the four broad categories utilised to sort the organisations into different performance levels – 1) World Class, 2) International Practices, 3) Host Country

*Table 5.1* Sample for manufacturing

| Organisation Code | Size | Home Country Region |
|---|---|---|
| TH01 | Large | North East Asia |
| TH02 | Large | North East Asia |
| TH03 | Large | North East Asia |
| TH04 | Large | Europe |
| TH05 | Large | South Asia |
| TH06 | Large | North East Asia |
| TH07 | Large | North East Asia |
| TH08 | Large | North America |
| TH09 | Small | Australasia |
| TH10 | Large | Europe |
| TH11 | Large | Europe |
| TH12 | Large | North America |
| TH13 | Large | North East Asia |
| TH14 | Large | North East Asia |
| TH18 | Large | Australasia |
| TH21 | Medium | Europe |

Compliance and 4) Non-disclosure. Following this, analysis will be undertaken on each of these different categories, with a particular focus on illustrating the highest level practices (what we determine as 'best practice') in utilising a corporate sustainability assessment from a World Class practices category. This will serve to provide valuable direction for other organisations seeking to be more fully engaged in sustainability through a systematic process within their international or domestic operations. Each step will conclude through looking at the general practices evident at the lower-level categories.

## Screening practices

When analysing the screening practices of manufacturing MNEs in Thailand and their performance against the overall sample, 19 per cent of manufacturing MNEs were adopting World Class practices. This is somewhat lower than the overall sample, which sits at 22 per cent. With regards to manufacturing organisations adopting International Practices, results indicate 75 per cent are within this category, which is slightly higher than the average for the Thailand sample at 65 per cent. Within the Host Country practices category, 6 per cent (or one organisation) from the manufacturing sector was operating at this level. This is less than half the average for the whole sample, with 13 per cent of organisations classified within the category. This is illustrated below in Figure 5.1, which shows the overall adoption of screening practices across both the overall sample and specifically for the manufacturing sector.

### *World Class Practices – screening*

With regards to World Class practices, 19 per cent of MNEs in manufacturing were performing at this level. This is compared with the overall sample, which indicates 22 per cent of MNEs were adopting these practices. While this is a

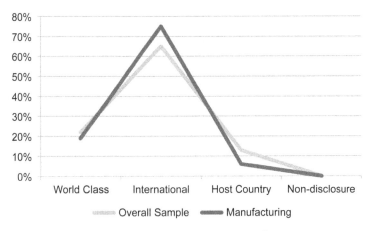

*Figure 5.1* Screening practices – Manufacturing versus all sectors

somewhat lower response, it indicates very little difference between the country averages and the manufacturing sector.

This indicates that 19 per cent of MNEs within the manufacturing sector are going far beyond what is legally mandated by the Government of Thailand. These organisations are attempting to adopt procedures and policies that address not only a core set of environmental, social and economic issues and impacts, but are actively seeking to engage with the community and local stakeholders to contextualise these issues within Thailand. Through the contextualisation and adaptation of existing processes, procedures and policies to suit the Thailand context, it is more likely that these organisations are able to identify issues and impacts of local relevance.

Looking at the specific standards and principles that these manufacturing organisations have adopted, two particular global guidelines were consistently evident for framing their practices – the Global Reporting Initiative (GRI) and the United Nations Global Compact (UNGC). These two global guidelines clearly influenced the broader consideration of sustainability related issues by these organisations. These principles and standards immediately provide a core set of issues and impacts that are specific to the manufacturing sector, directing the organisations to have a foundational basis for determining their broader impact on the local community they are operating within.

When examining the manufacturing sector more closely, it is clear that these organisations operating at World Class levels were also utilising principles, guidelines and standards from the World Business Council for Sustainable Development (WBCSD), the Carbon Disclosure Project (CDP), as well as a range of international standards including ISO 14001, ISO 50001, OHSAS 18001, SA8000. Two of these organisations were also part of the International Integrated Reporting Council.

The adoption of World Class practices is well demonstrated through the operations of TH12. Thailand manufacturing operations constitute their largest manufacturing base within the Asia Pacific region, with the remaining facilities and operations spread across the region mainly involving downstream (value chain) investments. Although starting from a smaller operation over 20 years ago, they now have expanded into a fully integrated manufacturing facility. From this, they are able to transform raw materials into either key production inputs for further downstream processing, or complete product development and production.

According to the executive in-charge of operations in Thailand (as well as the broader Asia Pacific) the sustainability screening process begins after the basic business fundamentals have been addressed – that is, good business acumen. They align all decisions with the corporate/business strategy of the organisation ensuring that it fits strategically with the intent and direction of their global operations. They then undertake more finite evaluations of the market conditions and ensure that there is an actual demand for their products. From this point, the evaluation moves on to determining whether the business conditions in the country chosen can support the standards and guidelines that the organisation implements in all of their global operations.

With regards to these standards and guidelines, it was emphasised that the organisation needs supportive government policies and logistics/infrastructure support to be able to implement their global practices in the chosen country. This includes their basic management systems, engineering standards, environment, health and safety standards, waste water and management systems, amongst others. This is a critical decision point for them in determining whether they are able to operate in a specific country (and whether they can adopt a globally consistent approach to their operations). The organisation has a policy to adopt the highest standards – be it theirs or the country in which they operate – through the use of global standards and guidelines informing their practices. It is always the case in the developing country context that this organisation utilises their global standards particularly around technology and engineering excellence.

Once the organisation determined that the core of their activities was able to be implemented in Thailand, and specifically the technology, engineering and operating systems, they then moved on to the evaluation of the particular sustainability issues that they will consider within their Thailand operations. This is interesting, as they delineate – to some extent – between specific sustainability issues and their business-related activities (which also include sustainability issues). This is reflective of the evolving business context in viewing core practices around health and safety, employee development, environment and waste management systems, as part of the basic business context and not general sustainability. This indicates the embedded nature of these issues within private sector decision-making processes.

Nevertheless, the specific focus on sustainability begins with a core global sustainability plan that the organisation has for their global operations. This sets the commitments of the organisation in terms of specific areas such as community outreach programs, waste management, waste reduction and energy efficiency efforts, amongst others (highlighted in Figure 5.2). This is a set range of goals that are consistent irrespective of the operational arrangements of the organisation (i.e. joint venture or wholly owned subsidiary), or the country of location. This funnels through all their sustainability activities and reporting they do on a global scale, and informs the communication with local communities in the areas in which they operate. These broader objectives and goals are considered by the organisation as the 'long-term license to operate', giving them the right (through working 'hard' to address these core objectives) to work within the community.

Their core sustainability plan and the key focal areas identified above are derived from utilising the materiality process as informed by GRI G4 Sustainability Reporting Guidelines (and earlier GRI standards). As a first stage of undertaking the materiality analysis, organisations – and in this case TH12 – are required to undertake dialogue and engagement with a range of different stakeholders to determine the importance of different sustainability issues for their stakeholders. For TH12, this process initially began with an internal, 'bottom-up' approach, in which the organisation went to functional experts across the

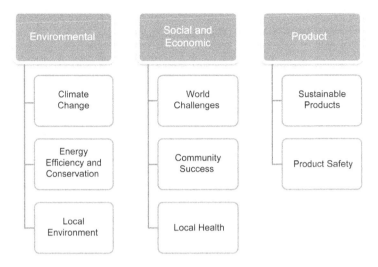

*Figure 5.2* Core global sustainability areas

organisation to determine the most important issues and then sought feedback from external stakeholders.

Since this point, however, the company has seen a substantial shift in their approach in line with the more recent GRI Reporting standards. This involves first conducting extensive stakeholder (both internal and external) interviews and focus groups from across their global operations. External stakeholders included academia, governments, environmental and sustainability communities, and customers. Internally, the organisation then turned to their sustainability committee members for input, extending this into senior leadership and employees of the company. This two-stage process then enabled the organisation to identify and scale the importance of the issue categories for internal and external stakeholder groups. This clearly had a greater emphasis on a participatory approach to engaging with their external stakeholders determining the meaningful sustainability issues that they should focus on.

Beyond their core sustainability goals, they build out a full range of different issues categories and associated impacts that they will consider and report on. These are aligned with significant and specific global initiatives such as the GRI, UNGC, CDP and Responsible Care. These different global initiatives often have a particular focus on what issue categories should be examined, and focus the issue identification process around these issue categories. For example, the CDP grades companies on their efforts to respect climate change and emissions disclosure for their activities. This specifically includes efforts aimed to reduce greenhouse gas emissions and climate change risks within their business operations.

| Society | Economic | Environment | Employment Related | Human Rights |
|---|---|---|---|---|
| ▢ Implemented local community engagement (%) | ▢ Direct economic value from revenues | ▢ Materials recycled (%) | ▢ New hires and turnover by age, gender and region | ▢ Employee training for human rights policies and procedures |
| ▢ Actual or potential negative impacts on local communities (%) | ▢ Defined benefit plan obligations | ▢ Energy consumption | ▢ Retention rates from parental leave | ▢ Number of incidents for discrimination and actions taken |
| ▢ Incidents of corruption and actions taken | ▢ Senior management from local community | ▢ Water recycled and reused (%) | ▢ Number of injuries and types | ▢ Significant risks for forced or compulsory labour |
| ▢ New suppliers screened for impacts on society (%) | ▢ Indirect economic impacts | ▢ Greenhouse gases | ▢ Average hours of training by gender, category | ▢ Incidents and actions taken on violation of indigenous rights |
| ▢ Number of grievances from society and mechanisms etc. | ▢ Policies and procedures for local sourcing | ▢ Waste etc. | ▢ Diversity and equal employment | ▢ Number of grievances about human rights |

*Figure 5.3* Extended issues identified

The culmination of drawing on the materiality analysis for their external engagement and identification of issues, as well as the selection of a range of leading global initiatives and guidelines, translated into both a comprehensive list of generic issue areas. These are associated with their normal business activities and a focused set of specific issue areas that accounted for the communities that they operate in. A sample of some of the main issue areas is detailed in Figure 5.3, extending beyond the core sustainability goals. This is not conclusive in terms of all their issue areas and indicators, but it provides an example of the extent to which this organisation is broadening the types of sustainability considerations when looking at their business activities.

### International Practices – screening

In terms of International Practices, a resounding majority of MNEs in the manufacturing sector are adopting these practices. This sits at 75 per cent of all manufacturing organisations, and is substantially higher than the Thailand sample averages which are at 65 per cent. What this indicates is that the manufacturing sector is much more likely to use a narrow range of corporate policies and procedures, international or industry standards, or their own home country regulations.

While these three categories of International Practices all exceed the requirements of host country regulations, they do not necessarily lead to substantially greater performance by the organisation towards achieving the holistic integration of sustainability within their operations. This is more likely to result in a very specific focus on particular sustainability dimensions, or a narrow range of industry specific considerations that are broadly acknowledged and accepted within the manufacturing sector.

A closer examination of organisations classified as adopting International Practices within the manufacturing sector show a broad application of ISO 14000, ISO 9000, ISO 26000, ISO 50001 and CDP. Five organisations (from North East Asia) had a particular focus on environmental issues with ad-hoc CSR programs covering their consideration of socio-economic issues. Three of the organisations openly acknowledged their use of GRI reporting, however evidence from the secondary data shows that they are not reporting on their performance in Thailand, and as a result, we do not classify them in World Class.

A great example to illustrate these international practice approaches by manufacturing organisations in Thailand is TH01. This organisation is from North East Asia, and although it began with a small level of investment some decades ago, it has since grown substantially through increased investment. It has also diversified its manufacturing base of consumer products in Thailand to cater for regional and global markets. Now it has operations across the entire global market, although it has a substantial manufacturing presence of products within the Asia Pacific region.

Like what was evident in the World Class practices, this organisation, first and foremost, focused on basic business principles in determining their investment choice and driving their business activities. As the Chief Executive Officer of the Thailand operations details through our interviews, the organisation looked at the basis of competitive advantage for their operations in Thailand including the general regulations and market conditions. The headquarter operations conducted a feasibility study, and from this they sought to get government incentives for their investment. It was after this point where sustainability considerations began to factor into their decision-making.

This organisation has a clear environmental focus within their operations, with early certification for ISO14000, which is focused on environmental impact. Throughout both the interviews with key decision-makers it was very clear that the focus of this organisation was identifying sustainability issues at the screening step that are associated with environmental issues linked with their production activities. This is apparent from accounts of when the organisation first established operations within Thailand. This has, however, evolved significantly with the organisation now identifying issues more broadly across a life-cycle assessment, showing a comprehensive examination of relevant environmental issues both direct and indirect to the business activities. For example, this includes R&D, product development, product production, distribution, sales and consumption of their products. Environmental issues are identified across the full spectrum of activities, including consumer use of their products.

Their consideration beyond environmental issues, is much more limited, with few issues identified across socio-economic dimensions. Their socio-economic issue identification appears to be driven by two factors. First, is the need for trained local labour that could supply their manufacturing facilities. In considering this, they evaluate local skills and capabilities, and more broadly across the region to ensure that they could access the right type of labour for their facilities. Second, another key focus was on identifying issues that they could address through CSR programs that they run internationally. These were not based on any systematic analysis of the local development issues, but rather programs that they could implement that would form a valuable promotion base for what the organisation was doing to contribute to the local community. This is perhaps a reflection of their focus on CSR reporting and alignment with ISO 26000.

Now while this organisation makes reference to the use of GRI 3.1 standards for reporting, it is clear from examining their screening of issues that this is not being adopted extensively throughout the organisation's international operations – rather it is more focused on domestic operations in their home country. There are considerable gaps in their reporting and there are indications that this has not been externally audited. Most of their alignment has been around the environmental aspect. Their social aspect appears to just be for CSR and community involvement, rather than meaningful engagement with social issues across their operations. There is no broad ranging set of issues identified around the socio-economic dimensions, but rather a series of ad-hoc social programs in a selection of countries they operate within, demonstrating an individual case of where they have donated a small sum of thousands of dollars to a local social cause.

More insight was gained from a senior-level manager who explained that socio-economic issues were not deemed important because of their location within an industrial estate. These matters were handled by a separate entity – and it is assumed that this would be a similar justification in other countries they operate within. They do emphasise throughout the interviews that they follow all local regulations, and that they adopt their International Practices for environmental issues. What appears clear from the interviews and secondary data is that this organisation has yet to move substantially beyond superficial coverage of socio-economic issues through ad-hoc CSR programs, however, they have comprehensive and very detailed analysis of environmental issues that far exceeds regulatory requirements.

This rationale approach and focus is evident in the majority of the organisations originating from North East Asia. However, similar insights were provided when looking at manufacturing organisations from other home country locations. A greater tendency to focus around the environmental impacts of their operations was evident, with more limited socio-economic issues being considered through the screening step.

### *Host Country Practices – screening*

At the Host Country Practice level, a very small percentage of MNEs within the manufacturing sector can be classified in this category. Only six per cent (or one organisation), fits within this category. This is less than half the average for the entire sample, with some 13 per cent of organisations within the sample classified at this level. This is a positive sign that the majority of organisations within the manufacturing sector are going above and beyond the regulatory requirements of Thailand – exceeding the minimum standards required for their operations.

In the strictest sense, the categorisation of an organisation at this level indicates that they are specifically aligning their business practices for sustainability with that of what the local regulations require. To be classified at this level, organisations would be emphasising the adoption of local laws and the requirements dictated there for the organisation's sustainability practices. In the context of Thailand, this means meeting all the investment, environmental, enterprise, employment and taxation requirements. Building from this, an organisation within this category would simply seek to identify the issues and impacts that are legally mandated for them to fulfil.

In the case of Thailand, one such example for foreign multinationals – and linked with their investment laws – is the required adoption of ISO 9000 and ISO 14000. ISO 9000 relates to a quality management standard through the International Organization for Standardization, which aims to help organisations improve the quality of the products they develop, particularly within the context of customer satisfaction. ISO 14000, also through the International Organization for Standardization, aims to support organisations that want practice tools for managing environmental issues.

From the two, obviously the ISO 14000 is more relevant and shows direct links with sustainability through enabling organisations to adopt more effective management practices around how they deal with environmental issues. Depending which of the standards under the broad classification of ISO 14000 are adopted, this standard can direct organisations towards identifying issues around their auditing systems for environmental management, life cycle assessments of products, climate change analysis, amongst others. This gives some foundation for the specific types of issues that are to be considered by the organisation.

These standards – linked through regulatory requirements – are, however, rather limited in their capacity to identify the breadth of sustainability considerations for organisations to consider in the screening stage. This is more likely to see a very narrow, singular, dimension – such as in this case with environmental management standards – of sustainability. It is also less likely to encourage full and active participation of the organisation with local engagement with stakeholders in identifying important issues of local relevance.

This is evident in the one organisation classified within this category, TH09. This organisation is classified as small and can be categorised as a simple assembly manufacturing organisation. Its operations in Thailand are limited, operating from an industrial estate, and entails the assembly of pre-made components into product outputs.

When looking at their operations, it is clear from the interviews that the organisation focuses solely on addressing local regulations to direct what is done in Thailand. According to senior executives both in the Thailand operations and headquarters, the operations in Thailand have minimal impact, as it is simply assembling components produced in their host country. There are no waste or pollution issues, because nothing is actually being produced in Thailand. There are no major social issues; with very small staffing required that places little pressure on the local labour force. All staff are either trained by headquarter staff in Thailand, or have been brought to the headquarters for dedicated training. It is perceived by the organisation that many sustainability issues are not relevant for their Thailand operations. Given the nature of their operations in Thailand, it was therefore expected that this organisation will have rather limited engagement with a comprehensive sustainability assessment evident in larger-scale investments seen in Thailand.

### Non-disclosure – screening

As indicated in the previous chapter on the overall sustainability practices of MNEs in Thailand, no organisations were classified within this category for screening practices. This is a positive indication of the willingness of MNEs in Thailand to – at the very least – meet local regulatory requirements. This was evident across all sectors examined, including the manufacturing sector.

## Scoping practices

Turning to scoping practices for the manufacturing sector, results indicate that there is relatively little difference between the broader sample of MNEs in Thailand and that of manufacturing organisations. With regards to World Class practices, 25 per cent of the manufacturing organisations were operating at this level, slightly higher than the overall sample (22 per cent). Seventy-five per cent of manufacturing organisations in the sample are operating within the International Practices category; which is relatively similar to the overall sample of organisations looked at, which sits at 70 per cent. This is illustrated below in Figure 5.4, which demonstrates that practices in the manufacturing sector do not differ significantly. Perhaps the most noticeable (although very minor) differences are across the adoption of International Practices, where the manufacturing sector again shows a greater prevalence of these practices. Likewise, minor differences are evident with the categories of Host Country Compliance and

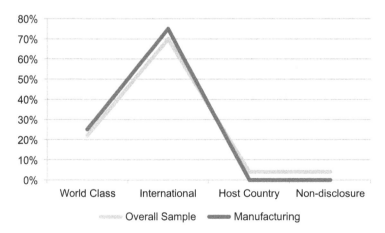

*Figure 5.4* Scoping practices – manufacturing versus all sectors

Non-disclosure, where it is evident that manufacturing organisations are not within each of these categories.

## *World Class Practices – scoping*

With regards to World Class practices, some 25 per cent of the manufacturing MNEs operating in Thailand were at this level. This is somewhat higher than the overall sample, which indicates 22 per cent of MNEs are adopting these practices. While this is a relatively little difference, it is still a positive indication that a quarter of manufacturing organisations are adopting these practices and that this is higher than the overall sample average.

With 25 per cent in this category, it indicates a broad engagement and participatory approach to scoping issues of local relevance. On face value, this result may appear contradictory with the earlier statements that screening is critical for this stage and should form the basis from which scoping occurs (and therefore, having a higher level of World Class standards at scoping may not make sense). This assumes that the organisations have already utilised World Class practices at the screening stage, and have a significant number of locally relevant issues to consider for prioritisation. However, the higher level of World Class practices here is due to these organisations using methods to engage and prioritise issues and impacts through participatory approaches.

So while these organisations might not have fully engaged with stakeholders in identifying the breadth of potential issues of local significance in the screening step, they are however using methods from which to refine the identified issues that may be classified as World Class. This is not a perfect process – which, if it was, would naturally assume that organisations have first identified, through screening, issues of local relevance. It is however a sign that organisations, at different points within their sustainability practices and processes, are willing to engage with both internal and external stakeholders to prioritise certain issues and impacts that the community in which they operate think are most important.

Therefore, the key basis in determining whether these organisations were within the World Class category was whether they were engaging with local stakeholders and undertaking some form of prioritisation of issues and impacts determined by this engagement. The key method to emerge from evaluating these organisations' practices was the use of a materiality assessment – which was developed through the GRI Organization.

Essentially, a materiality assessment is a process to find which issues and impacts have the most significance for stakeholders. There are a range of different methods for undertaking a materiality assessment – including through the use of different research methods (such as interviews, focus groups or surveys), and bases for determining significance for each stakeholder group. But generally, organisations following the GRI reporting guidelines weigh the significance attached by external stakeholders to different issues and impacts, versus the significance or importance attached by the organisation. This allows the organisation to maintain some coherence in their global and local strategies for the issues and impacts they focus upon (and provides some greater ease in reporting). It also enables the identification of the most important issues for local communities where they operate.

A materiality matrix is demonstrated in Figure 5.5, drawing from both the GRI technical protocols. This illustrates the weighting/significance of issues and potential impacts specific to stakeholders and the organisation, identifying priority areas in the top right-hand corner of Figure 5.5. It is assumed that the organisation will specifically address those issues in the top right-hand quadrant, which have both greatest priority for the organisation and the stakeholders. This enables a prioritisation to occur on the types of issues focused on by the organisation, and funnels through into later stages of the assessment included through monitoring and reporting of their performance in addressing these issues.

Perhaps the best example to demonstrate this process for the organisations in this category is through TH08. TH08 is a large investment (more than USD$100 million) that has been undertaken by a North American MNE, with a manufacturing joint venture based in Thailand supplying its products throughout the region.

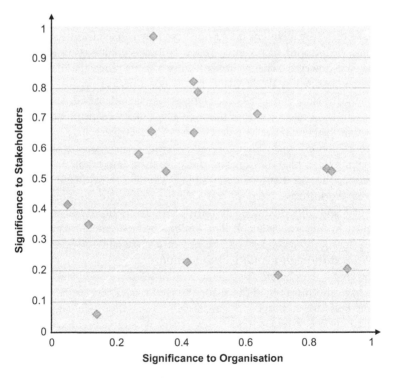

*Figure 5.5* Materiality assessment for scoping

Source: *GRI, Technical Protocol*[1]

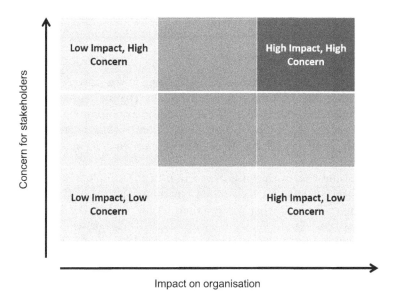

*Figure 5.6* Manufacturing materiality assessment
Source: *Adapted from TH08 and de-identified*

TH08 utilised the most comprehensive materiality assessment across the organisations in this World Class category. They delineated issues across the level of impact and concern for both external stakeholders and the organisation. This was scaled, due to the organisation undertaking annual audits to determine relative performance across each issue area, across nine boxes each detailing a different level of impact and concern – from high impact/high concern, to low impact/low concern.

This scaling mentioned above, either decreased or increased the relative position of different issues each year across their materiality assessment. The lightest grey boxes were examined by the organisation and issues were identified, however, they are not incorporated into the key material issues they examine or address through their business operations. Rather the four darker grey boxes in the top right of the table are focused on. Here, over 50 issues were identified, documented and incorporated into their ongoing sustainability assessment and sustainability management practices. As part of this, indicators, descriptors and general trends were detailed.

This approach extends and sits on top of their core sustainability issues linked with their core sustainability issue categories derived from global guidelines and standards, including GRI G4, UNGC and the United Nations Development Goals. It enables the organisation to involve a range of internal and external stakeholders to identify and prioritise those issues that are most important to them each year. In turn, it also develops a common basis for ongoing issues and impacts that will be addressed by the organisation in accordance with their international and global commitments.

### International Practices – scoping

In terms of International Practices for scoping, it was again evident that a resounding majority of manufacturing MNEs in Thailand are adopting these practices. Again, this sits at 75 per cent of all the manufacturing organisations within this sample. While this is a significant majority of organisations, it is relatively similar to the overall sample of organisations we examined, which sits at 70 per cent.

What became clear within this proportion of the sample was the tendency for scoping practices to be focused on environmental issues. This was commonly done far beyond what was required locally, with ISO 14000 focusing organisations on examining their environmental management systems, and what particular types of environmental issues should be therein focused upon. Building from this, however, these organisations had a significant tendency to adopt full life-cycle assessments on environmental issues and impacts, identifying both local and global environmental issues and mapping this across a life-cycle assessment. This included through the engagement with external and local stakeholders, as well as internally within the organisation. This indicated the tendency to go above and beyond the regulatory requirements of the Thailand government in how these organisations refined and focused the types of issues they focused on – despite having a focus on environmental issues, this was a positive indication of a proactive approach being adopted by these organisations.

A simplified life-cycle diagram is presented below in Figure 5.7 which shows five key stages of a product life cycle beginning from Development and Design through to Products (usage/consumption). This representation is quite typical, although with some variations depending on the product category and stage of production, across the majority of the manufacturing organisations in this category. In this diagram, one particular aspect of the product life cycle is evaluated – distribution – which

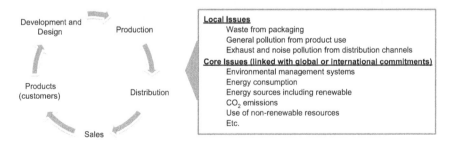

*Figure 5.7* Manufacturing environmental life-cycle assessment

Source: *Adapted from participating manufacturing organisations*

relates to the movement of their products from the manufacturing location to the end consumer. For the organisations within this sample, this tended to be conducted by business partners specialising in distribution and logistics functions. Despite this often not forming the basis of the core business activities for the organisation – that is, being implemented by a member of their supply/value chain – it was still typical for manufacturing organisations to map and address environmental issues created by their business partners, particularly those directly associated with their business activities.

This represents a good reflection of the types of assessments that organisations are doing when utilising a life-cycle assessment, with both local issues identified and core issues retained through their international or global commitments. This offers prioritisation and localisation to suit the local context in which they operate, but also leverage from the organisation's global activities and initiatives they are implementing throughout their entire operational network. It may also include organisations that are not owned or operated by the organisation, but only form part of their close network of suppliers or value chain partners.

Another significant tendency across the manufacturing sample classified as adopting International Practices was the use of broad and generic social and economic issues and impacts. These would often fall within the realm of CSR activities, and entail very limited consideration of important socio-economic issues of local relevance. This was despite the fact that six organisations out of twelve, or 50 per cent of the sample in this category attested to their commitment to the GRI standards.

On closer inspection of both interviews and archival data (including sustainability or CSR reports) there was no evidence to indicate the use of these guidelines within the context of Thailand. Rather, it was evident that these organisations selectively used the guidelines in specific locations, including with a heavy orientation on their home country operations. There was also no evidence that there was a systematic approach to engaging with local stakeholders to determine important issues across either the social or economic dimensions of their business activities.

### *Host Country and Non-disclosure Practices – scoping*

As indicated earlier in this section, no manufacturing organisations were classified in either one of these categories. It was clear that organisations were exceeding local regulations (Host Country category), and no organisation chose to not disclose their practices around issue and impact refinement. This is a more positive outcome for the manufacturing sector than the average for Thailand, with the overall results showing an organisation in both categories (from the service sector).

## Impact analysis practices

When looking at the comparison of the overall sample and that of the manufacturing sector, there appears to be minimal differences. It is worth noting however, that no organisations within the manufacturing sector were identified as being at the Host Country Compliance or Non-disclosure levels, with all organisations in either the World Class (31 per cent) or International Practices (69 per cent) categories. Of the organisations classified within the International Practices category, 55 per cent were from the North East Asia region. The remaining were from Europe and Australasia. Over 80 per cent of the organisations within the International Practices category were classified as large, indicating that size was not of importance in their ability to implement more comprehensive approaches to their impact analysis. This is illustrated below in Figure 5.8, which looks at impact analysis practices across the manufacturing sectors against all sectors

### World Class Practices – impact analysis

When examining World Class practices more closely, a more significant percentage of manufacturing organisations are adopting practices at this level for impact analysis than that of the overall sample. Although this is only narrowly above that of the overall sample, with 31 per cent (manufacturing) verses 26 per cent (overall sample), this is a positive indication for the types of practices being adopted by the manufacturing sector.

These results indicate that manufacturing MNEs operating in Thailand still have some way to go with their approaches to identifying, refining and localising the issues and impacts that they consider within their sustainability assessments. They are much more likely to adopt progressive and comprehensive methods for evaluating the issues and impacts that they have selected. This means the adoption of various methods in which they can analyse the issues and impacts identified through the previous two steps.

A common thread across the organisations identified at the World Class level was the adoption of the GRI reporting methods and UNGC principles. These

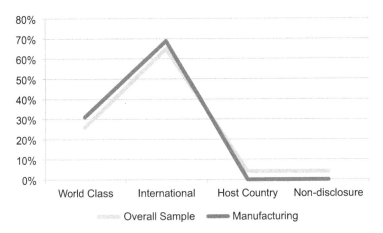

*Figure 5.8* Impact analysis practices – manufacturing versus all sectors

organisations had the tendency to identify a range of measureable areas and indicators aligned with a core set of issue areas across environmental, economic and social dimensions. While not all of these organisations utilised a materiality analysis to identify and refine issues of importance for the local community, they did however, demonstrate the breadth and coverage of common core sustainability issues derived from the GRI reporting guidelines, and also linked with the UNGC principles.

An interesting anomaly to emerge from looking at these organisations adopting global guidelines was the use of external auditing. All of the organisations in this category, except one, utilised some form of external auditing to validate their impact analysis methods and measurement. TH13, a major manufacturing organisation from North East Asia, failed to provide any information detailing their external auditing mechanism for their impact analysis area – rather referring to the fact that they are 'committed' to the GRI standards and the UNGC. We decided to leave this organisation within the World Class category due to the coverage of issues with specific measurable indices aligned with these. It is worth noting, however, that without appropriate auditing and transparency in place for the reporting of this organisation's methods, no conclusive judgement can be made on the accuracy of their reporting.

Nevertheless, all of these organisations also had a range of different international commitments directing them towards particular measureable areas attached with the issue categories and issue areas identified in the screening and scoping steps. This includes ISO 14001, ISO 50001, OHSAS 18001, ISO 26000, SA 8000 and the CDP, amongst others. While the majority of these international standards and guidelines do not provide specific reference to measureable areas required for impact analysis, they do require the organisations to address and report on very specific areas associated with sustainability.

An excellent example of an organisation within the manufacturing sample for undertaking World Class impact analysis practices is TH10. TH10 is a global leader in consumer products with more than 100,000 employees. Although its headquarter operations are based in Europe, over two-thirds of its workforce resides outside of its home country. Although Thailand is considered a small location for their regional operations in Asia Pacific, they still have substantial investments in the country. Entering the market over 20 years ago, they have established their operations largely within an industrial estate. While specialised activities are undertaken in Thailand, the organisation generally acknowledges the importance of the broader region for future profits and market development. Thailand is considered an important regional headquarter operations for Asia Pacific.

In discussing their approach to sustainability and impact analysis, a regional senior manager emphasised the consideration of local and regional regulations but, placed a caveat on this, pointing to the importance of the organisation drawing on a global approach to sustainability as it is a 'global player'. This meant that there was a consideration of local regulations to ensure that the organisation conformed to local requirements; however, it went significantly beyond this ensuring that its operations in Thailand and elsewhere in Asia were aligned with the global approach of the organisation and what it sought to measure.

The impact analysis of the organisation's operations is determined from this global approach, informed initially through expert advisors outside of the organisation, before being implemented and executed within the organisation. This includes both quantitative and qualitative approaches to impact analysis, linked in with a range of key matrices and metrics for what the organisation seeks to measure. In addition, while this is implemented through the organisation, it was very clear that there is a heavy reliance on external factors – including NGOs and outside experts – in developing and directing the data collection approaches and methods.

An important basis for the type and extent of impact analysis undertaken across the operations of the organisation is the matrices and international commitments the organisation has. The organisation recognises this through their international reporting, acknowledging the importance of the GRI and the ten principles of the UNGC on its measures and impact analysis. It is also committed to following the guidelines of the OECD and ISO 26000, as well as the Greenhouse Gas Protocol, the World Business Council for Sustainable Development and an industry specific, European standard. The issues and impact areas, as well as indicators, are aligned against the requirements of each of the commitments the organisation has identified. Like the other organisations evaluated, this is usually aligned through their annual reporting and in the appendices of their report.

Below, Figure 5.9, illustrates the shift from the broad issue areas, to the specific, demonstrating how eight key issue categories are delineated down to each issue area. From this, a range of specific indicators across each of these issue areas. Getting more specific, Figure 5.9 shows how eight broad issue categories aligned with sustainable development objectives are first set (this was informed through both their global commitments and their materiality assessment conduct in the scoping step). These are then broken down further into issue areas, and in the case of the example below, ecology issue areas are identified. From this point, each issue area is then further delineated into specific indicators that will be analysed by the organisation.

Examining the specific indicators further, indicators for water related issues are presented including the new water consumption, usage, discharges and emissions through water use. Net water consumption, for example is broken down to include the overall water consumption and the different sources as a percentage of the total consumed water (as illustrated in Table 5.2).

While this example is rather simplistic, when considering issues around water use such as the level of emissions released into water used by the organisation, it does nevertheless provide a good gauge of the level of analysis across different issue categories, issue areas and individual indicators being utilised. This is a common approach adopted across their different issue categories linked with their sustainable development report.

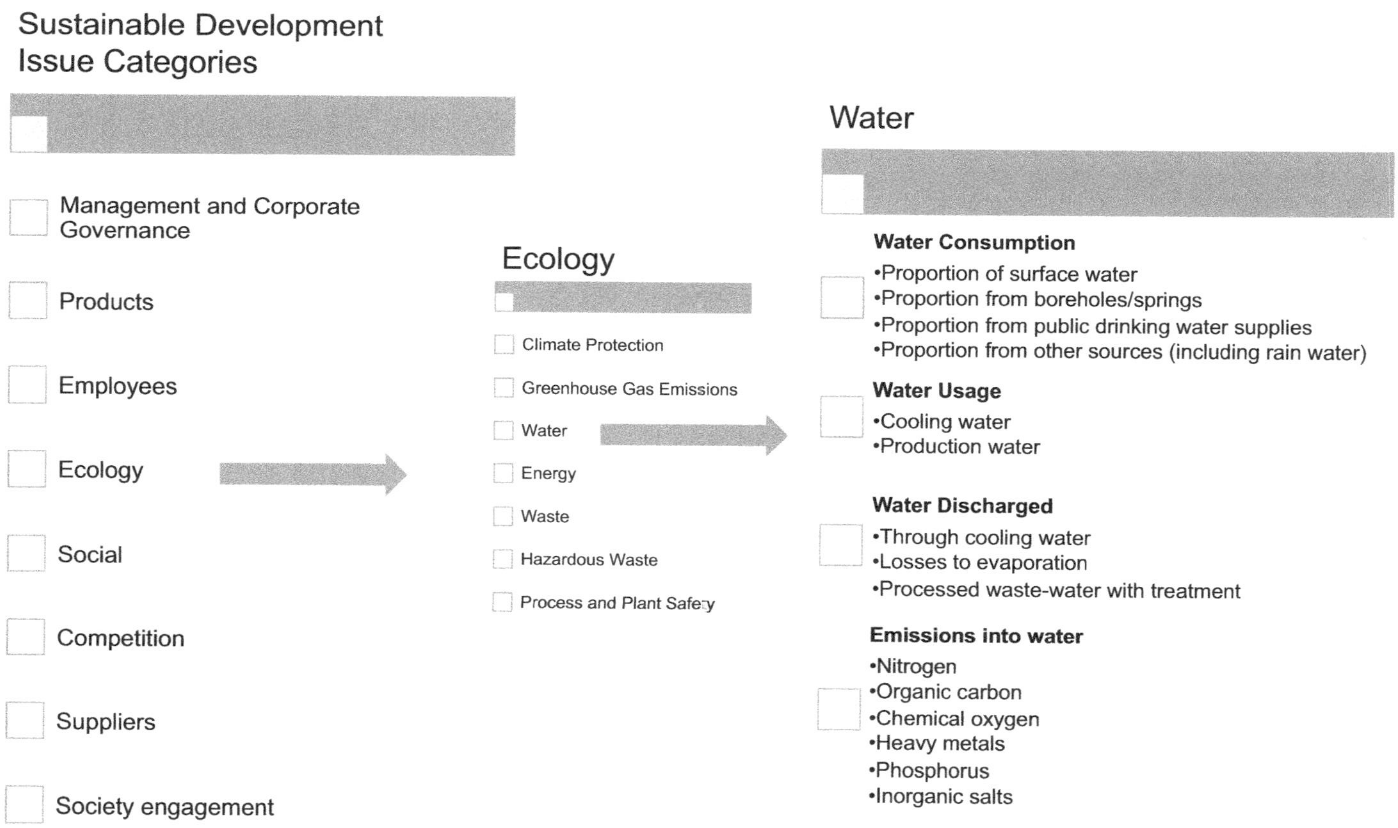

# Sustainable Development Issue Categories

- Management and Corporate Governance
- Products
- Employees
- Ecology
- Social
- Competition
- Suppliers
- Society engagement

## Ecology

- Climate Protection
- Greenhouse Gas Emissions
- Water
- Energy
- Waste
- Hazardous Waste
- Process and Plant Safety

## Water

### Water Consumption
- Proportion of surface water
- Proportion from boreholes/springs
- Proportion from public drinking water supplies
- Proportion from other sources (including rain water)

### Water Usage
- Cooling water
- Production water

### Water Discharged
- Through cooling water
- Losses to evaporation
- Processed waste-water with treatment

### Emissions into water
- Nitrogen
- Organic carbon
- Chemical oxygen
- Heavy metals
- Phosphorus
- Inorganic salts

*Figure 5.9* Issue categories, areas and attached indicators

Source: *Adapted from TH10 and de-identified*

*Table 5.2* Net water consumption and indicators

| Net water intake by source | Year XX |
|---|---|
| Water consumption | Number |
| - Proportion of surface water | % |
| - Proportion of public drinking water | % |
| - Proportion of other sources (including rainwater) | % |
| - Proportion of boreholes/spring | % |

Source: *Adapted from TH10 and de-identified*

For all of their issue categories, with specific issue areas and indicators aligned, the organisation utilises very clear and transparent reporting of the impacts that they are measuring, and linking this clearly with the standards, guidelines or principles that they are addressing through their international and global commitments. They also highlight the importance of credible reporting, with transparent and valid data, which is audited through a leading multinational accounting firm for ensuring that it is accurate. This accounting firm undertaking the external audit of the sustainable development report also uses a widely acknowledged approach using the International Standard on Assurance Engagement (ISAE) 3000, which is commonly used for organisations seeking to evaluate compliance with the GRI standards. This approach to impact analysis is also certified by an international body linked with one of the key global guidelines they report against.

*International Practices – impact analysis*

When looking at the level of International Practices for impact analysis, a significant number of organisations were again classified within this category. With some 69 per cent of manufacturing organisations within this category, it demonstrates the prevalence of these practices being adopted within Thailand. While this is somewhat lower than the 75 per cent of organisations in this category for the previous step (scoping), it nevertheless shows the dominance of these practices in framing what manufacturing organisations are doing in Thailand.

Of the organisations classified within this category, some 55 per cent were from the North East Asia region. The remaining organisations were from Europe and Australasia. This clearly shows the tendency of organisations from this region to be adopting International Practices when operating within Thailand. Moreover, over 80 per cent of these organisations were classified as large, indicating that size was not an important inhibitor or indicator of whether these organisations had the capacity to implement more comprehensive approaches to their impact analysis. Only one small and one medium sized organisation were in this category, and while these were the only small and medium sized organisations in the sample, it does not provide any firm indication of a tendency for size to be an important indicator of these practices.

Looking more closely at these results, however, there are some substantial links between what was seen in the earlier assessment steps, and particularly in terms of scoping. Organisations classified within this category tended to have very limited engagement with social and economic dimensions, but they did have comprehensive coverage of environmental issues. This coverage and consideration of their environmental issues often was approached through a full life-cycle assessment, charting the course of product development, through to consumption and disposal.

Approximately 80 per cent (9/11) of these organisations conducted full life-cycle assessments on the environmental issues and impacts that were associated with both their direct activities, and across their supply chain. A significant amount of quantitative and technical measures were used to capture their environmental impacts, including covering issues such as electricity consumption, water usage, $CO_2$ emissions, material usage (including raw material) and pollution. This was captured and modelled along the different activities needed to develop, produce, consume and dispose of their products. As noted above, this also went beyond just identifying the issues and impacts associated with the organisational activities, and sought to model the issues and impacts of the consumption. This was particularly interesting for organisations in the automotive sector, with many demonstrating that consumption was a major variable in determining the overall impact that was likely to occur through the product life cycle.

Like what was evident in the World Class category, organisations within the International Practices category also aligned their activities around impact analysis with different international standards and guidelines. A dominant theme was around the use of ISOs, which included those required through regulatory guidance of the Thailand government, as well as extending beyond these, with the inclusion of ISO 50001, ISO 26000 and the CDP measures. One organisation also highlighted the use of risk matrices, which was overlaid with identifying potential issues and impacts associated with the environmental systems of the organisation.

A common thread also in these organisations, which differentiated them from those organisations in the World Class category, was the limited coverage of social and economic dimensions in their analysis. It was evident that very few areas were covered by the organisations beyond the environmental aspect, with many only covering several health and safety related issues (such as lost time to injuries, or deaths) within their operations, or ad-hoc CSR activities (sponsoring local activities, community groups etc.). One organisation even had a CSR scorecard to demonstrate and elaborate upon their CSR activities they were conducting. However, consistently across these organisations was the tendency to only cover a very limited number of social or economic issues when conducting their impact analysis. This was shown in stark contrast to the depth of their consideration of environmental issues.

A final observation was that of these 11 organisations, three made reference to global guidelines in their reporting, including the GRI standards. It was clearly evident from analysing the activities of these organisations, through both the interviews conducted and the secondary data collected, that they were not adopting these practices beyond their headquarter operations.

### *Host Country and Non-disclosure – impact analysis*

As was evident in the scoping step, no organisations were classified within either the Host Country Compliance or Non-disclosure categories for impact analysis. This is again a positive indication of the manufacturing sector going beyond the minimum requirements set by the government of Thailand, as well as the willingness to be pro-active in addressing issues and impacts associated with their activities. This is despite the fact that only 31 per cent of organisations were in the World Class category.

## Alternative selection practices

When looking at the context of manufacturing MNEs in Thailand and their comparative performance against the overall sample, it appears that they are largely in alignment. The majority of organisations in both the overall sample and the manufacturing sector are adopting either World Class or International Practices. This was slightly higher for manufacturing organisations in both World Class (50 per cent versus 43 per cent) and International Practices (50 per cent versus 48 per cent), with only 9 per cent of organisations in the overall sample classified as adopting a Host Country Compliance approach. No manufacturing organisations were categorised in either Host Country Compliance or Non-disclosure categories.

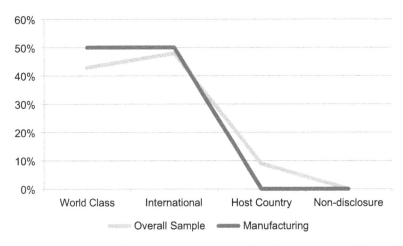

*Figure 5.10* Alternative selection practices – manufacturing versus overall sample

## World Class Practices – alternative selection

Looking more closely at the results, 50 per cent of manufacturing MNEs operating in Thailand were classified at this level. This is a very substantial number of organisations and exceeds the performance evident in all earlier steps. This indicates that these organisations, once they have identified the particular issues and impacts that they will focus on, undertake a comprehensive mapping of these to determine what alternatives they will implement. This is slightly higher than what was evident for the overall sample, which sat at 43 per cent.

So, despite the limitations evident in the earlier steps of the assessment about the extent of organisations operating at World Class levels, this step indicates a positive outcome for how organisations within the manufacturing sector are addressing the impacts that they are creating in Thailand. From the organisations within this category, the majority (75 per cent) were adopting both GRI standards and UNGC principles in directing how they addressed their impacts and the types of alternatives to be implemented.

Two organisations, or 25 per cent of the organisations in the World Class category, stated that they were aligned with GRI standards and making a shift in their reporting methods to conform with this. However, their sustainability reports still largely followed a CSR approach and were informed by a range of ISOs including ISO 26000 and the key categories that need to be addressed through this. This was also heavily influenced through their home country regulations, which were emphasised in the interviews with the key stakeholders as being critical in their approach to sustainability in Thailand. Despite this approach, it was still evident that they were adopting very comprehensive profiling and alternative selection to address potential impacts within their operations based in Thailand.

A good example of this is TH02. Current operations have expanded over the last 20 years to see Thailand emerge as one of their key global production bases. Their home country operations are in North East Asia, although the majority of their manufacturing operations have been shifted off-shore. In Thailand, the company identified as a large MNE with more than 10,000 employees in their Thailand operations.

In framing their sustainability activities, including their alternative selection and mitigation strategies, they identify the importance of industry standards set in their home country, which directs both their domestic and international activities. They also utilise two key ISOs, ISO 14001 (which is a regulatory requirement in Thailand) and ISO 26000 (which relates to CSR standards). This is also underpinned by a national law in their home country on the treatment of environmental issues. And finally, they align their sustainability activities – including progressively more in their reporting – to the GRI 3.1 standards.

Looking more closely at their activities in Thailand, it was reported by a senior manager that the majority of operational decisions and changes to business activities are based on the decision of the home country headquarter operations and specifically the board of directors. This was reinforced through reviewing the archival data, including the CSR reports of the company, whereby the company focuses on their home country perspective for setting global initiatives aimed at addressing sustainability. These initiatives are then adapted to the different countries according to cultural differences, including in Thailand.

It is clear from examining the activities of this organisation that their main focus is on environmental issues, and how this links with other social and economic considerations. This was evident in both the interviews with the subsidiary and headquarters operations, as well as the reports that the organisation conducted. Like TH10, this organisation worked from broad issue areas, to the specific, identifying different issue categories they focus on, issue areas within each issue category, before delineating down to indicators to measure the impact of their activities. From this point, they identified particular alternatives that could be implemented to address their performance across different indicators.

For example, in a recent operational expansion, the organisation identified a range of new technologies that could be utilised to better manage and mitigate some of their key environmental impacts (including all plant effluents and emissions). This includes addressing more broadly $CO^2$ emissions caused by their value chain, such as through their production related activities, the distribution of both production inputs and outputs, and the end user consumption of their products.

Another very interesting example is through the use of water within their production. Here the organisation maps how this is used both as an input, and what their outputs are across the different production activities. The use of local water, particularly from existing water supplies in developing countries, is often a critical issue due to the volumes of water consumption in large-scale manufacturing. This organisation is no different, drawing on water from local water supplies, industrial water, ground water, rainwater, spring water and river water. Here, the organisation utilises detailed impact analysis to determine and quantify the amount of water used, as well outputs through the production process.

For the waste water, the organisation initially determined the level of recycled/ reused water, the level of acidic or alkaline in the water, the chemical oxygen demand, the biological oxygen demand, the suspended solids and the o-hexane extracts within the water, amongst others. To address these different types of environmental issues with their water consumption and release, they developed processing equipment to address all of these water-related purification issues. The overall strategy implemented by the organisation has been to reduce (or eliminate completely) the environmental impact of their water consumption and disposal to zero, completely eliminating all waste water emissions.

This is illustrated in Figure 5.11 in a life-cycle assessment that is adapted from the organisation's external reporting processes, which details their waste water mitigation activities for production processes. The organisation implemented one solution – which was to completely mitigate waste water pollutants – that was able to address a range of environmental/water indicators around pollutants from their use of water throughout their production processes.

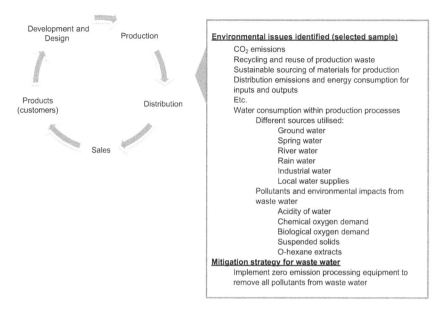

*Figure 5.11* Life-cycle assessment, environmental issues for production and mitigation strategy for waste water

Source: *Adapted from TH02 and de-identified*

This life-cycle assessment was also extended to different sustainability issues, including socio-economic. Although the organisation was focused on environmental issues as the dominant theme within their life-cycle assessment, they also considered socio-economic issues. They were therefore classified within the World Class category. Earlier examples of life-cycle assessment evident within the manufacturing sector had been primarily classified in the International Practices category due to limitations around the multidimensional nature of their assessment with a clear focus only on environmental issues.

## *International Practices – alternative selection*

As noted earlier, 50 per cent of organisations were classified within this category. While this is a significant number of organisations within the manufacturing sample, it nevertheless shows a dramatic decrease from what was evident in earlier steps where International Practices had dominated our classification of organisational practices. This is reflective of the higher number of organisations demonstrating comprehensive practices to address their organisational impacts.

Looking more closely at the organisations classified within the International Practices category, half of these organisations had their headquarter operations located in North East Asia, while the other 50 per cent were from either Europe or Australasia. These organisations were predominantly large, although one medium and one small organisation were also within this category. This again points to the fact that size is not necessarily an important predictor of organisational practices. Overall, however, the main characteristic of organisations within this category was the dominance of an environmental focus in their alternative selection and consideration or mitigation or enhancement strategies when looking at their impacts.

These organisations tended to adopt full life-cycle assessments of their environmental footprint, irrespective of their ownership or involvement in different activities. This life-cycle assessment had a predominant focus on mitigation/minimisation strategies, attempting to reduce all environmental impacts from their supply chain, to raw material usage, to product consumption. When evaluating their specific manufacturing activities, there was a significant focus on considering recycling and using resources more efficiently (this includes water, energy, material usage etc.), as well as looking at renewable resources that can be integrated into processes.

Looking beyond the environmental impact of their manufacturing processes, these organisations also focused on product adaptation as a major element of the alternative selection practices. This showed many organisations reflecting on a cyclical introduction of new technology to address issues right across the product life cycle but particularly in the consumption of their products. This was very evident in the automotive sector, where the most significant environmental issues – particularly with regards to $CO_2$ emissions – come through the consumption or use of their product. These organisations tended to therefore focus on how different changes to their products was having an impact at reducing or removing the environmental impacts associated with the consumption part of their life-cycle analysis.

Interestingly, the supply chain partners were also a pre-dominant focus on the strategies being implemented by these organisations to address their environmental footprint and linked with their alternative selection to reduce, minimise or remove their environmental impacts. One organisation, for example, had a very clear strategy about implementing their sustainability policies across their entire product life cycle through both their direct and indirect suppliers, setting ambitious targets for the level of compliance across all their partners for the full adoption of their sustainability policies.

Again, as was evident in the impact analysis step, organisations within this category – although implementing very comprehensive strategies around their environmental impact, and extending this along their product life cycle and supply chains – failed to comprehensively integrate social and economic considerations in any meaningful way. The most significant theme through these organisations when examining the alternatives being implemented for the social side related to employment conditions and workplace safety.

Some organisations even made reference to the importance of putting in alternative strategies to enhance the attraction and retention of staff from the local community, and had buffers in place to ensure the employment of these staff was not affected by down-turns in profitability or demand for their products. This included maintaining employment levels in the event of natural disasters, as was evident in Thailand in recent years with major floods affecting the production facilities of many manufacturing organisations. Reference was often also made to different training and development activities being implemented to address the safety of their staff. Despite these examples, however, organisations within this category generally had very limited consideration of social and economic dimensions for alternative selection.

### Host Country and Non-disclosure Practices – alternative selection

Continuing with the pattern evident in the two earlier steps, no organisations were classified in the Non-disclosure or Host Country Compliance categories. It was evident that all organisations were going beyond local regulatory requirements, and at the very least exceeding requirements around the environmental aspect of their operations when considering alternative selection.

## Monitoring practices

In terms of the results for the monitoring step, it is clear that there are relatively little differences between the overall sample and that of the manufacturing sector. Although, it is worthwhile to note a higher level of manufacturing organisations were classified in both the World Class and International Practices category. Approximately 44 per cent of manufacturing MNEs in Thailand were adopting World Class practices. This exceeded the overall average in the Thailand sample, which was 39 per cent. For the overall sample, there were approximately 13 per cent of organisations classified in the Host Country Compliance category; yet, no organisations within the manufacturing sector were classified as being in either the Host Country or Non-disclosure categories. This is demonstrated below in Figure 5.12, which looks at monitoring practices of manufacturing MNEs against all business sectors.

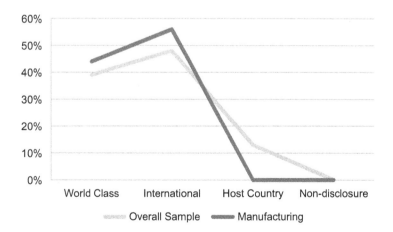

*Figure 5.12* Monitoring practices – manufacturing versus all sectors

## *World Class Practices – monitoring*

Approximately 44 per cent of manufacturing MNEs in Thailand were adopting what we classified as World Class practices. This is a substantial proportion of organisations, and again demonstrates the tendency of these organisations to be adopting comprehensive and sophisticated methods across different steps of the sustainability assessment. This is despite the lower level of participatory and World Class practices evident in the earlier steps of the sustainability assessment for manufacturing organisations, where we were specifically looking for local engagement and locally relevant issues being identified by stakeholders.

This level of World Class practices in the manufacturing sector also exceeded the overall average evident in the Thailand sample, which was 39 per cent. While only a nominal increase over the average for the sample, it is nevertheless a positive indication of the practices being implemented by these organisations in Thailand. The majority (71 per cent) of these organisations utilised either GRI standards or UNGC principles, with specific issues and indicators linked across their environmental, social and economic dimensions.

Two organisations within this category did not fully adopt GRI standards and UNGC principles. Both these organisations were from North East Asia, and both explicitly stated that they 'conformed' with, or 'aligned' to, standards set through the GRI. Despite this stated affiliation from these organisations, it was not clear that they were completely conforming to GRI requirements from their sustainability reporting. Indeed, both appear to still adopt largely CSR-based standards in their reporting. Having said this, it is clear that both these organisations should remain in the World Class category due to the comprehensive coverage of issues and impacts within their monitoring cycles.

Again, as we did in previous steps of the sustainability assessment, an analysis was conducted of interview and archival data on the activities that occurred at both the subsidiary and headquarter level. Within the latter, including news reports, annual reports and sustainability or CSR reports, the data were analysed to determine whether it was collected in Thailand as well as across the organisation's global operations.

Of the organisations within the World Class category, TH10 is a particularly good example demonstrating the comprehensive nature of the monitoring practices. Building from the earlier example of TH10 under the impact analysis step, here we extend the analysis of their activities as it demonstrates the approach of not only identifying but also measuring their issues and impacts along a longitudinal perspective. As noted earlier, this is a global leader in its market with operations across countries and more than 100,000 employees.

Providing an important underlying basis for the monitoring activities of this organisation is their commitments to undertaking cyclical assessment and monitoring through their association with the GRI standards, UNGC and CDP. According to one senior-level manager, this organisation has a key focus on long-term issues, and monitors their issue areas "very carefully". This is driven by the fact that the organisation is internationally recognisable, so it is very important for their reputation that they carefully monitor different issues associated with their business activities. The monitoring does not just occur on direct business activities, as one director emphasised the importance of also looking at their entire supply chain, amongst other areas, as it all determines how well they are able to engage in sustainability across their operations.

The senior-level manager emphasised the importance of the headquarters in regulating the practices that the Thailand operations adopt around monitoring methods and activities. The headquarters "collects [the data], monitors and controls" the processes that the subsidiary puts in place around monitoring. This has translated into a very strict adoption of a consistent set of processes across their global operations, irrespective of the country of operations.

Elaborating further, this manager pointed to the fact senior executives in the headquarters had a role in the development of some of the global sustainability initiatives, guidelines and standards that the organisation is committed to. This is an important part, therefore, of their philosophy that they are "an international company so that we have to cling. . . [to]. . . the world standard[s] that [are] globally accepted". Monitoring for this organisation does not simply translate into putting automated systems in place to capture data and send back to the headquarters for evaluation.

Rather, the subsidiary adopts a multilevel monitoring process, where the subsidiary monitoring activities are just the first step in determining the impact of their activities. These monitoring activities span the full scope of their operational activities from accounting and finance, to implementation of local tax policy and regulations, to ISO certifications and industry standards. In the implementation of systems for this monitoring, the senior-level manager points to a range of formal online procedures that were developed and implemented by the headquarters. This drives a lot of their monitoring activities and ensures compliance across a variety of internal and external sustainability commitments.

The director pointed to the fact that monitoring is not only through formal processes and automated systems, but also includes, for instance, the head or director of different functions within the subsidiary giving informal updates of their monitoring activities and performance. As part of these informal mechanisms of monitoring, the director articulated how this communication can not only help understand the relative performance of the subsidiary across their sustainability issues, but also aid in testing assumptions and mechanisms put in place by the headquarters and whether this is appropriate in the local context. It also ensures a flow of information from the different areas of the business operations to the key decision-makers to increase the capacity to rapidly act, should there be any issues around their performance.

Overlaying these monitoring activities, the subsidiary is then regularly audited, both internally and externally, with both the headquarter operations and independent and certified companies coming into the subsidiary to ensure they are collecting accurate data across their monitoring activities. This includes through international accounting firms that have the capacity to not only audit basic business activities, but also ensure the organisation is accurately measuring across all their sustainability activities for international commitments such as the GRI standards or CDP. Once this information is audited and the organisation is sure that the information is accurate, it is collated, analysed and included in the sustainability report produced by the headquarters. This is publicised through their websites, as well as provided through online mechanisms to local officials, including the Department of Environment in Thailand (where relevant).

In Figure 5.13, an example is extracted (and de-identified) of the monitoring conducted by this organisation across its global operations. This demonstrates the flow of issue categories, areas and indicators, informed through the screening, scoping and impact analysis steps into the monitoring step.

When looking more closely at occupational health and safety, while all these issue areas and indicators are not consistently adopted internationally, it is evident from examining archival data that a range of different measures are being put in place to capture what the organisation is doing globally. The clearest indicator selection adopted consistently within the occupation health and safety category is regarding the level of occupational injuries, lost work hours and fatal injuries. An example is demonstrated in Table 5.3, adapted from the organisation's reporting.

### *International Practices – monitoring*

When looking at the International Practices category, approximately 56 per cent of manufacturing organisations within our sample were classified within this category. This is slightly higher than the overall sample, but is also reflective of the fact that no manufacturing organisations were classified in the bottom two categories – Host Country Compliance and Non-disclosure. Overall, this result is very positive, with manufacturing organisations exceeding local regulatory requirements, demonstrating the voluntary initiatives that these organisations do to engage with sustainability.

However, the major difference in classifying organisations within this category, as opposed to that of World Class, is the breadth of coverage of non-environmental issues and indicators in their business activities. The organisations within this category utilised a comprehensive set of largely quantitative measures across a wide variety of environmental indicators to identify and measure their impacts. This included $CO_2$ emissions, electricity consumption, pollutions, chemical usage, recycling, material usage and waste management. These data were captured usually along a life-cycle perspective for monitoring potential impacts, looking from development to consumption and disposal of products.

While there was a significant limitation evident in the coverage of social and economic indicators, it was nevertheless evident that these organisations went beyond the regulatory requirements for their activities. Organisations were consistently referring to the requirement to undertake ISO 14001 as part of their environmental management systems, which was required by the government of Thailand. It was clear that their activities extended much further than

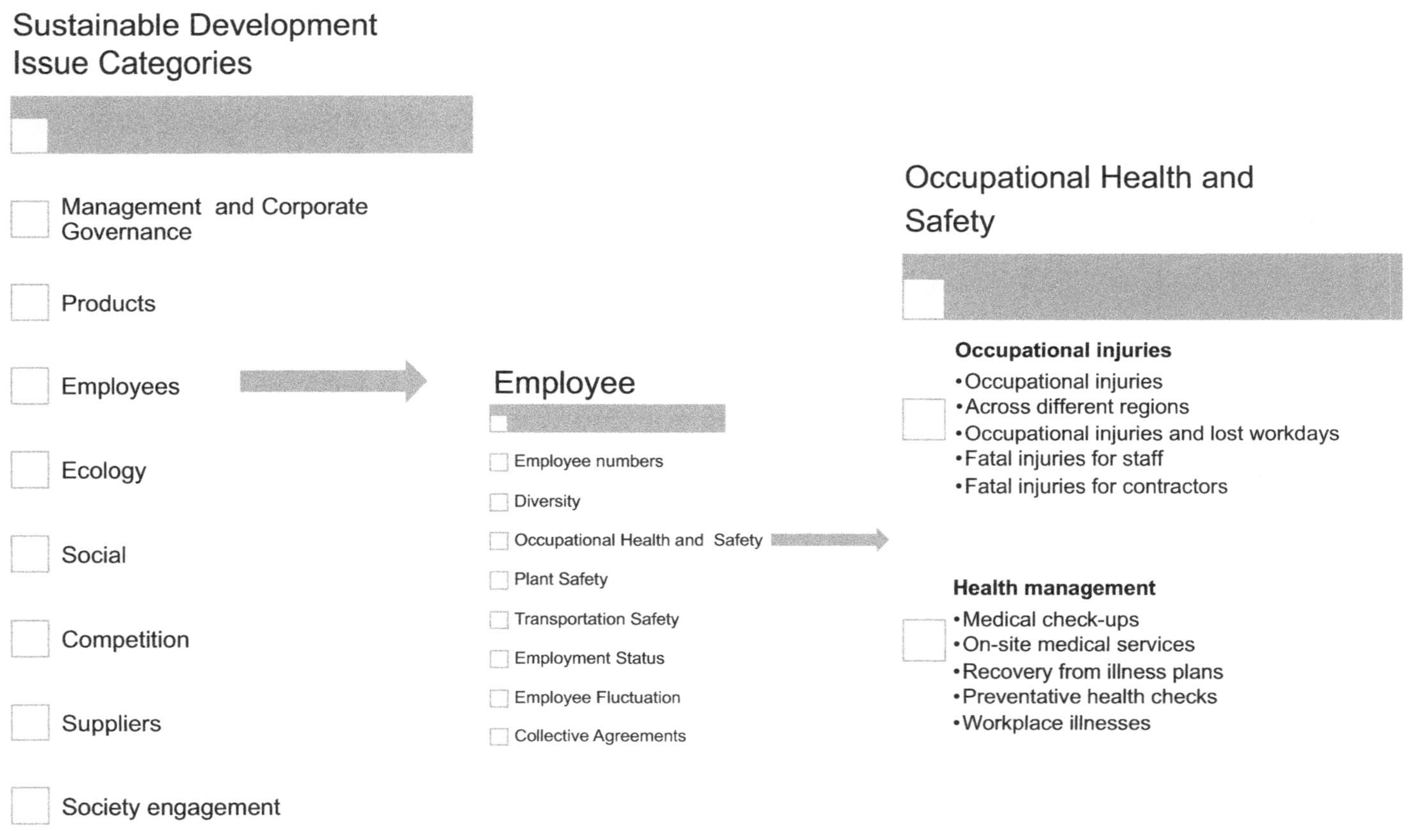

# Sustainable Development Issue Categories

☐ Management and Corporate Governance

☐ Products

☐ Employees

☐ Ecology

☐ Social

☐ Competition

☐ Suppliers

☐ Society engagement

## Employee

☐ Employee numbers

☐ Diversity

☐ Occupational Health and Safety

☐ Plant Safety

☐ Transportation Safety

☐ Employment Status

☐ Employee Fluctuation

☐ Collective Agreements

## Occupational Health and Safety

**Occupational injuries**
- Occupational injuries
- Across different regions
- Occupational injuries and lost workdays
- Fatal injuries for staff
- Fatal injuries for contractors

☐

**Health management**
- Medical check-ups
- On-site medical services
- Recovery from illness plans
- Preventative health checks
- Workplace illnesses

☐

*Figure 5.13* Issue categories, areas and attached indicators

Source: *Adapted from TH10 and de-identified*

*Table 5.3* Issue indicators and monitoring for occupational injuries

| Occupational injuries | Year X1 | X2 | X3 | X4 | X5 |
|---|---|---|---|---|---|
| Occupational injuries | Number | Number | Number | Number | Number |
| Occupational injuries with lost workdays | Number | – | – | – | – |
| Fatal injuries | Number | – | – | – | – |
| - Organisation employees | Number | – | – | – | – |
| - Contract employees | Number | – | – | – | – |

Source: *Adapted from TH10 and de-identified*

the requirements for certification here, with the adoption of very comprehensive life-cycle assessments. Other international standards were also commonly referred to, including the CDP, when looking at the environmental issues and indicators that these organisations were considering.

It was also evident that these organisations were monitoring these environmental indicators longitudinally, capturing data regularly and reporting on these against benchmarks and baseline points. This demonstrated a consistency in their approach to capturing data over an extended period of time, and was usually consistent across their broader international operations. As part of our analysis, we considered this from both the subsidiary and headquarter perspective, with evidence indicating that not only were the subsidiary activities directly influenced by the headquarter standards, but also that this was usually implemented as part of a global initiative for the organisations. These practices would often funnel into the practices of all operations irrespective of their location. It should be noted that there were some limitations to this for organisations that were from North East Asia, where it was not always evident that a global approach was being implemented and not all the highest standards implemented in their home country translated into the developing country context for their subsidiary operations.

Looking beyond the environmental focus for organisations within this category, it was also evident that these MNEs were addressing – to a lesser extent – some social and economic indicators. As has been demonstrated in earlier steps of the sustainability assessment framework, it was apparent that addressing health and safety issues of employees was one of the key methods for capturing any data around the social aspect of their operations. This tended to link in with monitoring injuries associated with work as well as fatalities. There were also several organisations that also implemented some significant measures for monitoring the training and development activities their organisation put in place to develop their workforce. This included identifying and measuring skills gaps in local workforces, monitoring and reporting on the level of training being implemented, and capturing measures around workforce diversity in management positions (within the development and employment of local personnel for management roles).

From the economic standpoint, this was by far the most limited area being addressed by these organisations. Most broadly, it was acknowledged by all these organisations about the importance of capturing and reporting important data about their operations to address regulatory requirements. Only two organisations sought to look beyond these requirements, and captured both some basic direct and indirect economic indicators such as employment creation and level of supply chain integration for local suppliers. This was very basic data being captured, with our analysis indicating the dominance of the environmental considerations in the monitoring activities of these organisations when going beyond regulatory requirements.

### *Host Country and Non-disclosure Practices – monitoring*

Building from the results in earlier steps, it was again evident that no manufacturing organisations were within the Host Country Compliance or Non-disclosure categories. This reinforces again the general willingness and pattern evident in these organisations to go beyond regulatory requirements and to undertake voluntary initiatives to address sustainability in their operations.

## Evaluation practices

An examination of the results for the evaluation step again highlight very little differences between the manufacturing sector and the overall sample. However, organisations within the manufacturing sector are classified at higher levels of performance, with all organisations in either the World Class (44 per cent) or International Practices (56 per cent) category. This is exactly the same as the monitoring step, and demonstrates how comprehensive monitoring practices are able to be translated into systematic evaluation processes. It is worth noting that while the manufacturing sector has no organisations within the Host Country Compliance or Non-disclosure categories, the broader sample had 4 per cent in

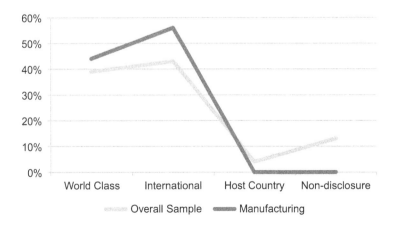

*Figure 5.14* Evaluation practices – manufacturing versus all sectors

the Host Country category and 13 per cent in the Non-disclosure category, driven by the services sector.

## World Class Practices – evaluation

When looking more closely at the World Class category for the evaluation step, 44 per cent of the manufacturing MNEs were classified within this category. This runs parallel to the monitoring results, and indicates a large proportion of the sample is adopting very sophisticated and comprehensive methods. This is true for not only collecting data across different points in time for their sustainability performance, but that they are also evaluating their performance against relative changes in their monitoring data.

To be classified into this category, we also looked for a more holistic integration of not only evaluating their ongoing performance based on their monitoring activities, but also considering how these results are anchored to benchmark or baseline data. Building from this point, it was also considered how these organisations set targets for improvement across these different indices or measures.

The organisations within this category were the same seven organisations that were classified within the World Class category for monitoring. There is a need within the evaluation process to establish a comprehensive baseline set of performance indicators to measure organisational activities over time. This assists when determining how well the organisation is performing. It makes sense that these two steps are inherently linked and we see the same organisations performing at World Class levels for both steps.

Again, like in the monitoring step, it was evident across these organisations that a comprehensive longitudinal analysis was being undertaken across a range of different issue areas and indicators. While two of these organisations from North East Asia appear to be adopting more of a CSR based approach – despite drawing reference and stating commitment to GRI standards – a comprehensive analysis was being undertaken on a full suite of indicators and measures. For the remaining organisations, it was clear that the GRI standards and/or the UNGC principles were playing an important role in the evaluation activities that they were undertaking. This was particularly through reporting and alignment of their performance against set issue/indicator areas elaborated upon through GRI reporting requirements or the principles from UNGC.

An excellent example of comprehensive evaluation techniques is TH11. TH11 is a major European MNE, with more than 100,000 employees worldwide and operations across the globe. The organisation is involved in component manufacturing, with a specialisation across consumer and industrial goods. Launching in Thailand some years ago, the organisation has continued to expand their operations and manufacturing facilities. Their Thailand operation serves as an important production point for their activities in the ASEAN region.

As is the case with many MNEs in the data set, TH11 takes strong strategic and operational direction from the headquarters country. One of the director's in Thailand elaborates, the subsidiary in Thailand "align[s] with the global vision, mission and value of the HQ, especially the value[s]". This headquarter perspective is an important determinant for when they establish operations in all countries that they operate in, with the initial investment decisions framed by whether they can follow all the protocols and requirements established by the headquarters. The next consideration is about the local regulatory requirements and how this changes or influences their activities in the country they are operating in.

In the context of Thailand, this necessitated the consideration of local regulations – such as undertaking an environmental impact assessment before establishing their operations – and then the implementation of the headquarter mandated guidelines across the environmental, social and economic dimensions of their sustainability practices. The underlying processes for evaluating their sustainability performance are set through the monitoring systems implemented by the headquarters, although they ensure that this is aligned with the regulatory requirements.

In evaluating their performance, the subsidiary has very specific targets and plans set, which it constantly monitors its performance against, and determines whether any changes are required to align with expected performance. According to one Thailand based senior manager, the standards and performance expectations are consistently applied internationally and are also informed through European standards and requirements. The monitoring systems are constantly enacted to identify issues with their performance, although this senior manager gave indications that the actual evaluation done by the subsidiary occurs every month.

When examining their monitoring and evaluation more closely, it appears a lot of this is enacted through the headquarters in automated systems. This includes through global data collection across a range of very specific sustainability indicators. These indicators are derived from global sustainability issue categories that are consistently applied in all operations, as highlighted by both their director and senior manager. Across these issue categories, the organisation derives a set of issue areas, which are then funnelled down further into specific issue indicators and measurable areas. This is illustrated in Figure 5.15, where an adapted framework is provided to highlight the flow from broader categories, into issue areas, and finally into the indicators that they are collecting.

The global approach this organisation adopts becomes more apparent when looking at how the data are collected across these different indicator areas. It is possible through their reporting mechanisms and online platform to delineate down into substantive regions the organisation operates within, where data are collected across foreign operations where they have a certain level of ownership. This is aggregated at the regional level, which, although obfuscating the ability to look at individual country performance such as in Thailand, it does nevertheless enable us to determine that these indicators and measurement approach are being adopted consistently.

Before turning to the specific evaluation approach that they adopt, it is useful to see how the organisation first establishes the monitoring measures. In

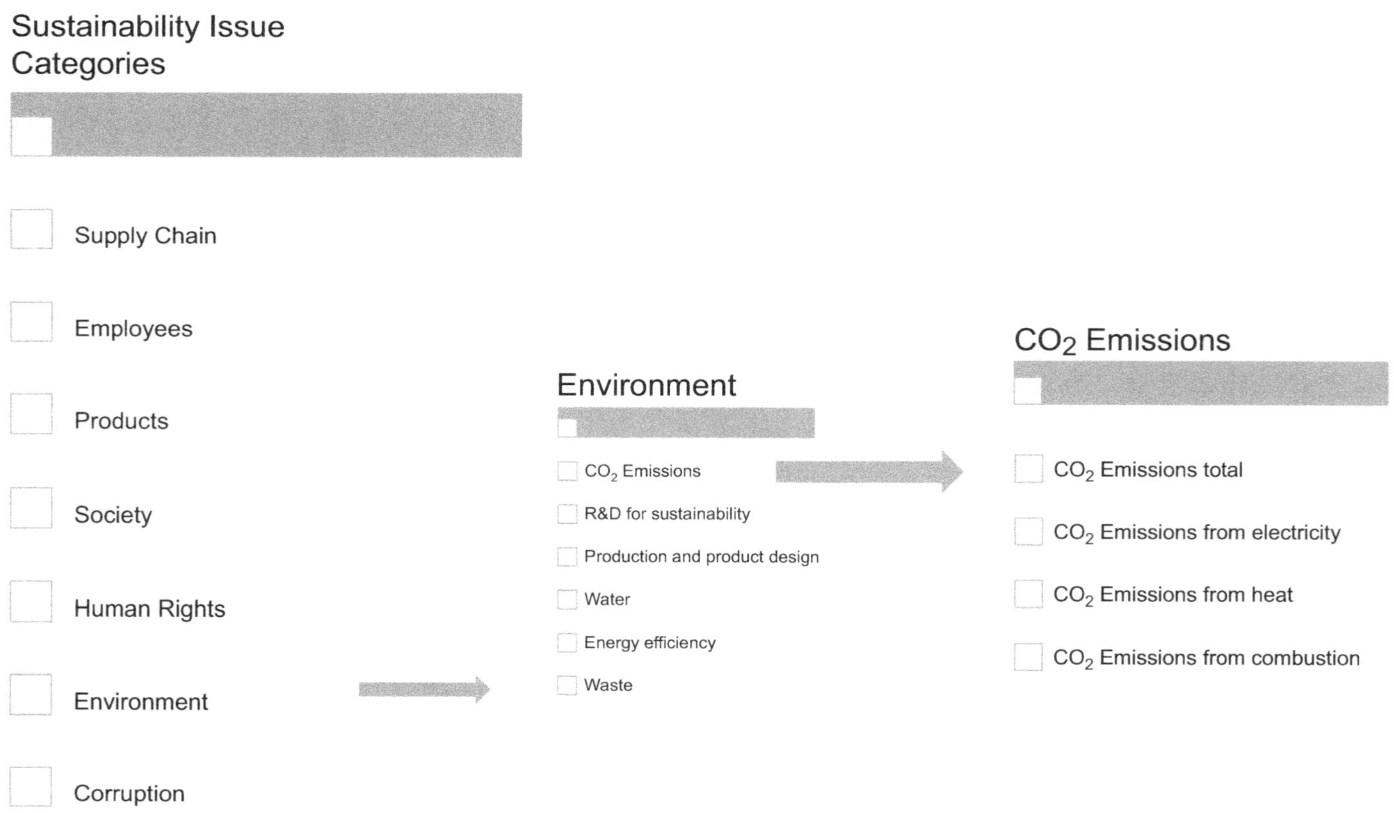

## Sustainability Issue Categories

- Supply Chain
- Employees
- Products
- Society
- Human Rights
- Environment
- Corruption

## Environment

- $CO_2$ Emissions
- R&D for sustainability
- Production and product design
- Water
- Energy efficiency
- Waste

## $CO_2$ Emissions

- $CO_2$ Emissions total
- $CO_2$ Emissions from electricity
- $CO_2$ Emissions from heat
- $CO_2$ Emissions from combustion

*Figure 5.15* Issue categories, areas and attached $CO_2$ indicators

Source: *Adapted from TH11 and de-identified*

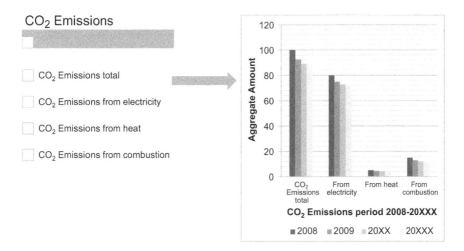

*Figure 5.16* Monitoring of $CO_2$ indicators
Source: *Adapted from TH11 and de-identified*

Figure 5.16, an illustration of the organisation's approach to capturing $CO_2$ emissions is demonstrated, and highlights how the data are presented using a longitudinal lens, visually showing how the organisation is performing. This, as noted above, is available at a regional level, as well as at the global level for overall performance on specific indicators. In presenting the regional/global context, it is easily possible to understand the performance of the organisation across these different indicator categories and regions that they operate in. A range of timeframes is presented, also demonstrating the longitudinal aspect of their monitoring systems.

From this monitoring data, it is possible through the sustainability reports the organisation makes available, to determine their relative performance across their sustainability indicators with articulated performance targets. In Figure 5.17, we provide the connection between these two different sources, showing how their monitoring activities can be linked with the overall targets that the organisation has set. While the organisation does not have a comprehensive set of quantifiable targets across all sustainability indicators, it does however identify set targets across all the major sustainability dimensions. For instance, in the example we present here, it has a range of targets for $CO_2$ emissions. It also identifies the activities (mitigation or enhancement strategies) it is implementing to improve its performance, and provides a judgement on how well it is tracking towards its targets.

While the approach taken to monitoring and evaluation requires some extrapolation and connection between different sources of data, it is clearly evident that this organisation is carefully considering how it is performing across different sustainability dimensions.

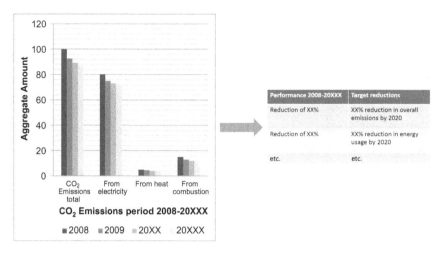

*Figure 5.17* Evaluation of $CO_2$ performance against targets

Source: *Adapted from TH11 and de-identified*

## International Practices – evaluation

As noted above, 56 per cent of manufacturing organisations within our sample were classified within the International Practices category. This showed a clear progression and link between both the monitoring and evaluation step – with organisations in both categories being consistently classified in the same level of performance. A part of this was due to the limitations and scope evident in the consideration of sustainability dimensions by these organisations when establishing their impact analysis, as well as their monitoring activities.

With regards to the breadth of sustainability considerations, as was evident in the monitoring step, organisations within this category had a distinct focus on environmental issues and indicators. While this focus was very comprehensive, often embedded in a life-cycle assessment of their products, from research and design through to disposal, and also from a longitudinal perspective, it was evident that these organisations did not have such a comprehensive system in place to measure, monitor and evaluate social and economic dimensions linked with their operations.

Despite this limitation, many of the similar types of procedures and processes were evident for organisations within this category as were those classified within the World Class category – with the primary difference residing in the scope of sustainability dimensions being covered. These organisations were using bench-marks and baseline data to tie their performance evaluation against, demonstrating the comparative differences in their performance. It was also consistent that these organisations had a range of different performance targets that they anchored their evaluation against, tracking their annual performance against expected improvements in outcomes.

### *Host Country and Non-disclosure Practices – evaluation*

Again, it was evident that no manufacturing organisations were in either the Host Country Compliance or Non-disclosure categories. Organisations had a clear sequence in their activities from the monitoring to evaluation steps, indicating the coherence and connection between activities around monitoring and evaluation for these organisations.

## Feedback and follow up practices

The results from examining the feedback and follow up mechanisms of manufacturing organisations shows a noticeable drop in the level of World Class practices. From some 44 per cent in the evaluation step, to approximately 33 per cent in this step, this shows some limitations in adopting a full cyclical process of addressing sustainability performance in these organisations. Having said this, it remains higher than the overall sample as can be seen in Figure 5.18, again highlighting the lower performance of the services and mining sector drawing down the overall sample. Despite this lower performance, there was an increase in organisations classified as adopting International Practices (with 63 per cent, compared with 56 per cent in the evaluation step), indicating the majority of organisations are still going beyond the regulatory requirements of Thailand. For the first time within the manufacturing sector there was one organisation – or 6 per cent of the sample – in this Non-disclosure category.

### *World Class Practices – feedback and follow up*

In considering the results more closely, the 33 per cent within the World Class category represents five manufacturing organisations out of the sample. This was two fewer than what was seen in the evaluation step. Despite this drop, this

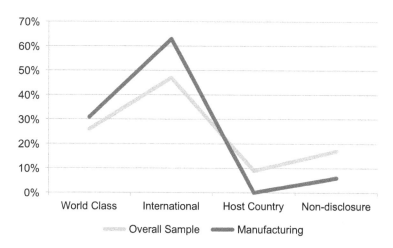

*Figure 5.18* Feedback and follow up practices – manufacturing versus all sectors

result is positive and indicates that these organisations are utilising the information and analysis from their evaluation step to adjust decision-making processes in how they address sustainability within their operations, including potentially adjusting or changing their alternative selection to enhance or further mitigate their impacts (depending on whether they are positive or negative).

All of these organisations within the World Class category had performed at this level for the proceeding steps within the sustainability assessment, and had generally performed at this level for the majority of the steps within the process. A consistent underlying commitment to the GRI standards was also evident in all these organisations, indicating again the importance of these guidelines in not only informing the sustainability practices of these organisations but also as an important predictor of those that will conduct more comprehensive sustainability activities as part of their business operations.

Building from the evaluation step, it is useful to leverage from the example of TH11 in demonstrating the link between an organisation's evaluation activities and their alternative selection activities (be it through mitigation or enhancement strategies). As noted earlier, TH11 is a very large MNE with extensive facilities in Thailand. In the preceding step, we demonstrated the flow from the broader sustainability issue categories established through the headquarter operations. This then was delineated down into issue areas and attached indicators for the substantive areas that the organisation was collecting monitoring data on.

Building from this point, we demonstrated how in the evaluation step the organisation anchored its performance against both baseline data and targeted performance. Moving beyond this evaluation process, we identified different mitigation strategies that the organisation identified through interviews and their sustainability reporting. In Figure 5.19, we extend from the earlier example in the evaluation stage and show how the performance of the organisation in addressing $CO_2$ emissions can be linked with different mitigation activities it is implementing.

As noted earlier, it requires some effort to link between the monitoring and evaluation steps, given the method the MNE uses to organise and present its

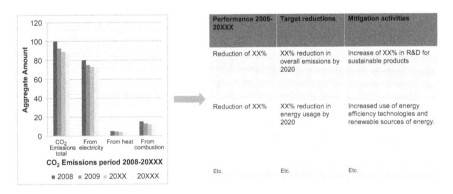

*Figure 5.19* Evaluation of $CO_2$ performance, targets and mitigation
Source: *Adapted from TH11 and de-identified*

data. This is a similar case with connecting the evaluation data with the alternative selection process and implementation of strategies to address their performance (in this case, a focus on improving their mitigation strategies and minimising the level of $CO_2$ emissions). This is perhaps reflective of the fact that one of the most difficult aspects confronting organisations is the attribution effects of different alternatives they are implementing and linking this with the overall performance it achieves across sustainability indices. This dilemma does not only complicate sustainability performance, but all aspects of research and attribution of cause–effect relationships. Our analysis shows that this is a consistent issue. Likewise, it is not easy for the general public to navigate an organisation's sustainability reporting, when they have to connect different data reporting from across different sources to determine what is happening.

## *International Practices – feedback and follow up*

With some 63 per cent of manufacturing organisations classified within the International Practices category, we see a dominance of these practices within the feedback and follow up step. While these organisations are going above the regulatory requirements of the Thailand government, showing broad-based engagement within voluntary initiatives, there are some significant limitations linked with this. Specifically, these organisations often had both an overarching focus on environmental issues and a limited integration of changes to their mitigation and enhancement strategies as a response to performance outcomes.

With regards to the environmental focus, this is not surprising given the results reviewed thus far. However, it does point to the importance of considering more systematic bases for addressing social and economic dimensions within the practices of organisations in the manufacturing sector. Our analysis tends to highlight difficulties for organisations looking beyond their direct impact on employees, basic contributions to employment generation and tax revenues when operating in the developing country context. It appears to be those organisations with a very proactive global approach to sustainability, commitment to leading global standards or guidelines, with a significant international profile and highly engaged executive leadership team, that are really taking steps to engage more broadly in a holistic approach to sustainability.

The other limitation associated with organisations within this category is the breadth and scope of adjustments being made to their operations as a result of their evaluation processes. In many organisations they were undertaking initiatives beyond the regulatory requirements to improve their environmental performance, or for engaging with their workforce more (such as through diversity management, training and development, local employment strategies or health and safety initiatives). However, what was less clear was how these organisations were engaging fully with their performance outcomes to adjust, enhance or mitigate their impacts through active engagement with stakeholders and the integration of new alternatives (be it enhancement or mitigation strategies).

### Host Country and Non-disclosure Practices – feedback and follow up

While there were no organisations classified within the Host Country Compliance category, there was one organisation within the Non-disclosure category. This represents 6 per cent of the sample, with this organisation classed as large based on a significant investment into Thailand. We were unable to determine whether they were adjusting any of their activities as a response to their performance evaluation. They had a range of strategies in place to address sustainability; however, there was no evidence to suggest that these were being integrated into ongoing operations.

## Conclusion

Concluding our analysis of the sample of manufacturing organisations, it is clear that the majority of these organisations are undertaking significant voluntary corporate initiatives to address sustainability that go beyond the regulatory requirements of Thailand. In only two incidences across the entire corporate sustainability assessment framework did we identify organisations at either the Host Country Compliance or Non-disclosure category, with the remaining organisations classified across either the International Practice or World Class category for all sustainability assessment steps.

This result is somewhat surprising, indicating laws and regulations – particularly in a developing country context such as Thailand – are not an important predictor of the likely behaviour of major multinationals. This is also irrespective of size and home country origins of these organisations' headquarter operations, indicating a certain level of acceptance to the need of implementing practices to address sustainability that are not determined by location or levels of investment involved.

Another overarching view on the current state of practices is the importance of global standards and guidelines. This includes those established by the GRI Organization, in directing and informing the types of activities organisations are implementing to address sustainability, particularly for those conducting rigorous practices across environmental, social and economic dimensions.

The final comment would be the clear dominance in the majority of manufacturing organisations to be adopting International Practices, which tend to be predominantly focused on environmental initiatives. This suggests that there remain some substantial areas for further improvement of existing practices of manufacturing organisations to more holistically engage with sustainability, beyond an environmental focus – despite voluntarily exceeding local regulatory requirements. From this point, we now turn to an examination of the services sample.

## Note

1  The Global Reporting Initiative released a technical protocol detailing the iterative process for incorporating stakeholder engagement into issue selection as well as the broader sustainability approach adopted by organisations. Sourced from: https://www.globalreporting.org/resourcelibrary/GRI-Technical-Protocol.pdf

# 6   Sustainability practices of service MNEs

*Jerome D. Donovan, Eryadi K. Masli,*
*Cheree Topple, Thomas Borgert, Masayoshi Ike,*
*Monica Van Wynen, Teerin Vanichseni,*
*Laddawan Lekmat, Lalita Hongratanawong*
*and Jirapan Kunthawangso*

This chapter builds upon the preceding analysis, providing a detailed analysis of the service sector organisations operating within Thailand. While there are constraints to the depth of this analysis given the smaller sample size for the service sector (when compared with the manufacturing sample), this chapter will provide some initial insights into the practices being adopted within the service sector around sustainability. Adopting the same process as has been followed in the preceding chapters, this chapter will again follow the general corporate sustainability assessment framework established in Chapter 3. In doing so, this chapter will be able to both contextualise the sustainability practices of service multinationals operating in Thailand, as well as provide some interesting insights into the differences in this performance relative to the broader sample of this study.

Building from this corporate sustainability framework will allow a detailed analysis of the service sector organisations and how they are addressing sustainability. This, to our knowledge, is one of the first studies that has sought to engage specifically with the service sector and how they are addressing sustainability through an impact assessment methodology. Often considered as a lower impact sector, we believe with the economic shift experienced in developing countries from labour-intensive industrial development to knowledge-intensive, service-based economies that this chapter provides some excellent insights into how sustainability is handled by organisations against a backdrop of shifting economic structures in Thailand. We also recognise that knowledge-intensive service organisations can have an important role in upgrading knowledge and skills within the developing country context, which may better enable development to occur.

From this point, this chapter will first begin by looking at the sample of service-based organisations in Thailand, contextualising this with regards to size and home country region. It will then proceed to examining the performance of these organisations across the seven key sustainability steps established in Chapter 3. Examples will be provided throughout this analysis to demonstrate the performance of these service organisations and the actual practices and processes they implement to address sustainability, with a particular focus on World Class practices.

## Service MNEs in Thailand – sample description

There are six organisations that form the service sector sample. The overwhelming majority are Australasian with 67 per cent (4/6) having their headquarters based in this region. The other regions are from North America and ASEAN representing 16 per cent (1/6) each. This is somewhat distorted with the dominance of Australasian-based organisations, however, it still captures an interesting cross-section of organisations.

With regards to the size of these organisations, a fairly large percentage of these firms was classified as being in the small to medium sized category (67 per cent, 4/6) with less than USD$100 million dollars invested into Thailand. A reasonable percentage of the organisations were large (33 per cent, 2/6), enabling insights into the role of size in differentiating performance within service organisations. With the tendency for larger organisations to have more significant or sophisticated systems of addressing sustainability, it is invaluable to have captured several large organisations to examine whether they do indeed have more comprehensive methods of addressing sustainability.

The service sample is illustrated in the Table 6.1, showing the breakdown of organisations across size and home country region, as well as the organisational code for de-identification purposes.

This chapter will now begin the evaluation of sustainability practices across these service sector organisations operating in Thailand. This will be done through looking at the individual sustainability steps and classifying the performance of these organisations across the four categories of performance – World Class, International Practices, Host Country Compliance and Non-disclosure. As noted above, examples will be provided throughout to demonstrate the actual sustainability practices of these organisations with a focus on World Class practices.

## Screening practices

When examining the results from the screening step for the service organisations operating in Thailand, there are significant differences against the overall sample and the manufacturing sector. First, organisations within the services sector

*Table 6.1* Sample for services sector

| Organisation Code | Sector | Size | Home Country Region |
|---|---|---|---|
| TH16 | Services | Medium | Australasia |
| TH17 | Services | Small | Australasia |
| TH19 | Services | Small | Australasia |
| TH20 | Services | Large | Australasia |
| TH22 | Services | Small | North American |
| TH23 | Services | Large | ASEAN |

appear to be performing better when compared against World Class practices for screening, with 33 per cent (2/6) of organisations within this category versus 19 per cent in the manufacturing sector compared to 22 per cent overall. This quickly changes when looking at the break down at the International Practices level, with significantly more organisations from both the overall sample (65 per cent) and manufacturing sector (75 per cent) within this category. Only 33 per cent (2/6) of service organisations were classified within the International Practices category. There was also a significantly higher percentage of service organisations classified within the Host Country Compliance category (33 per cent) compared with manufacturing (6 per cent) and the overall sample (13 per cent).

When looking at these results, it is evident that the manufacturing sector is driving the overall sample results for International Practices. This is both due to the larger percentage of the sample that are classified as manufacturing organisations (16/23, 70 per cent) and the fact that these organisations are also much more likely to adopt International Practices within the screening step. The differences evident in the Host Country category are also somewhat distorted by the high level of service sector organisations being classified within this category. With 33 per cent (2/6) service organisations in this category, and only 6 per cent (1/16) manufacturing organisations, it is clear that the overall sample (13 per cent) results are driven by the higher percentage of service organisations. While the numbers are relatively small for the service sector, the fact that 33 per cent of organisations are at this level indicates the greater tendency for these organisations to adopt Host Country practices.

Figure 6.1 illustrates these results, with the services sector relatively low across the first three categories and then dropping for the final category, Non-disclosure. The manufacturing sector spikes for the adoption of International Practices. The overall sample parallels the trends of the manufacturing sector and reflects the large percentage of manufacturing organisations within the overall sample.

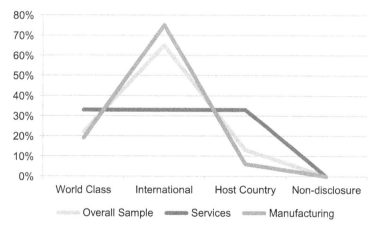

*Figure 6.1* Screening practices – Sector and sample comparison

## *World Class Practices – screening*

As noted above, service sector organisations are performing quite well for screening practices with 33 per cent (2/6) classified within the World Class category. While this is only indicative of a very small sample, it is nevertheless positive to note that several organisations are indeed adopting very comprehensive practices to identify a raft of sustainability issues and integrate these into their operational considerations. These organisations are putting in place procedures or policies that are aiming to identify a breadth of social, environmental and economic issues as part of their business operations.

When looking at the two organisations within this category more closely, it is immediately evident that they are very different in the type and scope of their operations. One organisation has a very large investment in Thailand, with a significant operational base for the region, while the investment by the other organisation is considered small with a focus on providing business services and marketing functions for their global operations within Thailand. This is interesting to note, as it is often highlighted within the extant literature that the scope of sustainability practices put into place by organisations is constrained by the resources, time and capacity of the organisation. Given that one organisation is small, and yet still classified within this category, indicates the capacity to still address sustainability holistically irrespective of the scope of investment undertaken.

Examining both of these organisations more closely, the role of international guidelines or commitments is only immediately evident in one organisation. The smaller of the two (TH22) is committed to the Global Reporting Initiative (GRI) standards, as well as undertaking significant adaptation to suit the local context for issues that need to be considered. A consistent approach is adopted by the organisation in how they approach all their international operations, irrespective of the size or location of their international operations. A senior manager and director within the Thailand operations made it clear that the headquarter policies and procedures are directing all their activities in Thailand, although there is extensive consideration for local laws and flexibility in adoption by local business executives.

While it was clear for TH22 about the role of international commitments and guidelines that the headquarters had set in driving sustainability activities, TH20, on the other hand, appeared to be driven in their sustainability activities from different motivations. Before divulging more, however, it is worthwhile providing some contextual background to TH20 before examining their practices for screening. TH20 is a large organisation with significant investment in Thailand, and originates from the Australasian region. It provides a range of key services along the value chain of other large organisations, with Thailand forming a key part of their operational activities within Asia.

TH20 is not openly committed to any international guidelines or standards (by that, we mean they do not identify clearly a range of commitments), beyond those required by Thailand regulations. However, in the interviews with the senior executives in charge of operations in Thailand, it is indicated that they have a corporate approach to addressing sustainability. Underlying this is the acknowledgement that they will identify the highest standards from their corporate policy, home or host country regulations, or business partners.

It appears that the role of the headquarter policies are critical in driving the practices of this organisation. While we would typically classify this organisation under International Practices due to this, a more discerning examination of data indicates they are indeed being driven by international guidelines and specifically the GRI standards. This is not directly linked through their commitment to these guidelines, but has rather been related to their corporate policy and linking in with business partners who have set this as a requirement for the organisation if it wishes to continue collaboration.

This translates into a comprehensive corporate strategy that has been developed to align with commitments that their business partners have and driven through the corporate strategy for the entire organisation. This includes conducting a comprehensive environmental, social and economic screening process to identify relevant sustainability considerations right across their entire operations. Looking more closely at this approach, the organisation identifies from the corporate headquarters a range of key sustainability areas that they will consider across product, environment, culture and people, and the economy. These categories have been extrapolated from their internal reporting, policy documents and objectives set by the headquarters (please see below, Figure 6.2: Core sustainability areas).

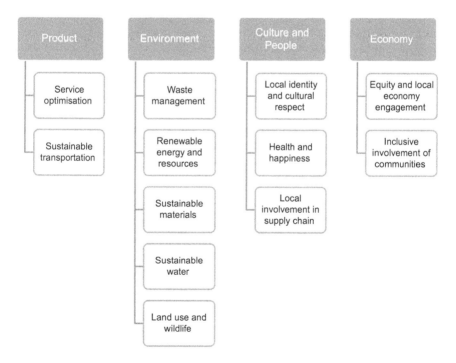

*Figure 6.2* Core sustainability areas
Source: *Adapted from TH20 and de-identified*

These key sustainability areas are further delineated down into different regions and countries that the organisation operates within. All of this is brought together in a risk register, where the organisation aggregates the key issues that they need to consider in their global operations. In this risk register, they have over 70 different types of issues across environmental, economic, social and operational levels of consideration – reflecting the integration of sustainability issues within their core business activities, rather than something that sits separate from their operational planning.

## International Practices – screening

Results indicate 33 per cent of service organisations within this category, accounting for two organisations. This is significantly below the manufacturing sector (75 per cent) and overall sample (65 per cent), indicating that service organisations are performing at substantially lower levels for their screening practices. This is despite the higher level of World Class practices (with services having 67 per cent in World Class and International Practices categories, versus manufacturing with 94 per cent).

The organisations in this category were substantially different in the nature of their activities, with one small organisation from the Australasian region specialising in more limited marketing, distribution and service delivery for their products within Thailand; while the other organisation was classified as large, from the ASEAN region and providing very specialised services to other organisations and key activities within their distribution network. With regards to the former, this organisation was particularly focused on looking at key environmental issues across their international operations, including in Thailand, with a focus on determining and addressing their environmental footprint along their supply chain. This MNE has identified a range of environmental issues linked with greenhouse gases, energy use and recycling. Beyond the environment, it tends to have a very limited focus on social or economic dimensions, with perhaps the greatest focus being placed on employee welfare and looking at issues around health and safety. Overall, it appears this organisation has far more initiatives around sustainability in their home country, largely due to the more limited size of operations in Thailand.

The second organisation appears to have more substantive processes in place for identifying different sustainability issues, although it also largely focuses on identifying a range of different environmental issues and occupational health and safety issues. The more systematic processes appear to be closely linked with different international standards that it has committed to, beyond what is required by the regulation in Thailand. Specifically, the organisation is linked with a range of ISOs including ISO 50001, OHSAS 18000 and ISO 26000. Many of the issues that the organisation discussed in interviews are directly related to addressing these ISOs and maintaining certification.

*Host Country Practices – screening*

The remaining two organisations within the services sector were both classified within the Host Country Compliance category. It was not clear from looking at either of these organisations that they were committed to any systematic process of screening for sustainability issues in Thailand. While their own domestic operations had much more comprehensive practices, it appears that both organisations had a very heavy reliance in identifying important issues of local context through reviewing relevant local laws related to the environment, social and economic dimensions.

## Scoping practices

The results for the scoping step indicate some differences occurring between the services sector and the overall sample and the manufacturing sector. As can be seen in Figure 6.3 when looking at the World Class category, it is comprised of only 17 per cent (1/6) of service organisations. Both the overall sample (22 per cent) and manufacturing sector (25 per cent) have higher rates classified at this level. While the overall sample is only slightly above the service sector, this result is mainly decreased through the lower level of service sector organisations within this category. More substantive differences are evident at the International Practices level with the manufacturing sector sitting at 75 per cent compared with the overall sample at 70 per cent, and only 50 per cent of service organisations in this category.

Clear differences are evident at the Host Country Compliance and Non-disclosure categories, with 17 per cent (1/6) of service organisations in each of these categories. This is compared with the manufacturing sector, where no organisations were classified in either category. The nominal figure (4 per cent) for the overall sample was driven by the service sector organisation in each of these categories.

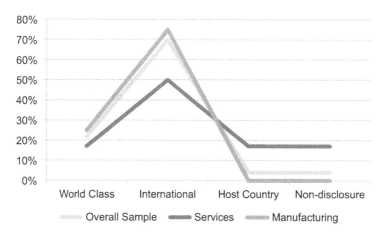

*Figure 6.3* Scoping practices – sector and sample comparison

While these figures are relatively low, it is again pointing to both the fact that the service sector is less likely to be classified in the higher categories (World Class or International Practices) and have organisations classified as only adopting Host Country Compliance or Non-disclosure. The following figure demonstrates these results for the manufacturing sector, the service sector and the overall sample.

### World Class Practices – scoping

As noted above, only one service organisation (17 per cent) was classified within the World Class category. While this is only slightly lower than the overall sample, this shows the limitations around service organisations conducting a systematic and participatory approach to engaging with their local stakeholders in refining the sustainability issues that they focus on as part of their operations.

This step assumes that organisations have already engaged with broader stakeholders through their screening step to identify relevant issues and impacts that potentially could be affected by their operations. This is the case with TH22, which is involved in consumer products and extended services to support this. They are a leading global organisation in their product category, based in North America, with their subsidiary in Thailand concentrating on providing a range of service offerings associated with one of their broader product portfolios. While this organisation is only classified as a small organisation due to the size of their investment in Thailand, globally, this organisation is very large with over 100,000 employees.

Like what was seen earlier in the manufacturing sector, the approach of this organisation to the scoping step was inherently linked with the international commitments of the global headquarters. The headquarter operations has made commitments for all their operations that they will abide by GRI standards for sustainability reporting. They also have a range of industry specific standards, CDP, and are committed to the Sustainable Trade Initiative. It is worth noting that this organisation has also made it a requirement for their tier 1 suppliers to abide by GRI standards and that they also provide sustainability reports to the organisation (as part of their broader supply chain auditing processes). They are also increasingly working through these tier 1 suppliers to target further along their global value chain, making it a requirement to check and audit the activities of tier 2 suppliers as well.

Looking more closely, however, at the scoping step, the commitments of the organisation to the GRI standards and particularly the materiality analysis had the most profound impact on their activities. While they identify the use of sector specific guidelines to account for the differences in their operations, drawing on a pool of key issues and impacts that they will address, they also undertook a global process of engaging with both internal and external stakeholders. This process of stakeholder engagement helped to identify those issues and impacts that were most important for their stakeholders when addressing sustainability throughout their operations.

The results of engaging with their internal and external stakeholders led to the development of 10 key sustainability categories to address, and within these sustainability categories that they prioritised, approximately 20 additional issue areas were linked into each to provide actionable areas to address. The key priority areas that they will address most broadly across their sustainability approach are identified below (please see Figure 6.4: Core global sustainability categories).

While this organisation provides detailed information around these material issues and commits to the implementation of an annual approach for updating broader sustainability areas as well as adjusting goals and targets, it is difficult to determine how the organisation weights these issues. Through our analysis it was unclear exactly how the materiality analysis is conducted, what are the most important issues for the organisation to engage with, and how this varies across operations.

It appears, rather, that this organisation identifies a range of key priority categories capped at 10 – and linked with their broader sustainability objectives – which are integrated and adjusted each year according to the new data and stakeholder engagement they undertake. In understanding their local approach more, it seems that the organisation sets these broader sustainability categories

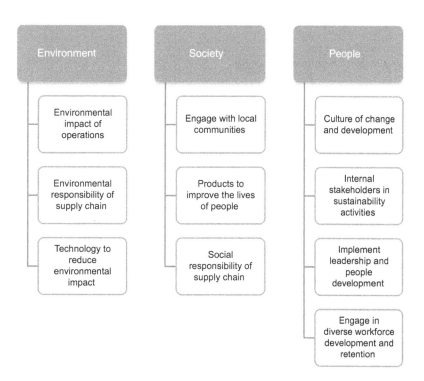

*Figure 6.4* Core global sustainability categories
Source: *Adapted from TH22 and de-identified*

as common priorities for all operations, however, at the local level there is variability in how some areas are implemented. For example, in engaging with the local community, the subsidiary has a range of options provided by a central committee in the headquarters for what they can undertake. It is then up to the local employees to propose, have approved and implement local initiatives. We would describe this as a glocal approach, mixing the global priorities of the organisation with local adaptation.

The approach implemented by this organisation seems to be quite common in a matrix structure for the coordination and control of subsidiary operations in major global organisations. Certain key functions are retained under central control by the headquarters, such as developing and implementing the corporate sustainability approach, and broad directives are given to local-level subsidiaries and employees that allow some adaptation to occur. Generally, it appears a common set of core categories and sustainability areas are adopted consistently across all operations – this is particularly with minimum global standards the organisation has around environmental impact or workplace health and safety standards. This is also reinforced in the common approach to organisations within our sample reporting on global operations rather than individual subsidiaries, reinforcing the need for comparable data and results across all their operations. Without some common standards or approaches, this would make comparability impossible.

### *International Practices – scoping*

With 50 per cent (3/6) of organisations within this category, it is clear that International Practices dominate the sustainability activities of service organisations when looking at scoping. While this is significantly below the levels evident for the broader sample, it nevertheless demonstrates the overall dominance of these practices across sectors.

Here, it is clear that all three organisations in this category are very much directed by the activities by the headquarter operations when prioritising the different sustainability issues they look at internationally, including within their operations in Thailand. This seems to be consistent, irrespective of the fact that these three organisations are providing very different types of services through their activities and are also characterised by both different home country locations and sizes.

Having said this, there appears to be some underlying motivations that differ across the three organisations. TH20 is clearly influenced by both the direction of the headquarters but is also influenced to a large extent by their business partners within their supply chain – emphasising the role of lead firms in determining the activities of other large organisations that they collaborate with. In this case, this MNE ensures that it adopts a comprehensive set of sustainability issues, yet the influence of the business partners in driving their activities towards scoping is limited and does not result in the use of a materiality analysis or other techniques.

On the other hand, TH19 appears to be driven by the selection and prioritisation of sustainability issues by their headquarter's orientation around assessing and addressing their environmental footprint. It also has some prioritisation around work conditions and the health and safety of their workforce. This cannot be linked to any clear ISOs or international standards, although the organisation is part of an industry association dealing with sustainability in their home country. It appears to be more motivated by the internal policies of the organisation in their home country to prioritise these issues across their international operations.

The final organisation, TH23, appears to be directed by their headquarter commitment towards certifying their business activities to a range of different ISOs including ISO 50001, OHSAS 18000 and ISO 26000. This leads to a distinct focus of the organisation when discussing which issues are the most important, which should be prioritised and how it engages in sustainability activities through their operational activities. This organisation, like the other two, clearly goes through some process of prioritising key sustainability issues beyond the regulatory requirements for their activities in Thailand.

Across the three organisations, however, these practices are not overly systematic or participatory. They do exceed the local regulatory requirements; however, it leaves significant latitude for improvement, with the clear need to implement some type of systematic process – such as through a materiality analysis – to address what the key sustainability issues are for their operations in Thailand.

### *Host Country and Non-disclosure Practices – scoping*

Within the final two categories, there was one organisation in both. For the organisation in the Non-disclosure category it did not appear to make any attempt to prioritise any of the local issues they might have identified through looking at local regulatory requirements. Rather, this organisation simply seems to adjust their business activities to also address local laws around sustainability, and made no attempt to prioritise these within their sustainability practices. The final organisation within the Host Country Compliance category appeared to have made some changes to their priorities in Thailand through leveraging from local regulatory requirements for ISO 14000 and ISO 9000. Although this was rather minor, it indicates that it had considered local issues when prioritising key issues, particularly when reporting to the local authorities.

## Impact analysis practices

When looking at the results for the impact analysis step across the overall sample, services and manufacturing sector organisations, the services sector is lagging behind in its performance. This begins with the World Class category where the services sector has an expanding gap with the manufacturing organisations and overall sample, with only 17 per cent (1/6) of service organisations within

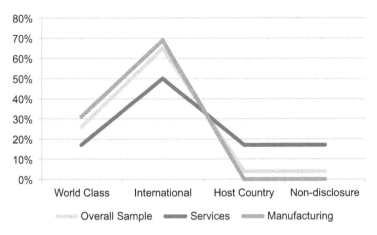

*Figure 6.5* Impact analysis practices – sector and sample comparison

this category. This is compared with the manufacturing sector that sits at 31 per cent and the overall sample at 26 per cent. International Practices almost replicate the result from scoping, with again 50 per cent (3/6) of the services organisations classified within this category. Both the overall sample (65 per cent) and the manufacturing sector (69 per cent) were substantially above this result.

Again, results indicate a common outcome for looking at the Host Country Compliance and Non-disclosure categories, with one service sector organisation (17 per cent) in each of the categories and no other organisations from the overall sample or the manufacturing sector within these categories. This is illustrated further in Figure 6.5; reflecting earlier results with the overall sample and the manufacturing sector having a large spike for International Practices, before dropping off at the Host Country and Non-disclosure categories. The services sector shows the lower performance across the first two categories and the continued higher level of Host Country and Non-disclosure categories.

## *World Class Practices – impact analysis*

Building from earlier results evident in the scoping step, again only one service organisation (17 per cent) was classified in this category. This is again below both the overall average and the manufacturing sector, indicating a very different level of engagement and coverage of sustainability within service organisations. Having said this, TH22 continues to provide a standout exemplar for service organisations in Thailand, despite being small in size, this organisation continues to perform at World Class levels utilising multiple sources of global compliance and a broad coverage of sustainability dimensions in their practices.

As noted earlier, this North American based organisation is a global leader in their product category, and the Thailand operations are quite limited and service orientated. Consistent with what was highlighted in the scoping step, the international commitments made by the global headquarters is a key basis for informing their sustainability practices across their global operations. This includes looking at their impact analysis practices.

Overarching all their impact analysis practices is their commitment to the GRI standards for sustainability reporting, where the organisation openly recognises the breadth of impact analysis areas and indicators that they have to address. This includes both through a dedicated report based on their performance in accordance with GRI standards. It does not stop there, however, with the organisation also committed to a host of other international guidelines and standards, including industry specific standards (set within their particular product category), CDP, and the Sustainability Trade Initiative, amongst others. Many of these commitments directly translate into measurable areas that the organisation must also measure and report upon.

Hence, the commitments made by the headquarters appear to be a key basis for the type of impact analysis the organisation undertakes globally, including through their operations in Thailand. When discussing the approach of the organisation in addressing their development and sustainability impacts within Thailand, a senior manager reinforced that the subsidiary organisation must not only comply with local laws but also all of the headquarter policies and procedures.

The headquarter operations has significant oversight over the activities of the subsidiaries, with teams regularly visiting to ensure that these policies and procedures are adopted and maintained at the same standard as the home country. Indeed, the senior manager highlighted the strict policy of the corporate headquarters to not be involved in any activity that will have "any harmful impact to the environment and community". While this leaves some scope for interpretation about what is classified as 'harmful', it is nevertheless clear to see through their reporting activities the full range of areas that the organisation addresses when determining the impact of their operations.

Running at the core of the organisation's efforts in their impact analysis is the global sustainability categories identified in the scoping step. These 10 categories are driven down into different areas with a host of indicators attached to these. This is demonstrated in Figure 6.6, which illustrates the engagement-related activities that the organisation has for diverse workforces. This is a particularly interesting area to examine, not just as an important element of addressing social issues, but also as it demonstrates a mixture of quantitative and qualitative activities that the organisation seeks to measure.

Looking more closely at the diverse workforce category, the organisation has sought to address major gender and racial dimensions in their workforce policies, capturing data around the percentage of their workforce that is within each category. As part of this, data is provided on locational differences, across the

## Sustainability Issue Categories

- Environmental impact of operations
- Environmental responsibility of supply chain
- Technology to reduce environmental impact
- Engage with local community
- Products to improve lives of people
- Social responsibility of supply chain
- Culture of change and development
- Internal stakeholders and sustainability
- Diverse workforce engagement
- Leadership and people development

## Diverse Workforce

- Women
- People of colour
- Asian
- Human rights

## Women

- Women in the workforce
- Women leadership programs
- Women advocacy and support groups
- Women education group

*Figure 6.6* Issue categories, areas and attached indicators

Source: *Adapted from TH22 and de-identified*

different regions the organisation operates. It also captures data around special interest groups, where different elements of the workforce can be mobilised along certain personal characteristics, such as gender or race, and can form support groups for each other. These groups are also used to introduce different initiatives such as leadership or education programs, where these elements of their workforce can put together strategies to mobilise and empower their group. This is illustrated in the Table 6.2.

Parallel to this quantitative data, the organisation also describes the way it measures the different activities associated with these indicators, including outcomes. This tends to be much more qualitative and descriptive, explaining through ad-hoc examples the different ways of measuring the impact of these activities. This is particularly done through mini case studies describing individual situations globally, for instance with employee X in country A, or employee Y in country B, and how this certain program affected their workplace interaction, engagement and satisfaction.

It is interesting to note that this organisation has also made it a requirement for their tier 1 and 2 suppliers to also abide by GRI standards and, for the former, to also provide sustainability reports to the organisation (as part of their broader supply chain auditing processes). This is also shown in their impact analysis, extending beyond the simple direct impacts of the organisation, to those of their suppliers and value chain partners. This was probably one of the better examples of organisations within the broader sample involved in doing this. While other organisations have, for example, implemented things like life-cycle assessments to capture the full impact of their products across all activities associated with producing, delivering, consuming and disposing of products, this is one of the few organisations that had a really comprehensive policy around auditing and evaluating their supply chain through the GRI standards.

*Table 6.2* Women engagement in the workforce

| Women | Year XX |
|---|---|
| Women in the workforce | Number |
| -   Proportion in region X | % |
| -   Proportion in region X1 | % |
| -   Proportion in region X2 etc. | % |
| Women in management positions | Number |
| -   Proportion in region X | % |
| -   Proportion in region X1 | % |
| -   Proportion in region X2 etc. | % |
| Women leadership group | % (involved) |
| -   Number of locations | Number |
| -   etc. | |

Source: *Adapted from TH22 and de-identified*

*International Practices – impact analysis*

Organisations within the International Practices category dominated the overall services sample again, with the same three organisations in this category as was seen in the scoping step. The 50 per cent (3/6) of services organisations within this category all exceeded the minimum standards set through local regulatory requirements; however, the breadth of coverage in their impact analysis for sustainability seemed to be more limited.

Specifically, a major common feature across the organisations within the International Practices category was the focus on environmental impact analysis. Despite the fact that service organisations typically have a significantly lower environmental footprint than other sectors such as manufacturing or mining, these organisations all had comprehensive approaches to determining the 'footprint' associated with their activities. They focussed on the most significant bases for determining environmental impact, including energy use, greenhouse gases, recycling and reuse of materials they use.

The other key issue with organisations in this category was the limitations on the impact analysis techniques put in place for broader social and economic issues. This was particularly the case with TH19, which focused on very few non-environmental indicators, unless they were required by local regulations. TH23 had a somewhat broader range of non-environmental indicators, but these seemed to be linked with both occupational health and safety and CSR based ISOs (OHSAS 18000, ISO 26000, respectively), which seemed to constrain the breadth of coverage beyond what was required for certification.

### *Host Country and Non-disclosure Practices – impact analysis*

In the final two categories, again one organisation was in each category. For the Host Country Compliance category, the organisation had set up impact analysis techniques to align with regulatory requirements. It was also clear from discussions that they did not seek to go beyond the mandatory requirements set by Thailand. For the final organisation classified within the Non-disclosure category, it was ambiguous whether they were putting in place any substantive impact analysis for development issues.

## Alternative selection practices

In examining the results for the alternative selection step, service sector organisations experience a performance increase from the preceding results. As can be seen in Figure 6.7, 33 per cent (2/6) of service sector organisations were within the World Class category, a jump from impact analysis. Despite this increase, the manufacturing sector was still substantially higher for the classification of World Class, with 50 per cent of organisations within this category. The overall sample was slightly lower, decreased by the performance of the service sector and the mining organisations. For International Practices,

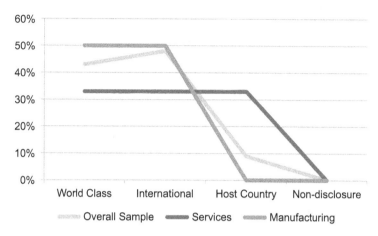

*Figure 6.7* Alternative selection practices – sector and sample comparison

service organisations still remained significantly below the overall sample and the manufacturing sector, with 33 per cent (2/6) or service organisations within this category. This compares with 50 per cent of manufacturing organisations, which resulted in 100 per cent of manufacturing organisations in either the World Class or International Practices category.

There were 33 per cent of service sector organisations in the Host Country Compliance category. While this is higher than the previous step, it is nevertheless a positive result, as no service organisations were classified within the Non-disclosure category. This is an improvement over the previous two steps, where one organisation was classified in the Non-disclosure category. The overall sample was, however, again influenced by the service sector with 9 per cent classified within the Host Country category, representing the two service sector organisations.

### World Class Practices – alternative selection

As noted above, two service organisations, or 33 per cent of the sample, were classified in the World Class category for alternative selection practices within their operations. This is, at least numerically, a substantial improvement over the previous step. However, given the limitations of the sample, this is still not indicative of an overall trend for a large number of service organisations to be actively engaged in changing their business practices to mitigate or remove their negative impacts, let alone enhance the positive impacts of their operations on the local community. Nevertheless, it is positive to see at least two organisations within this higher level category.

When looking across the alternative selection activities within the sector, the sustainability practices of these organisations is very much determined by the perception of the organisations developed from the headquarter perspective. Where these organisations are in pure services, we picked up a tendency for some organisations to be dismissive of their impacts, often conceiving of sustainability to be linked purely with environmental activities and more relevant if it is related to manufacturing or mining operations. However, the two organisations that are in the World Class category here clearly have a much broader perspective embedded through the vision and mission of the senior management in their home country headquarter operations that drives down into their activities in Thailand. These organisations both implement very comprehensive environmental analyses looking at reducing or completely mitigating their environmental footprint, and put in a host of socio-economic initiatives to address their business activities.

Shifting away from the example previously articulated for TH22 in the impact analysis step, we now turn to TH20, which offers interesting insights into the types of alternative section practices evident within the services sector. As noted above, this organisation also had a very comprehensive environmental focus, as what was seen in the manufacturing sector, looking at the full life-cycle analysis of their service delivery. This was particularly comprehensive and addressed not only a range of different types of issues and impacts, but considered significant adaptation and minimisation strategies to reduce or remove environmental impact, with a range of alternatives implemented to address their environmental impact.

Having said this, it is worthwhile to note that this organisation was not classified as being within the World Class category within their impact analysis step. This was mainly around the limitations in the transparency and reporting of their non-environmental indicators, with the measurement of environmental impacts dominating their activities. This organisation is adopting very comprehensive strategies beyond the environmental dimensions in implementing mitigation strategies linked with sustainability. This is across both the social and economic dimensions, and is particularly focused on workforce development within the developing country contexts that they operate within.

Perhaps most interesting, however, is the implementation of strategies to address human resource development and health and safety issues within the workforce. This is particularly around the health and safety issues within their workforce and business activities, with fatigue and stress identified as major issues affecting their workforce. As a result of identifying these issues the organisation implemented a whole host of programs and interventions to support staff. This includes, but is not limited to, screening staff based on personality profiles and characteristics; induction training when new staff are hired, including training on different techniques to handle stress and fatigue; workforce activities to continuously prevent injuries or health risks that are not limited to stress and fatigue, but also the general well-being of staff; and, even automated systems to determine changes in staff profiles with regards to health and well-being, stress and fatigue and overall performance.

The automated systems are particularly interesting in creating a workplace that is supportive of the well-being, health and safety, and general performance of staff. They have implemented a significant program of automation and systems to determine issues with their workforce. This enables the identification of issue areas as they emerge across their operations. A dedicated team that evaluates these data implements different interventions to address workforce conditions as they emerge – moving from a rather static annual process, to an interactive and technology driven system to support their workforce. This system is also inherently linked with their environmental performance, also allowing the organisation to track their environmental impact, and work through their employees to improve their performance in addressing environmental issues.

For this organisation, the focus on the well-being of their workforce is driven from the Chief Executive who has set ambitious targets aimed at improving the conditions for all staff. This clearly permeates data from interviews and company statements from both the headquarter operations and those business activities in Thailand. It is also clear from the corporate policies promoted online that the organisation has embedded this within their operational mantra, with their vision and mission accounting for this focus on their staff.

## International Practices – alternative selection

With 33 per cent (2/6) of service organisations within the International Practices category, we see a significant difference in the degree to which these practices are being implemented compared with both manufacturing (50 per cent) and the overall sample (48 per cent). It appears that there are some similarities between the two service organisations in this category and the overall sample, with both service organisations having a heavy environmental focus within the alternative selection strategies they implemented.

Specifically, both organisations appeared to be implementing a range of mitigation strategies beyond what was required through the regulations established by the Thailand government. These mitigation strategies were implemented for environmental impacts that they had identified, with one organisation looking at the entire life-cycle analysis of their service delivery, and the other organisation focusing specifically on their operational facilities and making changes to make these more 'green'.

While it should be noted that these organisations are exceeding the requirements of the local regulations on at least with one sustainability dimension, it is clear both organisations still fall short from adopting a range of mitigation or enhancement strategies that could holistically address all their sustainability impacts. It appears that the depth of engagement with social and economic impacts, particularly around enhancement strategies, is not being pursued widely within the services sector.

## Host Country practices – alternative selection

For the remaining 33 per cent of organisations within the service sector, these two organisations were classified within the Host Country Compliance category.

The major difference between these organisations and those in the International Practices category was the level of changes these organisations were willing to put in place to address their impacts. Both organisations were again focused specifically on the environmental dimension; however, it was not clear that either organisation would implement any changes unless it was required by the government. Both organisations emphasised through the interviews that they would adopt any changes required by the government in their annual audits and workplace visits, but did not provide any evidence for implementing any activities beyond this.

## Monitoring practices

On closer inspection of the monitoring step, a continued convergence happens for service sector organisations with the broader sample following the higher results in alternative selection. Specifically, 33 per cent (2/6) of the service sector organisations were classified in this category, compared with 44 per cent of manufacturing organisations and only 39 per cent of the overall sample. These are encouraging signs for service sector organisations and their monitoring practices, that is until we examine the level of International Practices. Here, service sector organisations perform quite poorly with only 17 per cent (1/6) of organisations classified within this category. This is compared with some 56 per cent of manufacturing organisations and 48 per cent of the overall sample.

This decrease in the overall performance is explained through a significantly higher percentage of service organisations being classified within the Host Country Compliance category. Some 50 per cent (3/6) of service sector organisations were classified in this category, providing an initial or are unwilling to implement in, or are unwilling to, implementing more sophisticated monitoring systems when compared against the broader sample and the manufacturing sector. As can be seen in Figure 6.8, no manufacturing organisations were classified in either Host Country or Non-disclosure categories.

With reference to Figure 6.8, the overall sample results show that 13 per cent of organisations were in the Host Country Compliance category, and this is representative of service sector organisations in this classification distorting the overall sample outcome. One positive note, however, is that no service organisations were classified as being within the Non-disclosure category, at least giving some indication about the willingness of these organisations to discuss the basis for their monitoring activities. The figure also captures the major fluctuations evident in the classification of service sector organisation's monitoring practices.

### *World Class Practices – monitoring*

Drawing upon the brief description above, there were 33 per cent of service organisations within the World Class category. This equates to two service organisations, and again is reflected by the performance of TH20 and TH22. This result remains below the overall sample and manufacturing sector (39 per cent and 44 per cent, respectively); however, it provides a good basis for continuing to explore more comprehensive practices within service organisations.

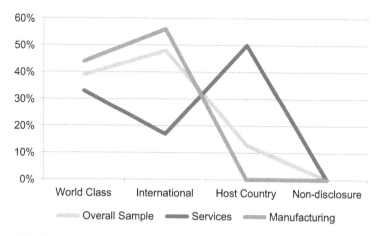

*Figure 6.8* Monitoring practices – sector and sample comparison

As noted in earlier steps, these organisations also provide an interesting counterpoint. With one organisation (TH20) being a large organisation with no explicit conformity to global guidelines or standards, and one small organisation (at least in terms of the investment in Thailand) with a range of different commitments to global guidelines and standards including the GRI standards (TH22). The classification of these organisations into this category indicates that they are implementing comprehensive monitoring systems collecting data across a range of issue and impact areas that are linked with sustainability. Threads of these practices have already been highlighted in earlier steps, demonstrating the breadth of issue coverage by both organisations across environmental, economic and social dimensions.

Building from the earlier details of TH22, this is an excellent example of an organisation implementing very comprehensive monitoring systems through their global operations. This is heavily linked with their international commitment to the GRI standards, with our interviews and collection of archival data both indicating the strength of this association and the importance of the headquarter commitments to this.

Perhaps the most interesting component of their monitoring systems was the extension of this beyond the direct activities of the organisation. Earlier we highlighted that the organisation was extending these considerations of sustainability performance and impact along both their direct and indirect supply chain partners (both upstream and downstream). This is particularly interesting to show the comprehensive nature of the monitoring activities that this organisation undertakes on a global scale, not just limited to direct activities (controlled by the organisation) in all the countries that they operate within.

Below (see Figure 6.9: Issue categories, areas and attached indicators), we provide a further elaboration of T22's impact analysis highlighted earlier in the impact analysis step. Here we extend their monitoring activities around their

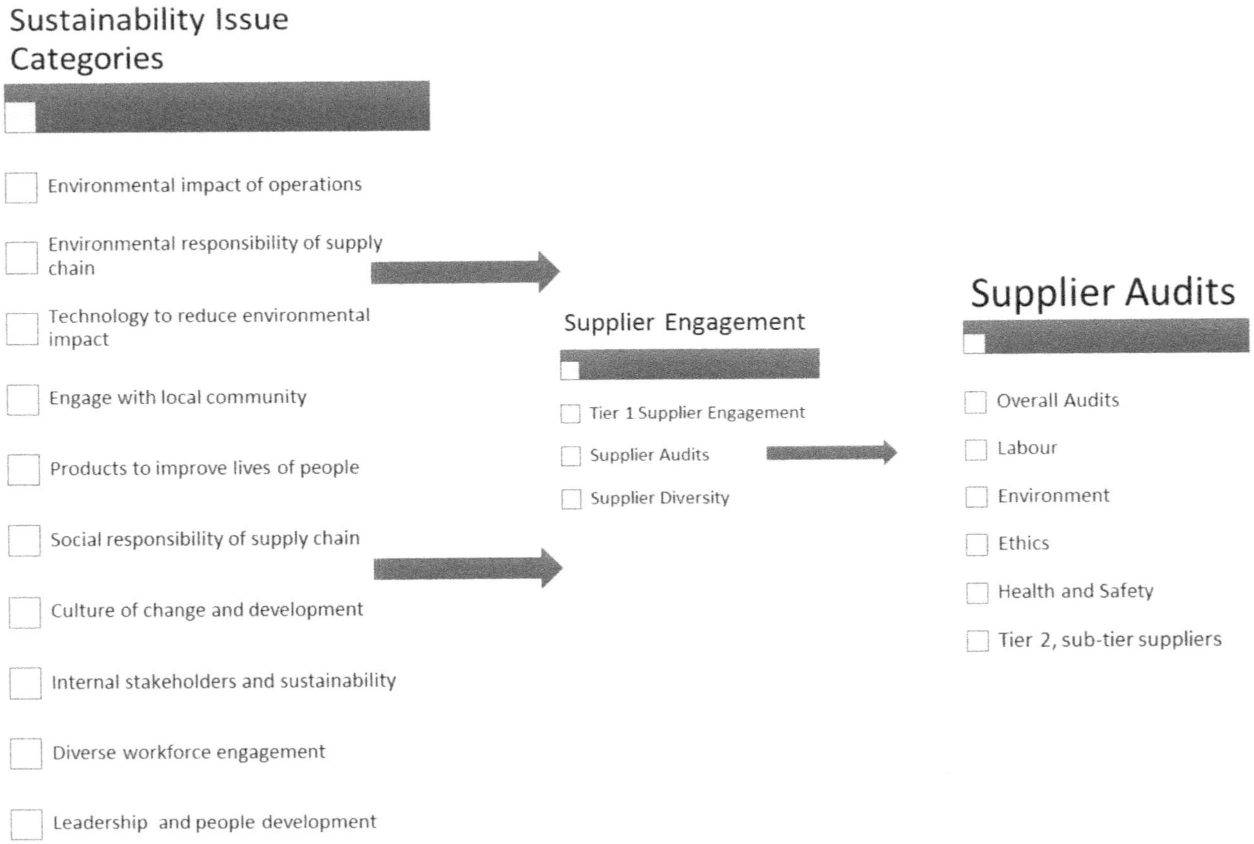

## Sustainability Issue Categories

- [ ] Environmental impact of operations
- [ ] Environmental responsibility of supply chain
- [ ] Technology to reduce environmental impact
- [ ] Engage with local community
- [ ] Products to improve lives of people
- [ ] Social responsibility of supply chain
- [ ] Culture of change and development
- [ ] Internal stakeholders and sustainability
- [ ] Diverse workforce engagement
- [ ] Leadership and people development

## Supplier Engagement

- [ ] Tier 1 Supplier Engagement
- [ ] Supplier Audits
- [ ] Supplier Diversity

## Supplier Audits

- [ ] Overall Audits
- [ ] Labour
- [ ] Environment
- [ ] Ethics
- [ ] Health and Safety
- [ ] Tier 2, sub-tier suppliers

*Figure 6.9* Issue categories, areas and attached indicators

Source: *Adapted from TH22 and de-identified*

supply chain. This is most broadly classified by the organisation under social and environmental engagement of their supply chains and industry. We have aggregated this below for the purpose of capturing overlapping activities of the organisation – with the actual auditing of their supply chain actually appearing to occur all at once, rather than delineated to social and environmental aspects.

Although the activities of this organisation are rather limited within Thailand, on a global scale it is clear that they implement and connect the consideration of their supply chain with determining the sustainability performance of their business activities. This appears to also be continually expanding to look beyond those supply chain partners that are directly associated with their operations globally.

When looking more closely at the supplier audits and how they measure the performance of these organisations, there is a significant focus first and foremost on their direct supply chain partners. The organisation indicates in their external reporting that these organisations are accounting for over 80 per cent of the support for their international activities and account for the majority of their direct impacts when measuring their sustainability performance. However, having said this, the organisation is extending this to sub-contracted, second tier, supply chain partners as they have determined this is where a substantial level of risk is associated with negative impacts.

In Table 6.3, we provide a snapshot of the organisation's monitoring measures for their supply chain, with specific reference to their direct, tier 1, supply chain partners. Here, it is focused around ensuring that the tier 1 partners are GRI compliant, that this is extending into other activities (such as specialist measures developed by CDP), and how it extends into other activities such as the number of audits they did to evaluate this, workshops for engaging with their supply chain partners around sustainability, and even the level of engagement/involvement for supply chain partners that are operated or owned by people from different groups (i.e. race and gender).

In our overview of the broader sustainability issue categories, areas and indicators for the organisation when looking at their supply chain, we also

*Table 6.3* Indicators and monitoring for supply chain engagement

| *Supply Chain Partners* | *Year X1* | *X2* | *X3* | *X4* |
|---|---|---|---|---|
| GRI compliance (%) | % | % | % | % |
| CDP compliance (%) | % | – | – | – |
| - Number of audits | Number | – | – | – |
| - Number of workshop | Number | – | – | – |
| - Supplier stakeholder engagement | Number | – | – | – |
| - Diverse suppliers (value of spending, US$ millions) | Number | – | – | – |

Source: *Adapted from TH22 and de-identified*

highlight that they are capturing specific measures for ethics, environment and labour, amongst others. We have not included this in the more detailed analysis of their monitoring activities, as this organisation appears to have only just begun extending their analysis into these specific areas with the introduction of new indicators. We rather focus on those areas and indicators where the organisation is capturing ongoing data to measure their performance, illustrating a longitudinal perspective is being implemented. We do not consider the more ad-hoc or newly introduced measures as part of a systematic basis for monitoring their activities.

### International Practices – monitoring

As noted above, a significant drop occurs in the overall level of practices being adopted by service organisations when reviewing the data for the monitoring step. Here, only 17 per cent, or one organisation, was classified within the International Practices category. This is significantly lower than the 56 per cent in the manufacturing sector, and when combined with the World Class category, it equates to only 50 per cent of service organisations in these first two categories (compared with 100 per cent for manufacturing).

When looking more closely at the results, it is clear a major point of differentiation is the level of transparency in place for the monitoring systems of service organisations. While it is clear from impact analysis and alternative selection that more organisations are exceeding Host Country Compliance requirements, in the monitoring step, the transparency in providing evidence of monitoring systems is sparse.

For the organisation we classified here, they exceeded the legal requirements of Thailand in collecting data around their environmental impact. The remaining components of their monitoring system seem to be focused either on what is required by local laws or through a financial/bottom line perspective on the relative success of their business operations.

### Host Country Practices – monitoring

With the remaining 50 per cent of organisations within this category for the services sector, it was evident that there were much more limited monitoring systems in place for organisations. It appears that these organisations do not go beyond providing relevant government departments with specific data required by law. As noted above, financial monitoring and reporting appears to be the key areas that these organisations are addressing through their monitoring systems of activities in Thailand.

## Evaluation practices

An examination of the results for the evaluation step, as captured in Figure 6.10, highlight a relatively high level of World Class practices within the services sector, with 33 per cent (2/6) of service organisations within this category. While

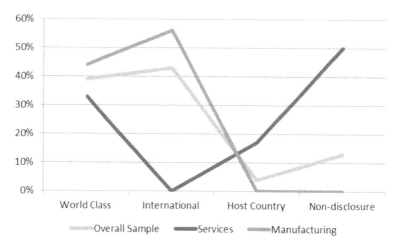

*Figure 6.10* Evaluation practices – sector and sample comparison

this is lower than the performance of the manufacturing sector with 44 per cent of organisations in this category, and the overall sample with 39 per cent, it is nevertheless a positive outcome for the services sector. This also parallels the results from the monitoring step with the same two organisations within the World Class category for both monitoring and evaluation.

Results from the International Practices category illustrate a different story though, with no service organisations classified within this category. This is compared with the manufacturing sector which sits at 56 per cent and the overall sample at 43 per cent. This initially suggests that while several organisations are performing well in adopting World Class practices to their evaluation processes, the same cannot be said for the International Practices category. This highlights a substantial difference in the performance of the service sector when compared against the manufacturing sector and overall sample.

As an extension of this, the remaining 67 per cent (4/6) of the service sector organisations have been classified within the Host Country Compliance and Non-disclosure categories. A particular concentration is evident within Non-disclosure, with 50 per cent (3/6) of service organisations within this category. This indicates that we were either unable to determine their actual practices around the evaluation step, or that they simply did not have any practices in place for evaluating their performance. Furthermore, the lower performance of service-sector organisations is illustrated across the first two categories before quickly increasing on the last two categories.

## World Class Practices – evaluation

As noted above, 33 per cent of service organisations, or two organisations, are classified within the World Class category. As what was evident in the manufacturing sector, the two organisations (TH20 and TH22) within the World Class category are the same as those within this category for monitoring. The evaluation function is clearly dependent on the data being collected within the monitoring step, providing the platform for organisations to systematically collect and then evaluate relative changes in its performance across different measures.

Building from the example provided within the monitoring step, we detail further the sequence between monitoring and evaluation steps utilising the example of TH22. Focusing on their evaluation activities around their supply chain engagement again, we are able to demonstrate the longitudinal monitoring of data relating to the sustainability activities of their tier 1 suppliers, as well as the organisation's ongoing evaluation of this compared with their baseline data and performance targets. In Figure 6.11 we highlight again the link between the general supplier audit indicators and the extension into specific indicators that the organisation captures data against.

We draw from the data collected as part of this organisation's monitoring activities in illustrating the charting of performance along a longitudinal perspective. The organisation does not provide a visual represenation of this data such as what we have done, but it is interesting to draw parallels with what has been done in the manufacturing sector for the capacity to map this data. There appears to be significant differences in the level of interactivity in the data presented by different organisations within our sample – with some providing detailed online platforms that allow data modelling, as opposed to others who selectively model data and primarily do this within their sustainability reports.

Similar to what was seen in the manufacturing sector, while this organisation sets both a clear baseline for its performance to be measured against and clear targets for what it wants to achieve, it is difficult to connect the disparate data from external reports. We have had to extrapolate from different data sources to determine the performance and also targets that the organisation is setting. Having said this, there are a range of quantifiable and clear indicators the organisation has established for ongoing monitoring and evaluation of how it engages its supply chain with regards to sustainability.

It is particularly worthwhile noting that the headquarter commitment to sustainability is driving changes within the broader supply chain of the organisation, showing the influence large, global, multinationals can have in spreading these practices internationally. Having a requirement for tier 1 suppliers to undertake GRI reporting, as well as an increasing focus on the activities of tier 2 suppliers, will expand the impact of the sustainability activities of this organisation across the entire product life cycle and will likely drive change in business practices across developing countries where this organisation outsources components of its value chain.

## *Host Country Practices – evaluation*

The limitations evident in the monitoring step flow through into the evaluation step, with 67 per cent of organisations in either the Host Country Compliance or Non-disclosure categories. As noted above, only one organisation was classified within

## Supplier Audits

- ☐ Overall Audits
- ☐ Labour
- ☐ Environment
- ☐ Ethics
- ☐ Health and Safety
- ☐ Tier 2, sub-tier suppliers

| Supply Chain Partners | Year X1 | X2 | X3 | X4 |
|---|---|---|---|---|
| GRI compliance (%) | % | % | % | % |
| CDP compliance (%) | % | - | - | - |
| - Number of audits | Number | - | - | - |
| - Number of workshops | Number | - | - | - |
| - Supplier stakeholder engagement | Number | - | - | - |
| - Diverse suppliers (value of spending, US$ millions) | Number | - | - | - |

*Figure 6.11* Indicators and monitoring for supply chain engagement

Source: *Adapted from TH22 and de-identified*

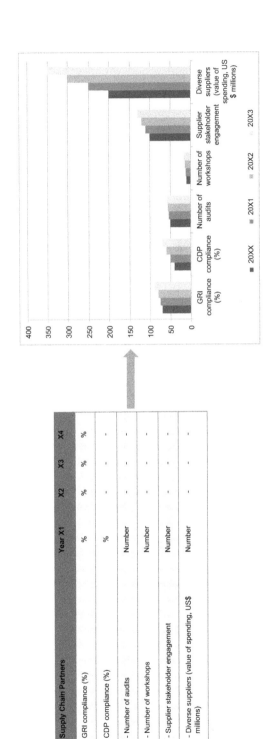

| Supply Chain Partners | Year X1 | X2 | X3 | X4 |
|---|---|---|---|---|
| GRI compliance (%) | % | % | % | % |
| CDP compliance (%) | % | - | - | - |
| - Number of audits | Number | - | - | - |
| - Number of workshops | Number | - | - | - |
| - Supplier stakeholder engagement | Number | - | - | - |
| - Diverse suppliers (value of spending, US$ millions) | Number | - | - | - |

*Figure 6.12* Monitoring data of supply chain engagement

Source: *Adapted from TH22 data and de-identified*

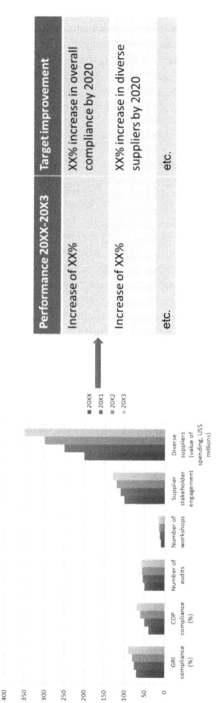

*Figure 6.13* Evaluation of supply chain engagement against targets

Source: *Adapted from TH22 and de-identified*

the Host Country category for evaluation. This organisation was also classified in this category for monitoring, and only indicated limited evaluation of their data on sustainability issues based on regulatory requirements. This was mainly around the environmental data, with the organisation highlighting the focus of the Thailand government on paying particular attention to the environmental impact of their activities, with a requirement to specifically address how well they are performing across a range of environmental indicators each year. Beyond this, there was not any evidence that the organisation was doing anything else to systematically evaluate their sustainability performance.

### *Non-disclosure Practices – evaluation*

By far the most prevalent level of practice for the evaluation step was Non-disclosure, with 50 per cent (3/6) of service organisations classified within this category. As highlighted above, it was clear the limitations around the monitoring activities of these organisations, along with the compliance focus, meant that unless it was required by law, these organisations were not going to undertake any systematic evaluation of their performance relative to changes in their monitoring data. It was clear through interviews that these organisations had felt compelled to collect certain key data for their reporting requirements to the Thailand government, but actually doing anything further than providing a static reporting function with this data was clearly not a priority.

## Feedback and follow up practices

With regards to the feedback step, Figure 6.14 shows that service sector organisations experience an ongoing shift towards the lower categories of Host Country Compliance and Non-disclosure. Only 17 per cent (1/6) of the service sector organisations

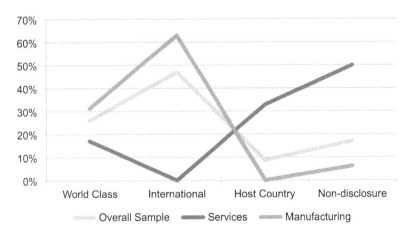

*Figure 6.14* Feedback practices – sector and sample comparison

were classified within the World Class category, and no service sector organisations were classified within the International Practices category. A comparison of these results with the manufacturing sector organisations shows substantial differences with 31 per cent of organisations within the World Class category, and 63 per cent within the International Practices category. So while the vast majority of manufacturing organisations are undertaking either World Class or International Practices for their feedback processes, it is only a small minority of service sector organisations.

Approximately 83 per cent (5/6) of service sector organisations were classified within the Host Country Compliance or Non-disclosure categories. This includes some 50 per cent (3/6) within the Non-disclosure category. Manufacturing organisations, on the other hand, only had 6 per cent (1/16) within the Non-disclosure category and none in the Host Country Compliance category. Figure 6.14 illustrates these results, showing the classification of service organisations across the four performance categories. It is clear to see the dominance of service sector organisations classified in the Host Country Compliance and Non-disclosure categories. In regards to the manufacturing organisations, there were a substantial number in the World Class or International Practices category.

## *World Class Practices – feedback and follow up*

As noted above, 17 per cent, or one organisation, was classified within the World Class category for the final stage of the sustainability assessment. Not surprisingly, it was an organisation that was at this level consistently across all the steps, with TH22, again being classified at this level. Here we see that TH20 was unable to demonstrate comprehensive activities for adjusting their activities consistently across environmental, social and economic indicators, based on their analysis of their sustainability evaluation step.

Looking more closely at TH22, we highlight again that this organisation has been firmly committed to a range of international standards and guidelines, including the GRI standards. Here we saw clear demonstrable evidence that this organisation – particularly through the headquarters – collects, analyses and adjusts their business activities in response to the sustainability performance. Building from the earlier example in the impact analysis step, we can see a sequence across the sustainability objectives that the organisation set for the broader international operations, through to the impact analysis data and the monitoring and evaluation techniques being implemented. For the majority of the key sustainability issue categories (detailed in Figure 6.15) we were able to sequence this through to the evaluation processes in how the organisation was performing across various sustainability areas.

Here we look at the earlier example focussing on the efforts to create a diverse and inclusive employment base within their organisation. We focus particularly on women in the workforce and efforts to promote gender equality within the organisation. It is clear that the organisation is adopting a range of different broad quantitative measures around gender employment and empowerment,

## Sustainability Issue Categories

- [ ] Environmental impact of operations
- [ ] Environmental responsibility of supply chain
- [ ] Technology to reduce environmental impact
- [ ] Engage with local community
- [ ] Products to improve lives of people
- [ ] Social responsibility of supply chain
- [ ] Culture of change and development
- [ ] Internal stakeholders and sustainability
- [ ] Diverse workforce engagement
- [ ] Leadership and people development

## Diverse Workforce

- [ ] Women
- [ ] People of colour
- [ ] Asian
- [ ] Human rights

## Women

- [ ] Women in the workforce
- [ ] Women leadership programs
- [ ] Women advocacy and support groups
- [ ] Women education group

*Figure 6.15* Issue categories, areas and attached indicators

although most of this data are aggregated, making it difficult to see the relative performance within their operations in Thailand. However, it is clear that they are collecting this information and evaluating their performance against both a baseline data point and a target for further growth and empowerment. We illustrate this below in Table 6.4.

Again, as has been evident across the majority of organisations, we need to extrapolate and sort information and data on what the organisation is doing. This remains a time-consuming process, which also indicates that stakeholders are likely to also struggle in determining exactly what activities are being implemented by the organisation. This is particularly the case with the enhancement strategies that the organisation is putting in place.

*Table 6.4* Evaluation of diversity performance, targets and mitigation

| Women | Year XX–X3 | Target | Performance Outcome | Enhancement Strategy |
| --- | --- | --- | --- | --- |
| Women in the workforce | Number | Increase number by XX by 2025 | Achieved XX increase (on track/ achieved etc) | More flexible workforce employment |
| - Proportion in region X | % | Increase % by 2025 | Achieve % increase (achieved) | – |
| - Proportion in region X1 | % | – | – | – |
| - Proportion in region X2 | % | – | – | – |
| - etc. | | | | |
| Women in management positions | Number | Increase number by XX by 2025 | – | Increase involvement in management training |
| - Proportion in redion X | % | – | – | – |
| - Proportion in region X1 | % | – | – | – |
| - Proportion in region X2 | % | – | – | – |
| - etc. | | | | |
| Women leadership group | % (involved) | Increase % by 2025 | Greater promotion through internal networks | |
| - Number of locations | Number | – | – | – |
| - etc. | | | | |

Some of these enhancement strategies are clearly linked with creating a more diverse workforce and empowering women, however, they are not always necessarily linked with specific performance areas captured within the organisation evaluation processes. This includes things like creating a workplace with flexible working hours and arrangements (i.e. location), creating programs to support employees returning from maternity leave, amongst others, which clearly have an impact on improving retention of female employees with families, and is likely to increase the attraction of new female employees.

Thus, our general conclusion is that the organisation is proactively engaging with the sustainability areas it has identified as priority areas; however, it is failing to provide this in a coherent and clear message to external stakeholders. Again, this is not uncommon for organisations within our sample with many organisations struggling around the attribution issue of making changes to their business activities and capturing impacts of this on overall performance. Perhaps the key issue here is around causality between actions and outcomes versus generating some relational links that may not be causal but rather indicative of adjustments being taken to address performance.

### *Host Country Practices – feedback and follow up*

As noted above, with only one organisation in the World Class category and none in the International Practices category, the remaining 83 per cent, or five, service sector organisations were classified within the Host Country Compliance or Non-disclosure categories. Thirty three per cent of organisations were classified within the Host Country category, indicating a very limited engagement with their evaluation outcomes. Specifically, both of these organisations only made reference to making changes as a result of their evaluation processes if it was required by the local authorities. No further evidence was provided to indicate any more substantive actions would be taken to address their sustainability performance within Thailand.

### *Non-disclosure Practices – feedback and follow up*

Building from the results in the evaluation step, the same three organisations provided no evidence of adjusting their activities in response to their sustainability performance. This is a logical conclusion, as the feedback and follow up step is meant to provide a closed loop to the monitoring and evaluation processes that organisations have implemented, allowing the organisation to adapt their practices to either further enhance or mitigate their impacts as determined by their performance evaluation. Without the evaluation of their monitoring data, it is clear that these organisations will lack the ability to adjust their activities.

## Conclusion

As opposed to the manufacturing sector, where it was clear that the majority of organisations in the sample were consistently adopting practices beyond what was required by local laws, the services sample showed significant limitations in the sustainability practices being implemented by these organisations. It should be noted that only tentative implications can be drawn from this sample due to limitations in the overall sample size, but it does give some clarity around potential activities and practices being implemented by these organisations.

Specifically, for the organisations that were in the World Class category, it was clear that global guidelines and standards had an important role in determining their practices both directly and indirectly. Direct, through the specific commitment of one organisation to global guidelines, and particularly the GRI standards. Indirect, through the pressure value chain partners had placed on the organisation to implement more comprehensive sustainability practices and report on these. It is clear for both organisations that were within this category that having a strong headquarter commitment towards addressing sustainability was an important precursor for this extending into their international operations.

With regards to the majority of other sustainability practices in place, it was evident that a range of industry standards and ISOs played a partial role in driving these organisations towards adopting specific practices to address sustainability. This was particularly around environmental or CSR based ISOs. Beyond this, however, it was clear these organisations would either revert to local regulatory requirements or simply not implement certain activities. This was most evident in the final stages of the sustainability assessment around the evaluation and feedback and follow up steps, with the majority of organisations in the Host Country Compliance or Non-disclosure categories. While we are hesitant about making sweeping generalisations regarding the service sector activities targeting sustainability in Thailand, it is clear that there are some major limitations around evaluation sustainability performance and acting on the outcomes of this evaluation within the sector.

# 7   Discussion and conclusion

*Jerome D. Donovan, Cheree Topple*
*and Eryadi K. Masli*

Building from the preceding chapters looking at both the manufacturing and service sectors, we reconsider in this chapter the corporate sustainability assessment framework established in Chapter 3. While we have utilised this framework as an organising theory for our examination of corporate sustainability practices, here we start the process of re-conceptualising how the private sector organises these steps.

Specifically, we look at establishing a clearer sequence of sustainability practices from an empirical basis. This includes adjusting the ordering and connections between individual sustainability activities we have seen within the corporate sector. Four distinct stages emerge from this, including 1) issue identification and prioritisation, 2) impact analysis, monitoring and evaluation, 3) alternative selection, and 4) feedback and follow up (please see Figure 7.1: Corporate sustainability assessment framework).

Within these stages we have also utilised our analysis from Chapter 5 and Chapter 6 to synthesise the activities of the corporate sector, drawing on the identified World Class practices. This provides a benchmark for current best practices when approaching sustainability from a private sector perspective, and a new organising theory from which to further examine the extent and application of these stages in different contexts, countries and sectors.

Before looking at these four stages in more depth, it should be noted that from a private sector perspective, we have captured a management decision-making process that is recurring. Organisations within our sample did not delineate between ex-ante (before investment) and ex-post (after investment or conclusion of operations) decisions. Rather the sustainability practices that we have categorised across these distinct steps and stages are embedded in their ongoing business activities.

Prior to beginning the operational activities in Thailand, organisations did however identify a range of key decisions that must occur. A recurring theme was the importance of first considering basic business acumen and business fundamentals. Organisations first decide on whether their business operations within Thailand were going to be feasible and generate sufficient outcomes to warrant the dedication of resources. Overlaying this was the importance of being able to implement broader systems and processes that are aligned with a global approach to business.

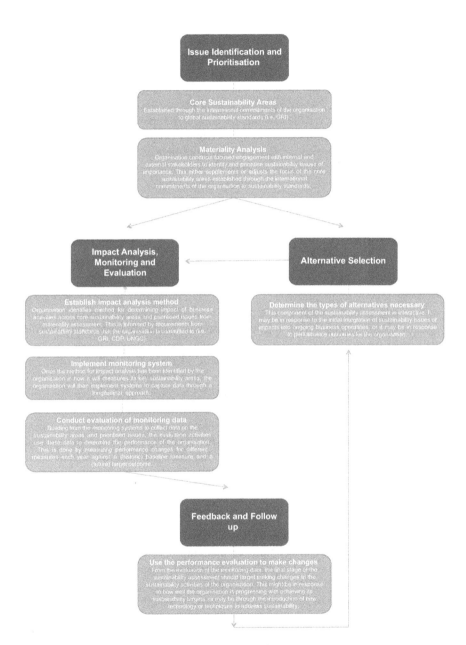

*Figure 7.1* Corporate sustainability assessment framework

Organisations often emphasised that an evaluation of the potential host country would include determining whether they could continue doing business in line with their International Practices – highlighting the tendency of the top performing organisations to approach their operations in a similar approach everywhere, irrespective of the development status of the country they are operating within. If organisations were not able to integrate their management systems, health and safety measures, environmental standards, technology etc., they would not enter into a country.

It was also flagged that prior to beginning operations, other impact assessments (and particularly EIAs) would be conducted, particularly if this was a requirement for the approval of their investment proposal to enter Thailand. But the sustainability practices we have captured here as part of the corporate sustainability assessment appear to provide the basis for a broader planning and management process for addressing sustainability within private sector activities.

## Issue identification and prioritisation

When examining the corporate sustainability framework against our data on leading edge practices being implemented by organisations, it is clear that screening and scoping practices are inherently connected. In fact, we would propose that these two steps are actually integrated into a common procedure whereby the identification of key issues occurs in parallel to the prioritisation of these issues.

Evidence suggests that the activity of issue identification and prioritisation should, however, build upon established commitments these organisations have made to various sustainability standards, which essentially form a key set of issue areas for organisations to concentrate on (similar to a checklist or matrix style approach). These sustainability standards, and particularly the Global Reporting Initiative (GRI) standards, form a key basis for many organisations when setting global sustainability areas and objectives that they will address across their international operations.

### Screening

Looking at this more closely, a key overarching theme evident when examining the screening practices of organisations was the importance of global sustainability areas and objectives for their entire business operations. This is clearly established through the headquarter operations, and is generally applied in a consistent manner across different operational and country contexts for organisations. As noted above, this approach is often directed through the international commitments that these organisations have made.

A recurring series of international commitments was evident, including from the GRI Organization standards, the United Nations Global Compact (UNGC) principles, the Carbon Disclosure Project (CDP) (around greenhouse gases) and often a range of industry specific sustainability standards or ISOs (International Organization for Standardization). These international commitments often form the basis for these organisations, directing the establishment of their sustainability areas and objectives across all their business activities.

Particularly important within the World Class category was the GRI standards that direct organisations to undertake a materiality analysis. This materiality analysis clearly connects both the screening and scoping practices, and directs organisations to engage with both internal and external stakeholders in identifying and prioritising the most important sustainability issues for consideration.

## *Scoping*

Building from the core set of sustainability areas and objectives established by the headquarter operations of these organisations, and linked with the international commitments that have been made, is the process of refining and prioritising key sustainability issue and impact areas (what is often referred to as scoping). This clearly builds from the processes organisations have established for engaging with stakeholders in identifying important issues within the screening process, and specifically through the materiality analysis.

This is where the delineation of these two steps becomes more difficult. While a majority of the extant literature has indicated the sequencing and independence of these steps, our data rather suggests that organisations build from their generic sustainability areas established by international commitments, and concurrently engage in a process of stakeholder engagement for both identifying and prioritising issue areas. The materiality analysis seems to dominate the practices of organisations looking to identify and prioritise issues in line with stakeholder expectations.

A materiality analysis can both build out the priority sustainability areas for these organisations to focus on (through identifying new areas of importance), as well as refining and focusing these organisations on those sustainability issues that are of most importance to their stakeholders. Clearly, this has elements of what we would define based on extant literature as being a screening and scoping step. Evidence, thus, clearly redefines and shifts how we perceive and conceptualise practices around screening and scoping from a corporate standpoint. Within our sample, we saw that MNEs used materiality assessments to identify another suite of issues and impacts that were then integrated with an existing suite of core issues and impacts identified in the screening step. So, rather than being a process to refine issues and impacts for the organisation, the materiality assessment provided an external perspective of engaging with stakeholders to identify meaningful issues and impacts to be considered by the organisation.

We would therefore propose that these two steps within the sustainability assessment process be connected more explicitly under a combined stage – issue identification and prioritisation. It is clear that organisations establish a global approach to setting sustainability areas and objectives that they will focus on across their international operations. This covers a set of core sustainability areas established through a range of international commitments, requiring these organisations to cover generic sustainability issues across environmental, economic and social dimensions.

The identification and prioritisation of activities within corporate sustainability practices appear to happen most rigorously through utilising GRI standards and the materiality analysis. Here, organisations extend beyond the generic areas established through engaging with both internal and external stakeholders to determine the relative importance of different sustainability issues – this may be through identifying further locally relevant issues, or through prioritising and further addressing the core areas identified through their international commitments.

In general, for the organisations performing within the World Class category, these activities lead to the development of core global sustainability categories that the organisation will focus on. From these, they will identify a range of associated areas that they will consider, and attached to these areas they will determine the different indicators that will be integrated into their assessment processes.

## Impact analysis, monitoring and evaluation

Building from the reconceptualised screening and scoping steps, we again see a different approach evident in the manner in which the framework is organised through our data. Specifically, there is a sequence between impact analysis, monitoring and evaluation whereby organisations do not necessarily implement these activities as discrete functions within their operations. Rather, organisations identify their areas and indicators of impact analysis, building from the process of issue identification and prioritisation and the established core sustainability categories, areas and indicators. Organisations align their tools and techniques against this, and capture data through a longitudinal approach, evaluating this against benchmarks (or baseline data) and future performance goals.

These activities intuitively sequence well from the issue identification and prioritisation stage, with organisations having identified their core sustainability objectives and goals, then they turn to determining how well they are performing across these different areas. Organisations within the World Class category had a very clear sequence across these different areas, although sometimes this requires an extrapolation from their data and reporting as targets for performance evaluation were often separated from the monitoring data.

### Impact analysis

As noted above, our results showed a sequence from the sustainability activities undertaken within the issue identification and prioritisation stage. This was particularly around the core sustainability categories, areas and indicators that the organisations identified, with clear alignment between their impact analysis and issue identification and prioritisation stage. Of particular interest, was the dependence on the corporate or headquarter strategy to direct the subsidiary activities around the methods and systems put in place for the organisation's impact analysis. This strategy for impact analysis also appeared to be informed by the international or global guidelines that these organisations used. Many organisations made specific reference to their international commitments to different sustainability standards, including through the selection of appropriate tools and techniques identified in these standards for measuring impact.

In doing so, these organisations often provided appendices to their sustainability or CSR reports, which broke down their impact analysis and aligned this against the different international commitments they had, showing where and how they were collecting data to match different requirements. Of particular prominence within the impact analysis approach adopted by organisations was the GRI standards with comprehensive measures across social, economic and environmental dimensions, as well as industry specific requirements. The most comprehensive presentation of impact analysis techniques and results were aligned across multiple sustainability standards, building from GRI requirements, to include UNGC, CDP, ISOs, amongst others.

For the integration of issue prioritisation into impact analysis activities, it was evident that many organisations within the World Class category were integrating impact analysis techniques to address material issues. It was, however, often necessary to make connections from disparate reporting techniques between different data these organisations collected and the material issues identified. Greater clarity is obviously necessary in defining the methods for how material issues, particularly those that are updated regularly, are reported upon.

## *Monitoring and evaluation*

An extension from the impact analysis step, organisations within the World Class category would collect these data regularly (monitoring) and evaluate the relative changes in their performance. This enabled a longitudinal perspective on the relative impact of the organisation across the key sustainability categories, areas and indicators they were focused on.

While extant literature often refers to these two steps as being discrete, albeit connected, it was clear that these steps were fully integrated into the impact analysis step whereby organisations identify the methods and measures for determining their sustainability impact. These three steps are clearly integrated when reviewing corporate practices, and aimed at offering a platform from which organisations can evaluate their sustainability performance against different targets and baseline measures. Most organisations within the World Class category provided both a baseline indicator, progress for each year and targeted outcomes that were usually linked with performance expectations in 2020 or 2025 (given a reasonable time horizon to achieve targets).

As mentioned in previous steps, the headquarter operations had a critical role in the type and extent of the monitoring being implemented. Across the organisations classified as World Class, the headquarter operations would implement the systems for collecting and analysing the information required for monitoring. These methods of monitoring and evaluating sustainability performance were also anchored against the different international commitments that these organisations had made to sustainability standards. GRI standards were the most significant international commitment directing the activities of organisations here, although perhaps the most reoccurring issue considered across all organisations was greenhouse gases and $CO_2$ emissions. This was evident across World Class, International Practices and Host Country Compliance categories. The techniques that organisations utilise in capturing different data tend to be largely from a technical or quantitative approach, with a heavy emphasis on the ability to quantify and measure their impact and performance.

So while extant literature would suggest a more discrete and separate consideration of these three steps, we would argue for connecting these three steps into one stage to reflect the processes of the private sector. These activities are inherently linked, are difficult to disaggregate from reporting and sustainability activities organisations implement, and usually the performance in one activity will fundamentally change that in the other two (i.e. poor monitoring practices inhibits the ability to evaluate performance). Furthermore, when it comes to the specific tools and techniques that these organisations utilise as part of this process, it appears that organisations have a focus on quantitative or technical processes to capture the data necessary for determining impact, capturing ongoing data and evaluating their performance.

## Alternative selection

When looking at the alternative selection step, this appears to be an interactive activity implemented by organisations. This can occur from the beginning of the process of sustainability assessment, with organisations considering the alternatives – be it mitigation or enhancement strategies – as a result of the issue identification and prioritisation, or can be integrated as a response to the monitoring and evaluation steps through the feedback and follow up process, with the organisation funnelling through changes to their mitigation or enhancement strategies. This may be due to not achieving targeted outcomes from their sustainability criteria, or it may be due to a desire to enhance certain outcomes.

Organisations within the World Class category also appear to be targeting their strategies towards mitigation for environmental issues and enhancement for social and economic issues. By far the most comprehensive practices were around the environmental dimension, with significant strategies implemented including along a life cycle and value chain analysis. Enhancement strategies appear to still be an area where even the most pro-active organisations are continuing to develop, with many alternatives implemented still focused on empowering employees.

## Feedback and follow up

The final stage of the sustainability assessment framework remains the feedback and follow up step. This step still remains the most difficult activity for organisations to comprehensively implement, demonstrating the response to performance evaluation through meaningful changes to the sustainability activities of organisations. Difficulties reside in the ability of organisations to attribute changes in their overall sustainability performance as a response to changes made through their activities and alternative selection process.

Despite this, organisations within the World Class category demonstrated an ongoing and cyclical set of changes to their sustainability activities in an attempt to improve their overall performance. This showed the willingness and engagement of these organisations in trying to improve their sustainability performance. This was most evident in those organisations adopting a broad range of international commitments to sustainability standards, such as GRI standards or UNGC.

## Future research and conclusion

While our study has some limitations, it does provide a useful basis from which future research can further extend. Specifically, we advocate for scholars to more fully engage with the empirical examination of impact assessment practice, particularly around developing theoretical frameworks for the private sector that capture and model current practices. This study has provided an initial large-scale study to further detail these practices, however, much more work is needed to further conceptualise private sector practices to address sustainability within their operations. Detail around more specific tools and techniques being utilised by the private sector will also help detail current practices, and potentially lead to further improvements in how sustainability is engaged with by the private sector.

Moving beyond the context of this study, into other developed and developing countries, will also continue to support the broader generalisations that can be derived from our corporate sustainability assessment framework. This might include a specific examination of different developing countries to determine whether there are common practices across organisations operating within this context, or extending analysis to a developed country context where many of the organisations within our sample are based. It will be interesting to determine whether these organisations are indeed driven by the headquarter policies and international commitments, or whether emerging regulations targeting the sustainability practices of these organisations is having a greater influence.

To conclude, we hope these initial efforts at reconceptualising the corporate sustainability assessment based on our empirical results offer a platform for future studies to further validate our results. Given this is, to our knowledge, the first study that has conducted a large-scale study, with multiple case studies, across the entire sustainability assessment framework, we hope this will provide a base to further understanding of pro-active and voluntary private sector sustainability activities, and also offer a platform from which to further improve these activities to lead to better sustainability outcomes.

We would advocate future studies continue to examine, identify and organise the sustainability practices of the private sector. Through this endeavour, it will be possible to further develop both the practical understanding of how to incorporate sustainability practices more comprehensively into business activities, and continue to contribute towards the theoretical development within this field, which remains constrained by the limited empirical studies in the area.

# Index